INSIDE

What really happened —

THE L.A.

and why it will happen again

RIOTS

*Essays and articles by more than 60 of America's
leading independent writers and journalists*

Published by the Institute for Alternative Journalism

The works that appear in this book are printed with permission.
A list of sources appears on pages 152 and 153,
which should be considered an extension of the copyright page.

The material published in this book represents the opinions of the authors
and not necessarily those of the Institute for Alternative Journalism.

Cover photo by Ted Soqui
Back cover photos:
Top, left to right: Ted Soqui, Ted Soqui, Michael Schumann/SABA, Ted Soqui
Bottom, left to right: Michael Schumann/SABA, Michael Schumann/SABA,
Maggie Hallahan, Ed Carreon/*Orange County Register*

Library of Congress Catalog Card Number 92-073103

ISBN 0-9633687-0-2

10 9 8 7 6 5 4 3 2 1

First Edition

Inside the L.A. Riots published by the Institute for Alternative Journalism

IAJ Editorial Advisory Board	Colin Greer, New World Foundation
	Kit Rachlis, *LA Weekly*
	Laura Washington, *Chicago Reporter*
	Mark Zusman, *Willamette Week*
Editor	Don Hazen, Executive Director, IAJ
Executive Editor	Sara Frankel
Art Director and Photo Editor	Daniela Gayle, Public Media Center
Managing Editors	Kate Kelly
	Julie Winokur
Associate Editors	Tiarra Mukherjee
	Laurie Ouellette
	Laurie Udeski
Production Assistant	Katherine Gibbon
Editorial Assistant	Megan Shaw
AlterNet	Margaret Engle, Director
	Cathy Cashel, Assistant Editor
	Kelley Culmer, Administrative Coordinator
Production	James Vowell, Publisher, *Los Angeles Reader*
	Denise Baker, Art Director, *Los Angeles Reader*
	Genevieve Leyh, Editorial Designer, *Los Angeles Reader*
	Melle Karakawa, Production Assistant, *Los Angeles Reader*
Board of Directors	Institute for Alternative Journalism
	Martin Linsky, Board President
	John F. Kennedy School of Government, Harvard University
	Kitty Axelson
	Valley Advocate
	Bruce Brugmann
	San Francisco Bay Guardian
	Patricia Calhoun
	Westword
	Gail Christian
	Pacifica Radio
	Katherine Fulton
	North Carolina Independent
	Florence Graves
	Independent Consultant
	Colin Greer
	New World Foundation
	Herb Chao Gunther
	Public Media Center
	Ray Hartmann
	Riverfront Times
	Kit Rachlis
	LA Weekly
	Jay Walljasper
	Utne Reader
	Laura Washington
	Chicago Reporter
	Nat Winthrop
	Vermont Times
	Mark Zusman
	Willamette Week

acknowledgements

Special thanks to

Kit Rachlis, editor-in-chief of the *LA Weekly*, and Dan Bishoff, national affairs editor of the *Village Voice,* as well as the help and support offered by their talented staffs.

Sam Weiner, the Angelina Fund; Colin Greer, the New World Foundation; Bill Moyers; John Passacantando, the Schumann Foundation; Harriet Barlow, the HKH Foundation; Dan Cantor; Barbara Dudley, the North Shore Universalist Veatch Program; Bill Bondurant, the Mary Reynolds Babcock Foundation; Martin Bunzl; and Marc Weiss. Without the support of these individuals and foundations, this project would not have been possible.

Bernard Ohanian, Andrea Torrice, Steve Brown, Hollie Ainbinder, Craig Marine and Fortunata Deborah Bueti; Jamie Morris, who helped us navigate the shoals of book publishing; Sara Frankel, Kate Kelly and Julie Winokur, who jumped in on short notice and worked intensively and with great professionalism; Daniela Gayle, who believed in the project and invested incredible time, skill and energy in making it happen; Marty Linsky, a supportive and understanding board chair; Herb Chao Gunther and the staff of the Public Media Center in San Francisco, for an immensely creative, helpful and above all patient environment; Ted Soqui, for the eloquence of his photographic vision; Margaret Engle and the rest of the AlterNet staff, for fast and dependable long-distance backup; Laura Sue Burstein for helping and encouraging in countless ways; and Colin Greer and Harriet Barlow, for their steady friendship and support.

— *The Editor*

Table of Contents

72 <u>making sense</u>

commentary

korean voices

who are the looters?

where's the leadership?

foreword

by Don Hazen

The explosion in Los Angeles of the most deadly and destructive riots in American history was almost a relief.

The riots were frightening and tragic, but they gave expression to years of pent-up frustration and anger about decades of forced urban decay, steady increases in poverty, a growing exodus of jobs as corporations have fled south in search of cheap labor, enormous cutbacks in every kind in government support and exponential increases in homelessness and violence. As one San Francisco looter explained, "The denial in this country about what is going on is so deep....The LA riots convinced me I was not nuts."

As the nation struggled to understand the explosion, exceptionally powerful reporting streamed out of the alternative and independent press. Most Americans viewed the riots from the perspective of news helicopters, disconnected from both what was happening on the ground and the actual causes of the unrest. In sharp contrast, the writing that emerged in dozens of regional newspapers and news-weeklies gave voice to people in the streets, put readers face-to-face with the anger and exhilaration of the rebellion and examined the real social and political causes of what took place.

This book was conceived when it became apparent that the mosaic of articles, when put together, offered a strong and moving representation of the Los Angeles story. We've published this book in six weeks to ensure that there continues to be an alternative view to the increasingly accepted official story — a version that, as writer Mike Davis observes, dismisses the riots as the mere expression of "black anger over the King decision hijacked by hard-core street criminals and transformed into a maddened assault on their own community." The truth of the riots is of course far more complex — and this book, through the perspectives of more than 60 journalists, writers and activists, offers a range of outlooks that provides a far more comprehensive view of events in LA and across the country.

Inside the LA Riots moves from the para-military world of the LAPD to the swap meets and immigrant enclaves of Koreatown. It examines the way South Central has been deliberately abandoned and written off by banks, corporations, social-service agencies and even one of its own representatives, Mayor Tom Bradley. It also looks at urban powder kegs in other parts of the country, including Atlanta, home of Martin Luther King, Jr.; Seattle, one of the country's seemingly model cities; and Las Vegas, where rioting for at least four consecutive weekends after the LA uprising offered powerful testimony to the frustrations of those in a boom-town who have been left out.

As in Las Vegas, where the media downplayed the disturbances, the mainstream press and the way it has shaped perceptions of the riots is a vital part of the LA story. The aim of the Institute for Alternative Journalism, publisher of this book, is to give voice to the ideas and opinions of those not otherwise being heard. Like the alternative press itself, it attempts to ensure that broad debate, representing a range of independent voices, continues to take place in this democracy.

The message of this book is clear. Calculated, cynical and well thought-out policies produced the LA riots; and these policies have set the stage for more eruptions as our cities continue to starve. There is little evidence that any of this year's presidential candidates possesses the commitment or the ideas necessary for genuine solutions to urban despair, though Bill Clinton shows signs of trying. At the moment, today's city-dwellers simply do not figure in any mainsteam political equation.

But the outlook is not completely dark. As we go to press, the Crips and Bloods remain at peace, police reform has been approved in Los Angeles and Daryl Gates has finally left the LAPD. This book ends with two visions: One, in the eloquent voice of Jesse Jackson, offers a plan to transform American cities, using the traditional arena of electoral politics. The other, outlined by Michael Ventura, argues that depending on voting in the hope of change indulges what he calls "a socially schizophrenic state of mind that allows one to vote for people in the hope they will behave as they have never behaved." Ventura urges a return to the politics of direct action: breaking down racial and economic barriers, working with neighbors, risking arrests to shape policy agendas. "History teaches over and over that government only changes when the people make it change," he writes. "And they usually have to get out in the streets to do it."

Though rarely covered by the mainstream media, such community-organizing efforts are already underway throughout the U.S., as neighborhoods band together across traditional lines of race and class to fight for better environmental, educational, housing and health conditions. As the riots abundantly demonstrated, if we want change, we're going to have to bring it about ourselves. ∎

Don Hazen is executive director of the Institute for Alternative Journalism.

introduction

by Kit Rachlis

What happened in a Ventura County courthouse and the streets of Los Angeles last week was a tragedy on a massive scale. And it should not have surprised anyone.

For 36 hours, the city was out of control. The social bonds that tie most of us together, as well as keep us apart, broke loose. This was neither the romantic uprising that some leftists have dreamed about nor the venal anarchy reactionaries have always feared. The Los Angeles riots contained both these elements — and considerably more. Fear, criminality, desire, horror, hope, nihilism, retribution, paranoia and need raced through the city, and took on a life — a pathology — of their own. The lid blew.

If you wanted, you could trace the source of that explosion to the arrival of the first slave ship, or to the failure of the Constitutional Convention to abolish slavery, or to 12 years of Reagan and Bush race-baiting, or to the Simi Valley jury that didn't just acquit four LAPD officers but sanctioned their behavior. Whatever line you draw, it arrives at the same point: American politics failed once again when it comes to race.

American history doesn't excuse the beating of Reginald Denny any more than it does the clubbing of Rodney King. It doesn't excuse the criminal contempt of Daryl Gates or the dazed paralysis of Tom Bradley. It doesn't excuse the economic devastation left by some of the country's largest corporations — Goodyear, Ford, Max Factor, others — when they abandoned LA during the last recession. But history, expressed as collective trauma, consumed a city that has made a fetish of escaping it.

What follows in these pages is not so much an attempt to write that history as an attempt to keep up with it. Taken as a whole, the articles in this anthology are full of loose ends and sharp opinions, shared experiences and private images. The pieces elbow one another aside and link arms; they reflect a common vision and deviate sharply from it. What they share is an insistence that there is no such thing as a single version of the riots, certainly not one that can be expressed in an institutional voice. Because what happened in Los Angeles cannot be contained — not yet, at least, and maybe not ever.

Why add to the flood of footage, soundbites and column-inches that have all but reduced the LA riots to just another media blip? For most Americans, not just the citizens of LA, the riots evoked intensely personal responses. The alternative press in this country remains one of the few journalistic venues where the subjective can not only express itself but is encouraged to do so: where ideas and opinions are not modulated into authoritative journalese. Reading the pieces in this collection, you get a sense of specific people having specific, complex — often contradictory — and intense reactions. By not claiming to speak for anyone but themselves, they're capable of speaking for all of us.

But the alternative press has another strength: an insistence that all events have a context, a public meaning, that can be teased out, examined and questioned. And that it is the reporter's — not the columnist's, not the editorialist's — job to suggest what that meaning might be. This is not the same as saying that everything is political, but that politics — that civic life — matters. That the decline of LA's industrial base, the departure of the black middle class from Watts, Proposition 13, Korean and Salvadoran immigration, the irregular distribution of federal funds, the LAPD's long history of racism, an overcrowded and underfunded school system — that all of these things affect one another. And that they shape those of us who live in Los Angeles and those who don't.

Like the alternative press itself, this anthology makes demands: that you supply your own context, make your own observations, arrive at your own opinions. And, most important, whatever your conclusions are, that you act on them. ■

Kit Rachlis is editor-in-chief of the LA Weekly.

the roots of conflict in LA: the real story

LA's State of Siege
City of Angels, Cops from Hell

by Marc Cooper

The city that the Los Angeles Police Department cruises has little to do with the bubble-gum colors, snake-haired blonds on roller skates and palm-tree sensibilities of Steve Martin's *LA Story*. With the city spanning 450 square miles (only a seventh of the entire urbanized metro area) and crossed by more than 500 miles of in-town freeway, the sunny, open public spaces of the past have been "containerized" into covered malls, corporate refuges and upscale cultural enclaves. The cross-pollenization of races found in other big-city public transportation systems doesn't happen in LA — we have no such network.

In white Los Angeles, there is an inbred fear of the crowd. Because the crowd, in a city where whites ceased to be a majority in the 1980s, is colored. And if it's colored, the city logic continues, it is poor. And, if poor, it must be dangerous.

Whites have abandoned the city's world-class parks as Latino families have come in to hold piñata parties. Dockweiler Beach, the only stretch of sand in LA county that permits open-fire barbecues, has been ceded to blacks and Latinos. White teenagers who live a straight-line 10-minute drive from the seashore will travel an extra 40 minutes to bask in the color-free sands of Malibu and Zuma. The 10 square blocks of restaurants and cinemas of Westwood "Village" adjacent to the affluent UCLA campus — the *only* pocket of Los Angeles with significant night-time foot traffic — is now considered a "rough" area because of the influx of black teens on the weekends.

Among 252 American cities analyzed by a recent University of Chicago study, Los Angeles was classified as "hyper-segregated." But segregation in this city is a function not only of race and the centerless geography, but also of social class. A new apartment complex in the suburban San Fernando Valley, one with a tenants' waiting list, boasts that it is connected by an underground tunnel to the Sherman Oaks Galleria mall, so "you never have to leave your apartment." From the airport-tram stops to the art museum gardens, most of LA's benches have been "bum-proofed," usually by making the seat round as a barrel, OK to sit on but impossible to lie on. Timed sprinkler systems scatter the city's 50,000 homeless from the few remaining public lawns, as well as from the doorways of chi-chi commerce.

"Los Angeles as a matter of deliberate policy has fewer available public lavatories than any major North American city," writes social historian Mike Davis in his *City of Quartz*. "On the advice of the LAPD, the Community Redevelopment Agency bulldozed the remaining public toilet in Skid Row....The toiletless no-man's land east of Hill Street in Downtown is also barren of outside water sources for drinking or washing. A common sight these days are the homeless men — many of them young Salvadorean refugees — washing in and even drinking from the sewer effluent which flows down the concrete channel of the Los Angeles River."

In the flinty eyes of the LAPD and the economically secure minority that cowers behind it, not only have open space and

Los Angeles: Ted Soqui

— God forbid — crowds become criminalized, but so have individual pedestrians and rogue motorists. If you're not tucked away in a fluorescent-lit office or security-gated condo complex, the cops want to know what you're doing out on the street.

The overwhelming majority of LAPD officers are white. Most are first- or second-generation immigrants from the South and Midwest. They look at the city they police today and they see it as a formidable, threatening, unpredictable, *foreign* land. They shake their heads in disbelief — and often in open disgust — at a city in which 60 percent of the kindergarten classes have Spanish as a first language; where the largest single racial group among UCLA freshmen is Asians; and where the most common name given to a male child born last year was "José." The LAPD had been making nationwide prime time for decades before the Rodney King video exploded into the country's living rooms: *Dragnet, Adam 12, Starsky and Hutch, S.W.A.T.* and even the doddering *Columbo* were based on the same depart-

ment, now run by Chief Daryl Gates. But as three baseball teams' worth of cops, 21 of them LAPD, swarmed in and systematically fractured Rodney King's cranium, ankles and arms, as they targeted his kidneys for dozens of blows from their two-foot-long solid aluminum Monadnock PR-24 batons, as they stomped and kicked him face down on the ground, while all the time the supervising officer took care not to break the two Taser wires that had each carried a 50,000-volt charge into King's body and were now dug into him like harpoons, millions of horrified viewers may have wondered what ever happened to those two nice clean-cut young men in Sears Roebuck suits, Sergeant Joe Friday and his sidekick, Officer Frank Smith.

But for those of us who were raised and live in this city — at least for those among us who cared not to sleepwalk through the last 30 years — the Rodney King beating is not the aberration Chief Gates claims it is, no loopy, David Lynch-like spin-off of Jack Webb's old black-and-white series. No way. Indeed, the pictures of white LAPD cops taking batting practice on King's black body are, for us, nothing but the outtakes from *Dragnet.*

Long before anyone had heard of Rodney King, our houses shook and dogs barked as squadrons of French-made LAPD helicopter gunships buzzed our neighborhoods. Thousands of our residential rooftops were painted with huge white numbers so the choppers could coordinate with computer-equipped patrol cars on the ground. Infra-red scopes mounted on the Aerospatiale helicopters could, after reading the heat signature of a single burning cigarette, guide the pilots to blind with 30-million-candlepower spotlights any lovers adventurous enough or tourists naive enough to attempt a midnight tryst on some of the most beautiful beaches in the world. Another wing of the LAPD air force, flying Bell Jet Ranger helicopters — just like the ones their U.S. counterparts fly in El Salvador — has been trained to ferry the elite SWAT troops swiftly into combat at any hot spot in the metro sprawl.

Five floors below ground level in a hardened bunker, the world's most advanced police communication network — the ECCCS, employing NASA-devel-

oped absolute-secure digital transmissions — links the LAPD command structure with mushrooming databases that keep tabs on an ever-growing, ever-more-suspect, ever-less-white metro population. Those who engaged in opposition politics during the Reagan era, those who (like myself) wrote about those activities, and even city councilmembers whose job it was to oversee the LAPD have found their names illegally gathered and coded in the files of the now-disbanded Public Disorder and Intelligence Division (PDID) — computerized information that was freely shared with ultra-right East Coast political lobbies. In the aftermath of the King beating, the few LAPD officers — all of them black — who had dared publicly to criticize Chief Daryl Gates were convinced that they were not only being followed by PDID's successor, the shadowy Anti-Terrorist Division, but that their cars were being vandalized by ATD operatives.

Our children regularly encounter LAPD officers in their classrooms as part of the so-called DARE anti-drug program. There kids learn of the ills of marijuana, coke and crack, often years before they've heard of the drugs themselves. As part of its "war" on crime — or maybe its "war" on drugs, or "war" on gangs — LAPD units routinely barricade off whole residential blocks, always in minority communities, and set up check points to search and question every motorist and pedestrian unlucky enough to wander into the newly designated "narcotics enforcement area."

While the media and the city administration ride the political horse of anti-gang hysteria, spurred by neighborhood house meetings addressed by police experts on "narco-terrorism," the LAPD's troop strength (and "troops" is the word used by the police themselves) has grown nearly 30 percent in just the last five years. While city social services shrivel, the LAPD budget balloons.

Unlike the cops in many big American cities, the LAPD has yet to surrender, remaining as fixed and committed to its steely vision of law and order as were those two blue-eyed virtuous rookies on *Adam 12.* This is a department that not only regularly beats the stuffing out of wise-ass car-chase suspects, it also floods the county court's office with Latinos picked up for drinking beer on their own front porches (a violation of the city's open container statute). It's a force that, along with county and local police departments, not only has racked up hundreds of police shootings in the last two decades, but every year takes the time to write more than 5,000 jaywalking tickets in a city where the nearest crosswalk can be three blocks away. In a single day it can "jack up" and sweep as many as 1,500 teenage "hoodlums" into holding cells and still have the energy to bust a ring of dart throwers caught making $5 bets *and* apprehend suburban housewife scofflaws who are feeding the jackpot kitty in their morning bowling league. We are talking the Mother of All Police Departments. Relatively free of corruption, strikingly efficient and aggressive compared with other metro forces, the LAPD uses the firepower of a mid-sized modern army to pry open the nooks and crannies of what it sees as a rotting civilization.

But it's a police force that, at least until the King tape became the most popular of America's Grimmest Home Videos, existed independent of any civilian or political control or scrutiny. While the city annually paid out $11,000 in damage suits against the LAPD 20 years ago, last year it shoveled more than $11.3 *million* into the hands of brutalized citizens. Police misconduct lawyers report more than 600 calls a year arising from run-ins with the LAPD. This reputation is as far-flung as any cop show rerun: While living in Europe in the 1970s, I can remember reading a stern warning in a French travel guide that went something like this: "The LAPD should not be confused with the Bobbies. Do not approach them on the street to ask for information or directions. Call upon them only in case of emergency."

In a city increasingly cleaved between rich and poor, white and non-white, between sparkling new Mercedes-Benzes and '74 Chevies, between $30-million mini-mansions and $600-a-month roach-infested apartments, the white minority that continues to exercise a monopoly over political power (with a compliant black mayor in office) asks few questions of the 8,300 cops charged with upholding civilization. The faceless, non-white,

increasingly foreign-born, ever-more-desperate underclass, in the wake of Reaganomics and the white-led taxpayers' revolt of Proposition 13, has been virtually abandoned by every arm of the state, be it local, regional or national. Proposition 13 was a clear message that the only public service that would be freely offered to minority communities was a shit-kicking police department to keep the lid on.

"The Rodney King beating is a watershed in the city's history," a Los Angeles-area cop-turned-writer said recently. "But not the way people think. A watershed not in revealing police brutality, but a historic turning point in the city's having to face the one problem it never does: race."

The South Central ghetto that runs the 20 miles from the Civic Center through Watts and Compton to dead-end at Los Angeles's garish post-industrial harbor has little, visually, in common with Harlem, Bed-Stuy or even Boston's Roxbury. There's plenty of gang graffiti on the walls and fences, but behind those barriers are fairly well-kept rows of single-family homes, with green lawns and trimmed hedges, far from the tenebrous tenements of the East Coast.

True, South Central spreads itself out on a plain of dense metropolitan flatlands in a city where residential prestige is associated with canyons, hillsides and beachfronts. But there are palms and gardens here, and even a few parks. One neighborhood, packed with post-war apartments backed by swimming pools set among banana trees and ferns, was lush enough to have been called "the Jungle."

But to the older LA police officers who grew up in the near-rural, all-white suburbs of the city, and to the recruits from Kansas lured to the force by $40,000 salaries, South Central is an exotic, harrowing, terrifying land inhabited by unruly natives. Today the cops still call that street of apartments "the Jungle," but not for its now-tattered tropical landscape. The Jungle today is the capital of West Coast crack traffic. "It's 'the Jungle,'" as one cop told the *LA Times*, "because that's where the jungle bunnies live." Or, as the police wisecracked on the night of the Rodney King

beating, "gorillas in the mist."

The economic devastation of this community, its badge of segregation from mainstream Los Angeles, manifests itself in the so-called commercial district. Its main artery, Central Avenue, which in the '40s cradled a raucous music scene (till the LAPD cracked down on multiracial night clubs) and in the '60s housed the headquarters of the Black Panthers (till the LAPD inaugurated its SWAT team by dynamiting off the Panthers' roof in a 1969 shoot-up) is today a seemingly endless road to nowhere. The stores that aren't boarded up are imprisoned behind iron bars. Used appliance stores, dingy pawn shops and, most of all, liquor marts — increasingly owned by Koreans — dominate.

Latinos have recently moved into what was a solidly black domain, attracting a few *pañaderavas* and *carniceravas*, but here there are none of the supermarkets, department stores or strip malls that clutter and entice the rest of the city. Even gas stations are scarce. The handful of businesses that have truly valuable merchandise on the premises — auto parts stores and used car lots — are protected not only with bars but also with the same coils of lethal razor wire used by Guatemalan oligarchs around the perimeters of their estates.

Almost half the black families that live in the ghetto flatlands fall below the poverty line. On a per capita basis, *less* government money has been spent on social services and job training in this part of the city than on the affluent, white Westside.

Against this background, along with the migration of well-paying manufacturing jobs to Mexico and Asia thanks to the "trickle-down" economic policies of conservative city, state and national administrations, LA's youth gang culture has grown into one of the most resilient in the Western Hemisphere. Estimates of youth gang membership in LA county range from a low of 10,000 to 10 times that amount, the most common figure being 70,000. What is certain is that an average of two gang-related murders a day take place in LA county.

The Cain Street Crips favor aquamarine Dodgers' caps. The Watts Grape Street Crips are into Lakers purple. The 118th Street East Coast Crips wax nostalgic in their Yankees hats. The Lime Avenue Bloods show off Celtics green.

The gang they have as a common enemy wears dark blue: the select units of the LAPD division known as CRASH (Community Resources Against Street Hoodlums). After a Japanese-American woman (LA's "most acceptable minority") was mistakenly killed by gunshots from a black gang in the predominantly white Westwood area in late 1988, cries for a crackdown on gangs issued forth from that neighborhood's liberal white city councilman. Within weeks, the LAPD, led by its CRASH division and under the banner of Operation Hammer, mounted full-scale retaliatory raids on the black community. In April 1988, 1,000 extra cops were sent into South Central, and in a single night they rounded up 1,453 black and Latino teenagers. Since then a state of siege has persisted in South Central, where each night — and often during the day — any teenager on the street is fair game for an

Los Angeles: Cynthia Wiggins

LAPD roust, "jack-up" or bust. An astonishing total of more than 50,000 youths have been detained in Operation Hammer's ongoing maneuvers. And, much like the tactics used by General Pinochet's militarized police as they rampage through politically unreliable shantytowns in Chile, up to 90 percent of the victims of Operation Hammer are released without charge — having been arrested in the first place as an act of sheer intimidation.

"The black community is under siege from the fall-out of racism, gangs, drugs and violence," says a 40-year-old black man I'll call William, an aide to an elected black official. "I *need* a protector. But if I'm walking down the street and see some gang-bangers on the one side and an LAPD

car on the other, I'm not really sure which group I'm more afraid of. But actually, I feel more threatened by the police. The gangs see me as a tall, powerfully built foe. To the cops, I'm one more nigger."

William, dressed in a three-piece suit, walks me through the Crenshaw Mall, the *only* full-scale enclosed mall in urban black America. Refurbished in the mid-'80s with city funds handed over to one of Mayor Bradley's white campaign contributors, the mall has an entire substation of the LAPD built into it. Even that was not enough to attract national retail chains, and today the shopping center is nearly empty.

"The LAPD now exercises authority to stop any black person in this community and subject them to any threat with

total impunity," William continues. "I mostly get stopped in white neighborhoods, twice last year. Let me tell you, I have been hassled by cops so many times that when I get stopped now, I shuffle, I shuck and jive! Those dudes are asshole motherfuckers. They *want* you to give them a reason to kill you. I may be 6-foot, 5-inches and 240 pounds, but when I get pulled over by the LAPD it is all "Yes-suh, no-suh, how-high-you-want-me-to-jump-suh?"

In the wake of the Watts riots and the black power movement, today's generation of black youth has assimilated rebellion. "It's an attitude that comes smack up against the torqued-down opportunities of Reaganomics," William argues. "It means we are now engaged in a day-to-day confrontation with the power structure. A confrontation we don't have the power to win." Black youth, he says, "will no longer do stoop labor, it wants the same opportunities that other immigrant populations that have been here seven, eight or nine generations have. Black folks no longer want to do what white folks want them to do to get ahead. We are not going to get up any more at 6 a.m. and put on a uniform for McDonald's. So how else do our youth achieve a sense of power without submitting to the rule of white society, other than by becoming outlaws? And that's where we meet the police."

In normal times, the LAPD operates under a code of silence. Reporters are viewed askance, as a mutant species akin to ACLU lawyers. And since the Rodney King beating became public, a siege mentality among the LAPD has almost hermetically sealed its members off from the press. But after an ironclad shield of anonymity was hammered out and guaranteed through mutual friendships, three veteran LAPD officers agreed to "give their side of the story of what it means to be an LA cop."

The three officers I spoke with are highly representative of the guts-and-glue core of the LAPD. All born to working-class families in Los Angeles, all white, all army veterans, all with more than 20 years on the job, all in their early to mid-forties, all members of an elite detail with city-wide jurisdiction, they are the typical "training officers" — the men who hone and shape incoming rookies, who in the privacy of the patrol car pass on the attitudes and rites from one generation of cop to the next, the men who will be there long after Gates is gone. For nearly three hours in the corner of a restaurant on the edge of downtown, for the first time since the Rodney King scandal unfolded, a group of LAPD officers spoke freely, for publication, with a reporter.

JACK: *I feel sad about LA. I feel we lost LA.*

GREG: *We at least used to have the mystique of Hollywood. Now you go up to the boulevard and you got the whores, the female impersonators, every runaway in the world.*

JACK: *We've had an influx of tens of thousands of illegal aliens who contribute something to the economy, I guess, but also clog it up. Take North Hollywood. Five years ago it wasn't a bad place to live. Now there are 20 illegals on each corner waiting around for a job. This open-border policy has got to go. We are getting all the world's rotten apples.*

GREG: *The hotel is full. Time to put out the no-vacancy sign. Too many people here. Too many of the wrong people.*

DOUG: *Yeah. You want to go downtown for a movie or play, OK. But getting there is the problem. I mean you're in the car, with your wife, and here are all these wetbacks everywhere peeing all over the buildings, drinking beer, throwing shit all around. To me LA is a place where I come to do a job and then go home where I can be safe.*

[As is the case with almost the entire LAPD, Doug, Greg and Jack live not only outside of the city, but outside of Los Angeles County — as far as a two-hour commute each way.]

DOUG: *I was raised like these two other guys here. Not from rich families. But you wanted something, you bought it, not stole it. The values we learned have turned to shit or are turning to shit because of the alien problem. They are going to ruin this city without a doubt. Economically, crime-wise, every which way. Two out of three people we stop are aliens. Drive 20 miles through this city and stop people at random, you won't find too many who can even speak English.*

MARC COOPER: *What do you feel when you work in the South Central section of the city, where the population is mostly black and Latino?*

JACK: *Fear and excitement. Life down there is very cheap. People are dying there while we are sitting here talking. One police division out of 18 in the city has more murders per year than all of England. Life's cheap. So there's a good chance there you'll get in a gunfight, see some violence.*

GREG: *It's really us against them. Not against blacks, really. But there is a lot of crime down there. You look at the guy on the corner and you know he's not working, he's waiting to rip off a purse. You got the dope dealers there in their nice cars.*

JACK: *The feeling we get from down there is what anybody else gets. Except we wear the badge. What you feel against you is hate. They hate us.*

DOUG: *The people committing the crimes hate us. And the good people don't understand us either. They don't understand what real life is about. They sit back and watch those [Rodney King beating] tapes and say, 'Isn't that just awful.' But is it really?*

JACK: *I'm not a sociologist, but the problem down there is no family structure. You see children having children with no fucking idea who the father is. In the black communities all the kids have different last names. All the mothers have six, eight kids and no fucking idea where they are. And they couldn't give a damn because they are too busy pumping out another kid. Picking up the government check. Every Cadillac and Mercedes you stop in the south end of town has food stamps in the glove box. They're on welfare and we're out here driving Volkswagens while they're driving Bentleys. I mean I saw a policeman dying in a car wreck once in the south end of town. Every resident and neighbor was out there while the paramedics were trying to give him CPR. But when he expired at the scene, the entire crowd cheered, clapped, whistled when they put the blanket over his head. This makes you cynical, bitter, makes you see life for what it is. Makes you see you are seen as the enemy down there. Makes you*

see maybe we really are an occupying force. When you clap when someone dies, to me that's not even a human being. You see the parents doing it and the kids watching and it makes you sick, pisses you off.

JACK: *Rodney King? Some dirty son of a bitch that was supposed to get two years and instead got six months. This whole thing shows you why people say it's us against them. Suddenly, there's an opening to take shots at the police and now everyone and his brother is a fucking expert on the police. No one gives a shit about the police officers. Everyone in America is against them! Bury them! They're gone, dead, fucked! But everyone knows Rodney King. Why don't the newspapers run the criminal records of the two guys who were riding with him? Lengthy records, I'm sure. No one knows the name of Russ Custer, a cop blown away by an illegal alien. But they know Rodney King. That's what makes it us against them. I hate to even say Rodney King's name.*

GREG: *We don't condone what happened out there, overkill.*

JACK: *It was a tragedy.*

GREG: *Definite overkill.*

DOUG: *From what I've seen on this job, I would venture to say that King and his buddies that night did some crime and we just haven't found the victim yet. No doubt in my mind, those guys weren't driving around just to be driving around at three o'clock in the morning. They were looking for a crime to do or coming back from one.*

JACK: *Too bad there's no audio portion on that tape. It's not as simple as it looks on tape.*

DOUG: *I think King wasn't doing what he was being told to do. They teach us to make people do what you tell them. If they don't, you escalate. Like they took the choke-hold away from us because a few people died. If we had the choke-hold, what you saw would have never happened.*

JACK: *That was the most humane way to put a guy out. You choke 'em out. Once you don't have that, your only option is to beat 'em. Maybe they beat him too long. According to the film, it looks like they did. Whatever. But if he's not complying with orders and he might have a gun or knife in his waistband or something, hey, you know.*

COOPER: *What do you think was running through the minds of the Foothill division cops who chased and beat King?*

JACK: *You chase a guy at high speeds in the night like that, it's like someone has a gun to your head and says, "I'm gonna kill you." Then he presses the trigger and it's empty. You're still going to beat the shit out of him anyway because he scared you to death. Like Saddam Hussein scared the shit out of us with chemical weapons and even though it turned out he didn't use the gas, we still made him pay the price. Same with Rodney King. You got to chase him through red lights not knowing if you are going to crash and then he gets out of the car dancing and strutting, not acting normal. And you say, yep, PCP. This is what went through the officers' heads. I can't condone what they did, but I know what I would have felt after the chase myself. Sad part of it is some of those young cops are going to go to jail.*

Fifty miles northwest of the LAPD's downtown Parker Center slumbers the glorified desert truck stop known as Castaic — home to Sergeant Stacey Koon, the supervising officer at the scene of the King beating and one of the four cops indicted on felony charges because of it. Numerous other LAPD officers live out here, as well in even more remote hamlets up the road toward Bakersfield. The mailing list of LAPD personnel is kept secret, for security reasons, but as many as 90 percent or more of the force is thought to live outside the city it is paid to police.

But in LA, there are no equivalents of Queens or Yonkers. Rather, a one- or two-hour drive away, in the desert or mountains — not in suburbs, nor even in what we have come to call "bedroom communities," but in that peculiarly Southern California-type cantonment known as "housing developments" — live most of the members of the LAPD. Spiritless, soulless, pre-fabricated neighborhoods with no history, not even an immediate identity beyond the huge signs that announce: "3 Bedrooms — 2 Baths — Security Gate — $119,000!"

Along a dusty half-mile stretch of access road along Interstate 5, the entirety of the Castaic business community sits as if at one big National Franchise Expo: a McDonald's, a 7-Eleven, a Del Taco, a Fosters Freeze and two chain motels. A single strip mall is the only reminder of urban life, and it's an hour away down the highway. At its center is a CB Supply store with a faded Confederate Stars and Bars hanging over the doorway.

Not much chance of any blacks living here. Or Latinos. Or Jews, for that matter.

On the hill above the mall are three residential developments, all filled with Spielbergian tract homes on loan from the E.T. set, all identical, all the same sandstone color, most with garages that serve as Saturday workshops. There's an extraordinary number with small boats in the driveways (I counted 13 in a quarter-mile).

Venice: Larry Hirshowitz

This is cop utopia. No minorities, no gangs, no crime (except for an occasional trucker's dust-up at the Country Girl Saloon) — "a great place to raise kids," as they say. A perfectly ordered uniformity and predictability. A whole town of compliance, if you will. Safely distant from the dystopia of the daily beat and its deviants, perverts, criminals and aliens, desert towns like Castaic are a perfect incubator for the LAPD's closed police culture.

"The problem with the LAPD is they recruit from the outside. All cops hate the city. But when you come from the outside in the first place, you *never* stop hating it. Who can be surprised, then, that these guys all live as far away as they can?" says former New York PD narcotics officer Bob Leuci, the celebrated "Prince of the City."

Another ex-NYPD officer, James Fyfe, now a professor at American University and a national expert on law-enforcement agencies, calls the LAPD a "closed society" of "rigid men of steel...a local variant of the FBI, with all of the same good and bad points. The LAPD is a national model for modern urban police departments, an aggressive, legalistic policing that allows the individual officer little personal discretion in the field. He merely follows an impersonal policy. That's why you can't talk your way out of a jam with the LAPD."

A certain dehumanization of the civilian, the potential enemy, festers inside the police culture. As American GIs went off to fight successive wars against "Gerries, Japs, Slopeheads, Gooks and Ragheads," the LAPD's "soldiers" have carried on

their war against "assholes." You can see the first glimmers of it in the old reruns of Sergeant Friday, who already, decades ago, was quick to demonstrate his Just-the-Facts-Ma'am impatience with his all-white interviewees; though they were all either innocent victims of crime or witnesses to it, Sergeant Friday would grimace and strain, barely tolerating their jabbering tomfoolery. They were, after all, just civilians. Or, in the officially unofficial locker-room lexicon of the boys in blue, mere "assholes."

"Burglars and rapists aren't necessarily 'assholes' in the eye of the LAPD," says Fyfe. "An asshole is a person who does not accept whatever the police officer's definition is of any situation. Cops expect everyone, including a stopped motorist, to be subservient. Any challenge — or the mortal sin of talking back — and you become an 'asshole.' And 'assholes' are to be re-educated so they don't mouth off again. The real cases of brutality come in the cases of 'assholes.' Cops don't beat up burglars. Last week I had a talk with a 25-year veteran of the LAPD who says he knows of no car chase that didn't end with the cops beating up the motorist once he was caught."

DOUG: *Yeah, in Houston they call 'em turds. In New York I think it's shitbird. Here we call them 'assholes.'*

JACK: *A good officer can weed out an asshole from the common citizen, say a white guy is working in a black area. If he's treated nice by a black person he'll come on back to him overly nice, because it's so rare you get treated nice down there.*

DOUG: *We treat people the way they treat us. Frankly there aren't a whole lot of cops* who feel much compassion anymore for some guy just because he's in a shitty situation. You just say, 'Hey, another asshole.'

DOUG: *That's why like 98 percent of the guys live outside the city. Not just that housing is cheaper and that you want your kids out of the LA schools where there's so much violence. You don't want to go to the grocery store and be in the checkout line standing next to the same asshole you arrested the night before. You just want to get in your car and get away from the shit you've seen all day, from the city where everyone thinks we are the assholes!*

GREG: *I remember a class at the academy some 20-odd years ago where the instructor says, 'Within a few years, you guys, your only friends are gonna be cops.' Everyone laughs and says bullshit. But you know, he was right.*

JACK: *The businessmen don't like you, the poor Hispanic doesn't like you, the blacks don't like you. So you retreat into a cave full of policemen, where you are understood. Where you can sit around and say, 'Hey, I saw an asshole on the corner doing such and such,' and everyone knows what you're talking about.*

DOUG: *That's right. When a guy walks into the bar you know he's an asshole, you just know it. And there are all the other assholes buying him a drink. It's a lot easier just to hang out with cops.*

JACK: *Yeah, but a lot of the overall togetherness on the job has disintegrated since I came on to the job. It's the problem with female cops, with the lowering of standards for minorities. I don't want to sound like a bigot, but when you lower the standards it's the black cop who suffers because people think he's got the job only because he's black. This has divided the department more than anything.*

DOUG: *You walk through the station nowadays, you don't say anything about females, about blacks, about whites.*

JACK: *We're not even allowed to talk about women. We can't even have a Playboy calendar on our desk. No jokes. No nothing. When I came on the job there were Polish jokes for the Polish cops, black jokes for the blacks cops, and everyone was still your buddy. That was the best part of the job. And you'd die for those other guys.*

GREG: *It's not just LA. It's the whole country. Now we have got to hire women, women who can't pass the physical tests.*

DOUG: *I resent the women.*

JACK: *Me, too. And he who pays in the long run is the citizen. Because you got a female [in a police] car and it's a non-working car. Money down the drain. There's been more shootings now by female officers*

because they are plain scared and can't handle the suspect any other way except to blow him away. Some guy you'd ordinarily get down with a nightstick, and now he's dead just because he got drunk. Not to say this about Hispanics, but you know Saturday nights are a ritual for them. They like to have parties and receptions and you know when the cops come you better get ready for a fight, nine times out of 10. When you work East LA that's just part of the game. One of those guys walks up drunk to a five-foot female, she's just gonna shoot because she knows there's no way to restrain him.

Newcomers to LA tend to equate the Westside of the city with the "white" part of the metropolis. Though it's a cliché, being white in Los Angeles is every bit as much a state of mind as it is a place of residence. There are, indeed, a few all-white neighborhoods, and they are for the most part (but not exclusively) on the Westside.

But the explosive growth of the city and the influx of immigrants from all social classes has hit like a blockbusting rain. The San Fernando Valley, for example, a 75-percent-white refuge 10 years ago, today is 42 percent minority.

As Angelenos of color overflow the traditional boundaries of the ghettos and seep into historically white enclaves, the Anglo population has been circling its wagons in ever-smaller, ever-more-checkerboard pockets of racial homogeneity. The white middle class, and, more accurately, the middle class of all colors, hangs on to its identity — and to its property values — by subdividing, remapping, chopping and splicing together wholly imaginary "communities." Their tools: simple two-by-five-foot blue-and-white "town" signs provided by the city Department of Transportation. Allow this example: When too many Salvadorans and Mexicans moved into the Los Angeles neighborhood known as Canoga Park, the better-off, mostly white homeowners on the western fringe of the area petitioned their councilmember to allow them to secede and form a new "community" called West Hills. With one phone call from the councilmember's office, the new — better — community was

born when a half-dozen of the Department of Transportation signs were posted around the newly delineated perimeter. Now, since everyone involved still lives in the city of Los Angeles, nothing had really changed — except West Hills property values doubled overnight.

That's People Power, LA-style. White, affluent, militantly organized homeowners. And while they might vote Democratic, and while on the Westside they are markedly "liberal," they are, nevertheless, pungently redolent of White Citizens Councils. These groups form the foundation of support for the LAPD.

JACK: *Chief Gates is a good administrator but let's just say he ain't no Norman Schwarzkopf out there leading the LAPD troops. The upper echelon of the LAPD has never had better troops in the street, but they live different lives than us. They don't even know our names.*

GREG: *They could bring another chief in tomorrow and to most guys it would just mean hearing a new name.*

COOPER: *So no big deal if Gates goes in the next few weeks?*

JACK: *I didn't say that! That would be very demoralizing. He goes and we get an NYPD here. To us, New York cops just show up for their paycheck and don't give a shit. All bullshitting aside, here in LA we go after criminals. And Gates did come up through the ranks, just like us, so in that way we do respect him.*

DOUG: *The main thing about Gates is that he's not Tom Bradley. Say what you want about Gates, but he's an honest man and Bradley isn't.*

GREG: *I think Bradley's dishonest. He took money from banks and claimed he didn't know what it was for. Come on! And he's going to investigate us? Now we got the FBI investigating 243 cops. I'm insulted. The asshole in the street — here we are back to assholes! — he's got more rights than we do. We can go up to the asshole and say, 'Hey, we want to talk to you' and they can say, 'Hey, fuck you.' He's got that right. But now they tell us the FBI can walk right into my house, in front of my wife, and interview me, and if I refuse, I can lose my job. It's just not right.*

GREG: *You want to fix this city? I say you start out with carpet-bombing, level some buildings, plow all this shit under and start all over again.*

JACK: *Christ, you'd drop a bomb on a community?*

DOUG: *Oh yeah, there'd be some innocent*

people, but not that many. There's just some areas of LA that can't be saved. And you are restricted by so many laws. Let me give a for instance. Say 20 years ago, every night I would put a lot of people in jail for not having their green cards. A lot of people.

GREG: *Yeah, we all did, it was a felony.*

JACK: *Take 'em right to immigration and right back on the bus to Mexico.*

DOUG: *Then we get a letter from some commander saying we can't do that any more. Now see what we got.*

JACK: *Actually anything that gets close to the answer would make this place look damn near like Nazi Germany. I don't think we are ever going to get there and I'm not sure I'd want to see it. But if you want to start with solutions, then I think birth control is a big part of the answer. The Catholic Church tells everyone to have babies and then these babies, when they are 16, start sniffing paint. Now I'm not talking about all the Mexicans. I'm talking about families of six kids that live on $8,000 a year and everyone is out there stealing stereos. It's a social problem. But our job is to arrest them. Anything you say along these lines is going to be construed as racism. I'm not talking racism. But I am talking about the black women having 80 percent illegitimate babies. In the black community you got Bill Cosby as the big role model. But what I see every day looks more like Sanford and Son. You say that in the newspaper, they say you are a bigot. You can't say anymore, 'Let's close the border down, let's take the army down to the border, do whatever you have to stop them,' because if you do, they say it's racism.*

When I grew up in this city there was a guy named Nick the Cop who lived in the neighborhood. He knew every one of us. Do something wrong and Nick would come up and slap you, send you home and call your folks the next day. We shit our pants whenever we saw Nick the Cop coming. But we respected him. He was a tough Mexican officer who worked by himself and if he needed to know something, he'd talk to you real nice. If you didn't tell, he'd get sterner. There were kids who stole cars and surrendered to Nick the next day because they figured he'd find out anyway. Things like that. But things like that are things of the past. ∎

Marc Cooper is the West Coast correspondent for the Village Voice, *where a version of this story first appeared.*

Los Angeles: Anne Fishbein

The Making of an American Bantustan

by Cynthia Hamilton December 30, 1988

Southward, beyond the high-rise towers of downtown Los Angeles, a symmetrical grid pattern of streets is barely discernible through the usual dim haze. These streets, stretching south to the horizon and east to west, are unknown to most white Angelenos. Crenshaw, Western, Normandie, Vermont, Hoover, Figueroa, Broadway, San Pedro, Main, Avalon, Central Hooper, Compton, Alameda, Washington, Adams, Jefferson, Vernon, Slauson, Florence, Manchester, Century, Imperial, El Segundo, Rosecrans.

These are the arteries of South Central Los Angeles. Hundreds of thousands of blacks move along these pathways daily. The fortunate go to places of employment in the metropolitan area, but for most the movement is circular, cyclical and to nowhere. These streets have become the skeletal structure of another "bantustan" in an American city — another defoliated community, manipulated and robbed of its vitality by the ever-present growth pressures of the local economy.

Los Angeles has never been an integrated community. The restrictive racial covenants of the pre-war years saw to that; the Ku Klux Klan based in Compton and Long Beach saw to it. Old timers will tell you about the days when they couldn't live south of Slauson, or they reminisce about their teenage years when it was an adventure to traverse the taunting white neighborhoods that separated the Central/

the roots of conflict in LA: the real story

Jefferson part of the black community from the black outpost in Watts. Those native to South Central have always known that blacks live south of downtown, Latinos to the east and whites on the Westside or in the Valley. In more than 40 years, this fundamental pattern has not changed.

Physically we are not talking about a "Bedford-Stuyvesant" that looks like the Warsaw Ghetto, with buildings bombed out. Rather, there is a different sort of emptiness and starkness, one caused by what appears to be a systematic pattern of displacement and removal of all the things that contribute to a livable environment and viable community. If one were to take the very long view, one would have to say that the larger society has denuded this community for the society's own long-term profitable ends. Much like the bulldozing of black encampments on the fringe of Johannesburg or Durban, it can be argued, South Central is inevitably slated by the historical process to be replaced without a trace: cleared land ready for development for a more prosperous — and probably whiter — class of people.

For the larger, unspoken malady affecting South Central stems from the idea that the land is valuable and the present tenants are not. This "bantustan," like its counterparts in South Africa, serves now only as a holding space for blacks and browns no longer of use to the larger economy. The area is simply home and neighborhood: many neighborhoods, centering around churches and schools.

These supportive environments, however, have become only a shadow of what they once were, as recently as 30 years ago. Many residents recognize the negative changes and deterioration that have taken place over the years, but the specifics are not easy to identify. People speak of it as a sort of undistinguishable malaise. "Yeah, man...things are really getting bad." Drugs, gang-bangers, homelessness, unemployment....Like the push of a bulldozer

against a shanty wall, the pressure is constant.

The housing stock in the area is older than most in the city. Forty percent of the housing, according to the United Way, was built prior to 1940; only two percent of the housing was built after 1970. The vast bulk of those who are employed must commute outside the community to work each day. For the more than 20 percent who are unemployed, survival is a function of subsistence inside the area. With no jobs, the underground economy takes over — that is, crime: theft, drugs, prostitution.

A cursory view of health conditions is equally shocking. The data on blacks in Los Angeles is consistent with the general deterioration reported for blacks around the country. The U.S. now ranks 17th in infant mortality among industrial nations. For every 1,000 births in 1986, 9.8 babies died; the mortality for black babies, by contrast, was 18.2 per thousand, and in parts of South Central the rate was 22 per thousand. South Central also suffers a higher death rate due to cancer and heart and liver diseases, as well as a higher rates of pneumonia and influenza than other parts of the city. And yet the LA County Board of Supervisors has slashed health-care budgets and closed trauma centers throughout the area.

More needful of social services than other communities because of the lack of jobs, South Central in fact gets less, and many are from agencies outside the traditional government apparatus. Basic needs are not being met by state, county or city agencies. Some sections of the Ninth District have never been visited by the Bureau of Sanitation's regular weekly trash trucks and street sweepers. This is a neighborhood where individuals and families try desperately to solve their problems alone because there is little or no help. Little for elderly grandparents tending to mentally impaired adult grandchildren, no help for the elderly or youthful handicapped as they struggle to take care of their own shopping and cleaning, no assistance for those on Social Security who spend hours on the third day of each month trying to get their checks cashed and get home safely, no help for

mothers who work and must leave their children on their own because of a lack of day care.

The explanation given — and accepted — is that conditions of severe poverty routinely plague the "underclass," a group separate from the general population and one whose problems are largely a consequence of their own cultural past and habits. "Underclass," of course, is simply the latest rationalization for the racism and neglect of the larger society. It conditions both residents of South Central and the public at large to accept government passivity, corporate hostility and citizen apathy to conditions of homelessness and unemployment. Furthermore, it prepares the population to accept repressive legislation — everything from the LAPD's regular sweeps to the mayor and police chief's order to sweep the homeless away from downtown business fronts.

Los Angeles has become the model American city. It exemplifies the corporate growth that all urban areas have sought to achieve since World War II in an effort to overcome industrial flight to the suburbs. Cities have relied on urban-renewal strategies to transform and transplant the old residential communities that in another era encircled downtown areas. Growth has become the primary concern of government.

When communities such as South Central are physically dismantled, political transformation is automatic and social justice is denied. Far more than a reference to a physical space, "community" is a source of identity, of values, of socialization, of strength; it is created and sustained by its residents. Communities therefore will not resist change and growth, if it is indigenous. If it helps to sustain, communities adjust. But alas for South Central, corporate conceptions of growth have excluded the poor — and indeed growth has been predicated on the community's eventual destruction. ∎

Cynthia Hamilton is associate professor of Pan-African studies at California State University-Los Angeles. A version of this story first appeared in the LA Weekly.

the killing of
South Central

Los Angeles: Michael Schumann/SABA

Police Power *by Joe Domanick* February 16, 1990

The raid on Dalton Avenue began on an August evening in 1988 with the whirl of a circling helicopter and the beam of its spotlight shining directly into the South Central living room of a heavyset black woman named Rhonda Moore. Startled, Moore, 24, peered outside and saw an LAPD patrol car pull up and an officer jump out with his gun drawn. "Uh-oh," she thought, "they're after someone." Then, at about 8:30, the street lights went dark.

Johnnie Mae Carter, who lived two doors down from Moore in a similar tiny duplex, was settling in to watch *Jake and the Fat Man*. The show was just getting interesting when Carter and her granddaughter, Amber Green, 15, heard some noise. As they turned, their door burst open and five or six LAPD officers, guns in hand, rushed in.

"Get up," one of them commanded. Dazed, Carter and Green were quickly handcuffed and ordered onto the floor. Carter, 60, overweight and recovering from an appendectomy, followed the officers' instructions exactly. Their voices had that tone.

The street lights going out had signaled the start of a raid by the Los Angeles Police Department on four apartments in two small buildings on a well-maintained block on Dalton Avenue not far from the Coliseum. As neighbors watched in awe, nearly 80 officers carrying guns, sledgehammers and crowbars stormed the apartments looking for drugs. Rushing through Rhonda Moore's door, police began kicking her, while a visiting friend named Tommy was knocked to the floor, handcuffed, and then thrown like a cord of wood through the open door and onto Moore's brown, parched front lawn.

Carter and her granddaughter, mean-

while, were led outside and ordered to sit on the stoop. Their lawn, like Moore's, was already overflowing with residents of the raided apartments and with passers-by randomly netted by the police. Most had been handcuffed and were now lying facedown where they'd been thrown. One was Carter's son, Raymond, 21, who'd been dragged from his car with his four- and five-year-old nephews as they returned home with pizza. Crying, they ran to their grandmother, who could do nothing but tell them to hush.

Among those manacled on Rhonda Moore's lawn was her upstairs neighbor Gloria Flowers, who'd been grabbed naked from her bathtub by onrushing police while her young children watched. Clothed now, she was lying not far from Carl DeLoach, a passer-by whom Moore and her sister particularly noted because the police had "kicked in his mouth so much that there was just blood all around him."

For the first half-hour, Carter was conscious of what was taking place. Then, hearing the shattering of her second-floor rear windows as her possessions were

thrown through them, she went blank. During the next several hours, Johnnie Mae Carter, Rhonda Moore, Gloria Flowers and the others watched while their homes were systematically destroyed.

Compared to breaking bones or blowing up houses on the West Bank, or setting an entire city block afire as the police had done in Philadelphia, the raid on the Dalton Avenue apartments wasn't much. Nobody, after all, was killed or seriously injured. But there was nonetheless something chilling, something grossly out of proportion, something not quite comprehensible about the methodical damage caused by more than 80 officers as they searched through four apartments looking for drugs on a tip.

All the toilets, for example, were broken to pieces and torn from the floor, leaving water running everywhere. The plaster walls were smashed in with sledgehammers, and so too were bedroom and living-room sets, televisions, VCRs and typewriters. Couches and chairs were cut and slashed with knives, jars of baby food and bottles of wine were emptied onto clothes and bedding, dishes and glasses were shattered, light fixtures were destroyed or torn out, phone wires were cut and frozen food and furniture were sent crashing through windows. Finally, before leaving, the officers spray-painted — gang style — some graffiti on a large board down the street. "LAPD Rules" and "Rolling 30's Die" were among the slogans written.

Then 33 people were brought to the Southwest Division police station, and six were booked on various misdemeanor charges. While there, according to eyewitness Hildebrandt Flowers, brother of Gloria Flowers, whose home had been destroyed, they were forced to whistle the theme from the old Andy Griffith television show, and to run a gauntlet of police officers who allegedly struck them with fists and steel flashlights. Moore, Carter, Flowers and the others later learned that their apartments had been targeted for the raid after a series of gang-related shootings in the neighborhood. But no gang members lived in the four apartments, and eventually only one person — from outside the neighborhood — was successfully prosecuted. Moreover, no weapons and no drugs except for a small amount of cocaine and marijuana were ever found in the apartments. "They told me later," says Johnnie Mae Carter, "that they was looking for drugs. And I remember very clearly saying back to them that the only ones acting like they was on drugs that night was you."

I n the late '70s, the LAPD became the city's biggest story, as tales of almost daily shootings of unarmed, mainly black citizens by the LAPD began appearing in the *Herald Examiner* and the *Los Angeles Times*. Those stories, in turn,

Los Angeles: Ted Soqui

competed with others concerning the department's use of deadly chokeholds that would allegedly kill at least 15 suspects (the LAPD will confirm only one) in seven years, and the LAPD's illegal spying on its critics as well as on more than 200 lawful groups, including the National Organization for Women, the Southern Christian Leadership Conference, Operation Breadbasket and the National Council of Churches.

What was particularly striking were the killings. It wasn't just the high numbers. Many deaths at the hands of police are, given the violent nature of the United States, both understandable and justifiable. No, it was the kinds of killings, as well as the department's dismissive explanations of them, that I found so extraordinary.

There was, for example, Reuben

Cortez, 37, who was taken hostage and forced at gunpoint to chauffeur around a deranged man, and was then shot to death by LAPD officers during a high-speed chase. Afterward, his wife and two children were awarded $300,000 in an out-of-court settlement with the city. And Donald R. Wilsson, a naked man who was choked to death while handcuffed and manacled. And there was Kenneth Ramirez, 19, shot dead in the head as he strolled toward an LAPD patrol car, and Larry Morris, 29, who was choked to death in his apartment after exchanging taunts from his balcony with officers passing by; and John Moore, who, while in custody, lying face down on the ground with hands cuffed behind his back, was shot to death by an officer as he rolled on his side after officers had engaged in a gun battle with another suspect; and Robert Ian Cameron, 32, a passenger in a car stopped by LAPD officers who then allegedly attacked them with a hairbrush and was choked to death; and Martin Brantly, 53, who raised a typewriter as if to throw it at officers and was shot to death. Subsequently, 80 of Brantly's neighbors signed a petition protesting "the senseless, unnecessary killing." And Herbert B. Avery, a black doctor who saw his son stopped by police officers and walked over to ask what the problem was. Without provocation, he was severely beaten with a nightstick and choked until he passed out. A jury later awarded him $1.3 million.

All of these incidences, as well as scores of others involving the killing of unarmed civilians by the LAPD (one in three civilians shot by the LAPD in the late '70s would prove to be unarmed) had, of course, extenuating circumstances: PCP in the bloodstream; a struggle with police before the typewriter was raised to be thrown; the fear of an officer who'd just been involved in a shoot-out. But all were characterized by an angry, defensive attitude toward anyone who questioned the circumstances surrounding the killings, and a bending over backward to justify the actions of the officers by a department investigating itself. In time, the self-serving rationale the police department would issue after every controversial killing would engender the devastatingly accurate South Central parody: "Subject reached into his waistband and pointed a black, shiny object at the officer, which subsequent investigation proved to be his finger."

The best way to get a feel for the Los Angeles Police Department prior to 1950 is to take a look at some old B movies from the '30s and '40s — the ones with, say, Ward Bond as a crooked, muscle-headed cop who'd kick your ass as soon as look at you and would sell the department for a dime, and Bogart as the private eye filled with cynical contempt who constantly outsmarts him.

That's what the police of LA were like before William H. Parker. Before the man who was to transform the Los Angeles police force from one of the most incompetent and corrupt in the nation to the Golden Boys of American law enforcement. No longer, after Bill Parker became chief in 1950, would LAPD officers systematically operate curbside courts where they'd shake down bribes from erring motorists. No longer would the department be a strong-arm extension of the Merchants and Manufacturers Association, striking fear into the hearts of union organizers. No longer would former Los Angeles policemen try to organize illegal gambling into a statewide protection racket. Bill Parker was on the job.

The dramatic changes that Parker would institute did not take place in a vacuum. Half a century of scandals had brought about city-charter reforms that were to make the chief of police of Los Angeles a uniquely powerful position chosen through a civil-service process rather than by appointment by the mayor.

Modern chiefs were thus freed from the influence of corrupt politicians, or, for that matter, the effective influence of any outsiders. Much like federal judges or tenured professors, they couldn't be ousted except for cause. Bill Parker would take that statutory autonomy and transform it into reality. After him, the police chiefs of Los Angeles couldn't be removed without, in effect, violating the penal code in a very provable way. That violation — barring resignation — would then have to be followed by a public trial, which, given the LAPD's intelligence files, could prove more embarrassing to a mayor, police commissioner or city councilmember than to a chief.

With Bill Parker, the chief of police of Los Angeles came to be in the position of being largely unaccountable save to a board of part-time civilian commissioners constricted by competing geographic and political interests and their lack of law-enforcement expertise. Politicians would come and go, but the Bill Parkers and Ed Davises and Daryl Gateses, all unelected, could play the law-and-order card and stay as long as they wished.

Most police departments, of course, want to be independent. But Bill Parker actually achieved it. "The police commission doesn't run the police department," he would tell an interviewer, "I run the police department." And Ed Davis would say in the mid-'70s: "I don't want to be mayor of this city. That position has no power. I have more power than the mayor."

Out of such strength there developed in the department an attitude that its critics were not only wrong, but a traitorous fifth column who had no right to criticize it. "The department didn't see itself as part of the city's political or social fabric," says former New York cop James Fyfe, now criminology professor at American University, "but regarded itself as something apart." So it was no surprise that Bill Parker would prove particularly resistant to any constraints on his men but his own.

In August of 1965 came a more direct affront to Bill Parker's world. It started, as the chief later put it, when "one person threw a rock, and then, like monkeys in a zoo, others started throwing rocks." The Watts riots had begun. Before their conclusion, 34 people would die.

Like many other departments, the LAPD had always had a tough, brutal reputation among African-Americans; and the high percentage of men on the force from the South and Southwest was said among blacks to make it particularly racist as well. "Many times," veteran South Central community activist Ted Watkins once told me, "I've seen a white policeman drop-kick a guy and laugh and say, 'Well, this is the first nigger I've kicked today.' I've seen that with my own eyes."

But the Irish, Italians and others who made up the many Eastern police departments had never been known for their benign racial attitudes either. As Patrick Murphy, who's headed the police forces of New York, Detroit and Washington, D.C., has pointed out, "The all-white, mostly male police in most cities were really there to enforce an informal but very real system of segregation."

So perhaps what was most notable about the LAPD's relationship with its city's black community was the public message Bill Parker sent to his troops. During the Watts riots, Parker would speak the unspeakable, and say for all to hear on a local TV show what would never again — in the post-civil-rights era — be so frankly uttered by a public official. "It is estimated that by 1970," said Parker, "45 percent of the metropolitan area of Los Angeles will be Negro; if you want any protection for your home and family...you're going to have to get in and support a strong police department. If you don't do that, God help you." ∎

Joe Domanick is the author of the forthcoming book To Protect and to Service: The LAPD and the Legend of the Golden Boys. *He is a contributing writer to the* LA Weekly, *where a version of this story first appeared.*

the killing of South Central

Malign Neglect

by Ron Curran

December 30, 1988

At the heart of South Central's problems is, quite simply, profound poverty. As many as 230,000 of the community's 630,000 residents — more than one of every three — live at or below the annual income poverty threshold. While South Central is home to just 18 percent of LA's families, 37 percent of the city's families in poverty are concentrated there. For South Central residents, quality of life and pride in community have been eroded, with the ensuing dead-end despair manifested only most visibly in the area's gang problem.

The existence of South Central poverty is, of course, not news to local government leaders. In fact, city officials supplied these poverty statistics. Why then haven't anti-poverty, anti-gang and other social programs been made to work better? What happened to ensure that, even after the intense attention focused on the community's problems following the Watts riots in 1965, progress wasn't catalyzed? Why, in a city whose citizens and politicians are so sensitive to crime, wasn't a common agenda developed to head off the social and economic devastation that encouraged South Central's cycle of drugs and crime?

The answers are truly saddening. In part, they can be laid at the doorstep of LA's self-absorbed — and often self-aggrandizing — economic power structure and elite. That power structure, liberal on its surface, whose voice has been the *LA Times*, saw both enormous profit and general city boosterism in the development of a downtown Los Angeles that could be an office mecca for corporations operating on

Los Angeles: Cynthia Wiggins

the Pacific Rim. With the willing assistance of Mayor Tom Bradley, who had himself been raised in South Central and served as one of its council representatives, that power structure pushed through a development plan that not only left LA besieged by a traffic explosion, a polluted environment and a large and mounting affordable-housing shortage, but also forced off the table serious consideration of alternative development models for the city.

One of these alternative models was the idea of converting South Central and downtown into a working-class enclave of light, non-polluting industry and sturdy and attractive low-income housing, one interlaced with a strong infrastructure of schools, health establishments and social-service and community organizations. Instead, politically weak and, in the eyes of many local activists, abandoned and co-opted by Bradley, the South Central community saw city resources funnelled into an LA of high-rise office buildings benefiting the existing white financial establishment and big-money developers.

Bradley: The Early Years

When Tom Bradley was elected mayor in 1973, he was a former South Central policeman who had just served 10 years as City Councilman for the community's tenth

District. Bradley's reputation as a "good liberal" was borne out by his active support at the time for federal anti-poverty and community-development funds. In those early years, as now, most of the money reaching South Central was in the form of block grants for community services and development from the federal government to the city. Bradley pledged to do more to bring in such money.

As mayor, especially in the early years, Bradley proved to be aggressive and creative in seeking to maximize the city's shares of federal anti-poverty monies. Community organizers still praise him for raising the level of child-care money available from federal sources, for generating so-called Section Eight housing subsidies to the city and for obtaining goodly amounts of Model Cities program money.

Bradley, however, was no progressive. As the first black man to come to power in one of the 10 largest American cities, he surrounded himself not with activists from his own community but with white liberals from other parts of the city. The difference was crucial. Black neighborhood leaders, backed by white progressive allies across the city, had argued that real structural change could alleviate the blight, with a significant shift of city resources into the most impoverished communities such as South Central. Money should be found, they argued, to build up the schools and job-training networks, to improve the housing stock, to provide additional police services (under the control of neighborhood organizations, to minimize the violent racism for which the LAPD was infamous), for development loans to start businesses within the community, and for tax breaks to lure businesses that could provide meaningful employment in the community. If money for these projects had to come from higher taxes or development "linkage" fees in the wealthier parts of the city, it was argued, then so be it.

But Bradley adopted an agenda that wasn't nearly as ambitious. Its main component was to get the state and federal government to provide more money primarily for remedial services, not for radical restructuring of the community, and to jawbone with the corporate community for whatever other aid was possible. Bradley discovered, as did other mayors elsewhere, that such private-sector aid usually amounted to crumbs.

When Bradley did act aggressively to change the community-development delivery system, critics say it was dramatically to the disadvantage of South Central. One of his first major mayoral moves, one that would have enormous consequences, was to disband the city's Community Development Advisory Committee, a progressive group of grassroots organizers who had been grappling with the city's development priorities under Bradley's mayoral predecessor, Sam Yorty.

"We were euphoric when Bradley became mayor, because he seemed like a true reform candidate," recalls Clara Gorenfeld, one of several South Central representatives on the committee. "Tom had been a good councilman, darn it. Tom was the guy we used to run to. He broke all the rules, stepping on other people's districts to get help for South Central. I was very close to Tom, and by the time he was elected, we had cleaned all the Yorty people off the committee so it was all ready to go for Tom.

To this day impassioned on the subject, Gorenfeld said she and others were overwhelmed when, shortly after Bradley was first elected, they were suddenly informed that they were no longer wanted. "We had been a hell of a group, very caring, very committed, with a 'big picture' view. We were shocked, and a lot of our people left politics because of that. Tom just broke their spirit."

Defending Bradley

Mayor Bradley is not without his defenders, however. Within South Central he is backed particularly strongly by what local insiders call "the minister mafia" — the Baptist Church elite whom Bradley has wooed with favors, attention and some programs. Members of this group cite the housing and shopping malls Bradley has helped steer to the community and the jobs blacks have obtained throughout the city bureaucracy (though, notably, few in Bradley's inner circle). "To say that I am pro-Bradley takes second place to saying that the facts are pro-Bradley," said the

Rev. Cecil L. Murray, senior minister of the First A.M.E. Church. "[Bradley] presided skillfully over the most unique metropolitan challenge in modern mayoral history: the channeling of over 90 different ethnicities into a cohesive force and stimulating the black economy through such developments as the Watts Shopping Mall and the recently constructed Baldwin Hills Crenshaw Shopping Center. [And] Bradley has brought more women and minorities into the city work force at every level than was accomplished in the 40 years prior to his administration."

Another minister, the Rev. Joe B. Hardwicke, noting that the city had helped the church construct a 200-unit apartment complex, said flatly that Bradley has unquestioned support in the community. Of the accusation that Bradley sold out to the city's monied interests to maintain city-wide support, former mayoral aide Maury Weiner has said, "Tom Bradley never does anything for political reasons. He only does what he thinks is right. I've never seen him do otherwise."

Nevertheless, Bradley, his critics argue, could at any point have used his Westside liberal base and black community support to mobilize a city-wide anti-poverty effort or to amend the charter. Not given to thinking as a progressive, however, he chose instead to rely on what some of his critics call "trickle-down" anti-poverty money. He stood by this approach even after 1982, when Reagan began to savage urban and anti-poverty monies. Activists recall trying desperately to meet with Bradley in those years to demand from him and his officials some programmatic response to the federal cutbacks. But they say their requests were ignored, and South Central's suffering mounted accordingly.

The Bigger Problem

A deeper and tougher issue than manipulation of statistics lies at the heart of the shortchanging of South Central: The city's overall anti-poverty and community needs are vastly greater than the resources allotted. Examined closely, very few of the projects funded elsewhere in the city by the Community Development Department can

be said to be unwarranted. Every councilperson has a big shopping list for his or her district. For any city administration, the expedient thing to do — if not the correct thing — is to divide the scarce money in a manner that appears to cover the political backsides of the individual councilmembers. This avoids war with individual council people and, as Bradley's critics note, lets him give the impression that he is mayor to all the people.

The same critics note that neither the council nor Bradley ever made much effort to expand the resource pie by developing systematic, non-regressive ways the city could contribute, and thus the neglect of South Central and the resulting crime and poverty crisis have been magnified. As a community organizer from another city remarked recently after a stay in Los Angeles, "The most striking thing is that no one seems to be in charge. There's no leadership at all. The city is just a great big buck-passing operation. The black poverty areas get deprived because no leader has broken through the muck, and you can't expect a City Council whose members have to keep their own constitutents at bay to think of the overall city needs without leadership."

According to both city administration insiders and Bradley critics who recently reviewed Bradley's 15-year tenure, the mayor and his office have rarely intervened to steer more money toward South Central, despite its critical needs, or to expand the pie. As a consequence, the average amount of money spent per person-in-poverty in LA is now significantly lower than in New York, Chicago, Boston or San Francisco, all of which supplement poverty funding with much more money from their own municipal coffers.

Many of LA's activists note that poverty rates in LA, as elsewhere in the country, came down dramatically in the early years of the country's anti-poverty effort, reaching a national low of 11.1 percent in 1973. They have gone up since, with cutbacks in anti-poverty funding being a major contributing factor — particularly, not surprisingly, in Los Angeles. ∎

Ron Curran is a longtime political writer for the LA Weekly, *where a version of this story first appeared.*

Congresswoman Maxine Waters

The Way Out

by Cynthia Hamilton

December 30, 1988

Compared to many of the major political battles of the 1960s, which were fought against violations of civil rights, the culprits of the 1980s who are responsible for dismantling communities are more elusive. While the 1960s government, especially the federal government, was an ally in the black struggle, today government is the cloak behind which the real adversary, corporate interests, hides. In the 1960's laws beneficial to blacks and the poor were passed and old constitutional interpretations were modified and transformed. Today, corporations use the courts to protect their private-property rights at the expense of the human rights of many. Therefore the new national agenda for communities must be drafted at the neighborhood level first — one area corporations don't control. Our major political objective must be to take back the decision-making apparatus from corporate special interests. Government must be made responsive once again to the people rather than to campaign contributors.

In sum, residents of Los Angeles must resist the corporate philosophy of isolation and individualism. It is only through group efforts that the new apartheid can be overcome. ∎

Testimony Before the Senate Banking Committee

by *Maxine Waters* May 14, 1992

Mr. Chairman, members of the committee, it is a privilege to be here today. The riots in Los Angeles and in other cities shocked the world. They shouldn't have. Many of us have watched our country — including our government — neglect the problems, indeed the people, of our inner-cities for years — even as matters reached a crisis stage.

The verdict in the Rodney King case did not cause what happened in Los Angeles. It was only the most recent injustice — piled upon many other injustices — suffered by the poor, minorities and the hopeless people living in this nation's cities. For years, they have been crying out for help. For years, their cries have not been heard.

I recently came across a statement made more than 25 years ago by Robert Kennedy, just two months before his violent death. He was talking about the violence that had erupted in cities across America. His words were wise and thoughtful: "There is another kind of violence in America, slower but just as deadly, destructive as the shot or bomb in the night....This is the violence of institutions; indifference and inaction and slow decay. This is the violence that afflicts the poor, that poisons relations between men and women because their skin is different colors. This is the slow destruction of a child by hunger, and schools without books and homes without heat in the winter."

What a tragedy it is that America has still, in 1992, not learned such an important lesson.

I have represented the people of South Central Los Angeles in the U.S. Congress and the California state Assembly for close to 20 years. I have seen our community continually and systematically ravaged by banks who would not lend to us, by governments which abandoned us or punished us for our poverty, and by big businesses who exported our jobs to Third-World countries for cheap labor.

In LA, between 40 and 50 percent of all African-American men are unemployed. The poverty rate is 32.9 percent. According to the most recent census, 40,000 teenagers — that is 20 percent of the city's 16 to 19 year olds — are both out of school and unemployed.

An estimated 40,000 additional jobs were just lost as a result of the civil unrest the last two weeks. The LA Chamber of Commerce has said that at least 15,000 of these job losses will be permanent. This represents another 10 to 20 percent of South-Central LA's entire workforce permanently unemployed. Keep in mind, our region had one of the country's highest unemployment rates before the recent unrest. It is hard to imagine how our community will cope with the additional devastation.

We have created in many areas of this country a breeding ground for hopelessness, anger and despair. All the traditional mechanisms for empowerment, opportunity and self-improvement have been closed.

We are in the midst of a grand economic experiment that suggests that if we "get the government off people's backs," and let the economy grow, everyone, including the poor, will somehow be better off. So what have we done the last 12 years?

•We eliminated the Comprehensive Employment Training Act (CETA) and replaced it with the Job Training Partnership Act. In this transition, the federal commitment to job training has shrunk from $23 billion in 1980 to $8 billion now.

•General Revenue Sharing, a program designed to assist local governments to cope with their own problems, was eliminated entirely. Another $6-billion abandonment.

•Community Development Block Grants (CDBG), a building block program for local economic development, was also severely cut. In 1980 the program sent $21 billion to localities; it's now less than $14 billion.

In housing, the federal government virtually walked away from the table. Overall federal support for housing programs was cut by 80 percent.

And Reagan-Bush tried to do more — by trying to eliminate the Job Corps, VISTA and Trade Adjustment Assistance.

The results of this experiment have been devastating. Today, more than 12 million children live in poverty, despite a decade of "economic growth," the precise mechanism we were told would reduce poverty. Today, one in five children in America lives in poverty.

The number of children in poverty increased by 2.2 million from 1979 to 1989. This was true for every sub-group of America's children. White child poverty increased from 11.8 percent to 14.8 percent. Latino children's poverty went from 28 percent to 36.2 percent. And black child poverty increased from 41.2 percent to 43.7 percent.

While the budget cuts of the eighties were literally forcing millions of Americans into poverty, there were other social and economic trends destroying inner-city communities at the same time.

I'm sure everyone in this room has read the results of the Federal Reserve Board's study on mortgage discrimination that demonstrates African-Americans and Latinos are twice as likely as whites of the same income to be denied mortgages.

High-income blacks are more likely to be turned down for a mortgage than low-income whites. These trends were true in all regions of the country and in every bank surveyed.

In Los Angeles, a group called the Greenlining Coalition did its own study of the Bank of America — the area's largest bank and the primary financial institution in South Central Los Angeles. As you know, the Fed recently approved the merger of Bank of America and Security Pacific — the largest bank merger in history. One of the criteria for approval of that merger

was the CRA rating of the Bank of America. BofA had earned an "outstanding" CRA rating. Despite this, the Greenlining Coalition's study revealed some startling figures:

•Only 2 percent of all of BofA's loans were made to California's 2.5 million African-Americans.

•Of these, only a trivial number, 156 loans, were made to low-income African-Americans. That comes to only one-fifth of 1 percent of all loans for low-income African-Americans.

•It is estimated that as little as $8 million was loaned to low-income African-Americans, or one-tenth of 1 percent of the $8 billion in home mortgages lent by the bank.

•Only $20 million was loaned to low-income Latinos, and one-fourth of 1 percent of Bank of America's loans went to low-income Asian-Americans.

•In total, only 4 percent of all Bank of America loans were made to low-income Californians.

● ● ● ● ● ● ● ● ● ● ● ● ● ● ● ● ● ● ● ●

Number of banks in South Central LA, 1991: 14

Number of savings and loans in South Central LA, 1991: 5

Number of these institutions affected by post-verdict violence: 3 damaged; 1 destroyed

"...The paucity of bank branches in lower-income neighborhoods pushes government-benefits recipients into using check-cashing stores, whose rates are as high as 10 percent of the checks' face value."

(Source: *LA Weekly*, 5/8/92)

In law enforcement, the problems are longstanding and well-documented as well:

•In a system where judges and lawyers remain overwhelmingly white, blacks account for a share of the prison population that far outstrips their presence in the population as a whole. According to The Sentencing Project, black men make up 6 percent of the population, but 44 percent of inmates.

•A *USA Today* analysis of 1989 drug-arrest statistics found that 41 percent of those arrested on drug charges were black, although blacks are estimated to be only 15 percent of the drug-using population.

•A *San Jose Mercury News* investigation last year of almost 700,000 criminal cases found that "at virtually every stage of pre-trial negotiation, whites are more successful than non-whites." Of the 71,000 adults with no prior criminal record, one-third of the whites had their charges reduced, compared to only one-fourth of blacks and Hispanics.

•A Federal Judicial Center study this year of federal sentences for drug trafficking and firearms offenses found that the average sentence for blacks was 49 percent higher than for whites in 1990, compared to 28 percent in 1984.

Is it any wonder our children have no hope?

The systems are failing us. I could go on and on. All we can hope for is that the President, his Cabinet and Congress understand what is happening. We simply cannot afford the continued terror and oppression of benign neglect — the type of inaction that has characterized the federal government's response to the cities since the late 1970s.

In conclusion, I congratulate this Committee for having this hearing. We're all working overtime trying to formulate a quick and effective response to the crisis that engulfs us. With leadership and commitment, I hope we can succeed. ∎

Maxine Waters is a Democratic member of Congress whose district includes South Central Los Angeles.

The 1980s, according to people like Ed Koch, were supposed to be the years cities came into their own. Instead, it was the decade they fell off a cliff. Despite pockets of gentrification, cities across America found themselves playing host to more poor people than ever before, laying off employees, slashing services, emitting Oliver Twistian appeals for help from unsympathetic state governments and the feds.

Although Republicans accuse Democrats of fostering a debilitating welfare dependency and Democrats accuse the GOP of taking an ax to social programs, the fact is that anyone trying to get to the bottom of why U.S. cities are in such desperate straits can't help concluding that the mugging of urban America has been very much a bipartisan affair. Both parties have slashed social benefits. Both now emphasize such punitive measures as more drug arrests, more prisons and more welfare cuts for unwed mothers. Even more important, both parties are more devoted than ever to the pursuit of costly middle-class investment programs whose effect on cities has been akin to the RAF's attack on Dresden during World War II.

Contrary to liberal dogma, the problem is not too little government spending but too much — or, to be precise, too much spending of a certain kind. A century ago, when the federal government consisted of hardly more than a Post Office and a Coast Guard, cities in this country boomed. They were among the fastest growing in the world — the most crowded, the wealthiest and the most dynamic. Arriving in New York immediately prior to the Russian Revolution, Leon Trotsky called it a "city of prose and fantasy, of capitalism, automatism...the fullest expression of our modern age."

Within five or six decades, however, the noise and tumult had given way to windblown streets, boarded-up storefronts and eerie silences punctuated every now

Los Angeles: Michael Schuman/SABA

The Killing of the American City
by Daniel Lazare

and then by the wail of police sirens. What happened? In a nutshell, America turned a corner from an economy based on coal and steel to one based on petroleum and asphalt. Instead of trains and trolleys and compact towns and cities growing up around harbors and rail hubs, the U.S. almost literally turned itself inside-out in pursuit of a hyper-decentralized development pattern based on highways, suburbs and mass-produced automobiles. Far from dying of natural causes, as Republicans would have it, American cities are succumbing to a process of planned de-urbanization that began early in this century, took off after World War II and accelerated at a madcap pace under Reagan and Bush.

Although de-urbanization is commonly thought of as a post-war phenomenon, the earliest signs were evident by the 1920s. With more motor vehicles than any other country in the world (twice as many per capita as Canada and New Zealand, nine times as many as France and Britain and 40

times as many as Germany), America saw the first auto-based suburbs and witnessed the first signs of middle-class urban flight. In Newark, NJ, for example, 54 percent of the officers and directors of the city Chamber of Commerce lived in Newark as of 1916. By 1929, the number was down to 36 percent. A few decades after that, it would plunge to near zero as all but the very poorest deserted Newark *en masse*.

If the government had wanted to be even-handed, it might have required auto manufacturers to ante up for roads and highways just as rail companies were expected to build and maintain the tracks their trains rode on. Barring that, it might have tried to reduce taxes on railroads or lighten the burden of government regulation. Ultimately, it did neither. Railroads were taxed to the hilt, government regulation grew increasingly encumbering and motorists got highways for free. The results were completely unsurprising. Traffic grew, while the rail system withered and died.

There's nothing covert about this process. Rather, in countless laws passed by Congress and innumerable policy decisions by administrative agencies, it's been open and above-board. Since the turn of the century, anti-urbanism has been at least as fundamental to American culture as racism. Cities are crowded and jumbled, matrices of political ferment and new ideas. Since the Middle Ages, they've been a nonstop threat to the political order. Suburbs are the opposite. Specifically designed as havens from urban tumult, they're places where people go to spend and own — not to rebel. From the point of view of the ruling class at the birth of the auto age, they opened up new opportunities for mass consumption and political control. America, once a country of clanging trolley cars and husky, brawling cities, was promptly redefined in terms of the vine-covered cottage and two-car garage.

the roots of conflict in LA: the real story

Rather than debating such changes, Republicans and Democrats cheered from the sidelines. The former promised a car in every garage, while the latter under FDR expanded federal infrastructure investments to include not just highways but suburban housing. During the '40s, Truman jump-started post-war suburbanization by having the Veterans Administration pass out mortgages literally for free, while in 1956 Eisenhower gave the go-ahead for the 41,000-mile interstate highway system, the largest public works project in history. This was the era of Levittown, hot rods and having fun, fun, fun till your daddy takes the T-bird away.

Yet what was a godsend for suburban developers was a catastrophe for the urban economy. Almost immediately, cities began pitching downhill. By 1955, *The Blackboard Jungle*, with its scenes of black and Puerto Rican juvenile delinquents rampaging through a seedy New York City high school, was playing to packed movie houses — just the sort of thing to make suburban parents thank God they lived out where the subdivisions were spacious and the schools squeaky clean. A decade later came Watts and Newark, followed by the 1970s New York City fiscal crisis and, in the '80s, homelessness, crack and AIDS.

As the problems multiplied, the political euphoria of an earlier generation faded. The problem was particularly acute for the Democrats, traditionally the party of the urban masses, who now found themselves begging for suburban votes. During Lyndon Johnson's Great Society, the solution was to shower benefits on both constituencies in the form of more highways, subdivisions and government-insured mortgages for the suburbanites, plus additional programs for the impoverished urbanites all this government-subsidized prosperity had left behind. But largesse on this scale soon fell victim to the staggeringly expensive war in Southeast Asia and, later, persistent 12-digit federal deficits. The Democrats' tasks were made more difficult as a result. The party had somehow to straddle the enormous class divide separating the cities from the middle-class 'burbs (a divide they had contributed to as much as anyone else) by promising favors to both sides and hoping no one would ask too closely how to pay for it. The wider the divide, the more precarious the balancing act — until the Democrats were left shaking and wobbling like leaves in a storm.

Not that the latest round of urban crises has left the Republicans in much better shape. With his do-nothing domestic policies so reminiscent of Calvin Coolidge, and his Panglossian faith in the free market to solve all ills, Bush was clearly shaken by this spring's explosion in LA, which caused his image incalculable damage in the polls. A president who insists things are getting better when they're obviously getting worse is not one who inspires public confidence. At the same time, it's not as though the riots were of enormous benefit to anyone else — except perhaps H. Ross Perot. A billionaire businessman of generally right-wing politics, he appeals to a middle class whose way of life is crumbling, which despairs of a solution yet clings to the hope of an easy way out. He's the ideal candidate for people who realize that the status quo is untenable but are hoping for a strong man to cut through the Gordian knot.

What needs to be done? What would actually help bring together the sharply polarized landscape created during the last 50 years? First, social spending should be increased to alleviate the most obvious symptoms of social distress: homelessness, long-term unemployment, children who grow up being shuttled from one welfare hotel to another. Second, a truce should be declared in the drug war so that addiction can be treated as a public-health issue by doctors, nurses and therapists, rather than as a criminal matter requiring the attention of prosecutors and cops.

Third, America should get over its deep-rooted obsession with home ownership, with its inherent anti-urban bias. According to a recent White House estimate taking into account various tax breaks, private housing subsidies cost the U.S. Treasury more than $60 billion a year, completely dwarfing the $2 billion or so that the feds grudgingly dole out for public housing and programs for the homeless. France, Switzerland and Germany all have significantly lower home-ownership rates, yet no one would be foolish enough to argue that their quality of life suffers as a consequence.

Finally, America should begin working down some of its enormous subsidies for the private automobile. Between the costs of highway construction and maintenance, growing dangers resulting from pollution and global warming, not to mention the deaths and injuries as a result of accidents and the countless person-hours lost sitting in traffic, the toll is enormous. Brian Ketcham, an environmental consultant, estimates that auto and truck travel costs American society a whopping $860 billion per year over and above what the government collects in highway taxes. This is a subsidy for suburban development that makes the farm subsidy look like small change. Until America tries to even the score by imposing more reasonable, European-style gasoline taxes, suburbia will continue sprawling ever outward, while cities will be left high, dry and economically isolated.

Simple, huh? Of course, the chances of America actually doing anything along these lines is — at least for the moment — slim to non-existent. A Congress that couldn't muster the courage to impose a five-cent hike in gas taxes in 1991 is obviously in no shape to take on deeply imbedded highway subsidies which, according to Brian Ketcham's study, amount to somewhere in the range of $6.50 a gallon. Sadly, after seven decades or so of continued urban decline, the immediate outlook is for more of the same.

Within days of the RAF's devastating incendiary attack in early 1945, Dresden began struggling back to life. So did Hamburg and Tokyo, Hiroshima and Nagasaki. Following Vietnamese liberation from the fanatically anti-urban Khmer Rouge in 1979, so did Phnom Penh. Yet it is hopelessly naive to imagine a devastated metropolis like Detroit coming back under anything like current conditions — or, for that matter, a Camden, an East St. Louis, or a South Central LA. One thing that can be said for America: When it kills cities, it kills them dead. ■

Daniel Lazare is the New York editor for In These Times. *He writes about urban affairs for the* Village Voice, Dissent *and other periodicals.*

SIMI VALLEY

Stunned silence reigns for the first few moments after the verdict. Even the most hardened reporters in the cramped courthouse media room stare at each other wordlessly before running toward the entrance of Judge Stanley Weisberg's courtroom.

The onlookers — an uneasy blend of inner-city activists, Simi Valley Anglos and trial junkies — file out slowly, many with dazed looks on their faces. They linger in the hallway, the reporters crowding around. And then it starts. Tears stream down an African-American woman's cheeks. "You go through the system, and it screws you," she says, cradling her one-year-old son, who stares at the collection of microphones in front of his mother's face. Another black woman starts shouting, "I grieve for America! I grieve for America! I grieve for America!"

The reporters don't know where to head next; everything is happening everywhere. An exhausted Terry White is mumbling about retrying Powell. Powell's sister cries with joy during a live TV interview. A vengeful crowd of about 75 is chasing down LAPD Sgt. Stacey Koon as sheriff's deputies hustle him to his lawyer's Mercedes-Benz. A gray-bearded man in a flowing white robe sounds a long ceremonial horn from the bed of a pickup in the parking lot and calls out, "The only justice comes from God! And there is no justice here today!" Compton Councilmember Patricia Moore, a media beacon in her bright red dress, resignedly tells her community through the cameras: "Do what you have to do." Shouting

Riot Scenes *by Rubén Martínez*

matches erupt in front of the courthouse. "That man was drunk, and he didn't obey orders," a peroxide blonde tells a black woman from South Central. "Fuck you, white bitch!" is the sister's response.

The afternoon sun shines strong, and a warm Simi desert wind makes the Navy, Army, Marine and Air Force flags of the veteran's memorial adjacent to the courthouse snap to attention. The crowd

around the courthouse grows and splinters into more bickering factions. Another black man, who'd told me earlier in the day that he would personally kick Powell's ass if the jury let him off, yells at the growing crowd — at the white housewives and World War II veterans, at the Anglo hip-hop teens and visitors from South Central, at the media, at all of Los Angeles — "Burn, baby, burn!"

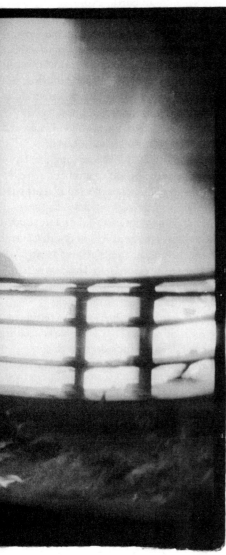

Los Angeles: Ted Soqui

FIRST A.M.E.

The banner at the entrance to the First African Methodist Episcopal Church reads, "Brother, Come Help Us Stop the Madness." It is nearly sunset, and the west-facing stained-glass depictions of the Passion are aglow. The black leadership of Los Angeles parades to the pulpit. The politicians, pastors and activists look out over the pews. Dozens of "Yes On Prop. F" (the police-reform bill on the June ballot) placards bob up and down in the past-capacity church. "God is alive! God is alive! God is not dead yet!" calls out First A.M.E. pastor Cecil Murray.

In the makeshift press box in front of the pulpit, our eyes are glued to the bank of small TV monitors carrying live shots of truck driver Reginald Denny sprawled on the asphalt at the intersection of Normandie and Florence.

The leaders: "We're not going to lose our head. We're not going to lose our cool. We're going to hang on for justice." (Rev. Frank Higgins) "We're not going to tear down our community to prove no point." (LA City Councilmember Mark Ridley-Thomas)

On TV: "All officers in the city have been instructed to put on riot gear... "

The leaders: "I want to ask you, have you ever seen a more morally bankrupt jury verdict in your life? Pass Proposition F!" (Melanie Lomax) "We want you to express all your anger, your frustration.... I was shocked, I was stunned, I had my breath taken away [upon hearing the verdicts]. We have come to say tonight that we've had enough, and to encourage you to express your outrage verbally." (Tom Bradley, who is received with boos, catcalls and general restlessness)

On TV: A line of riot gear-clad LAPD officers faces off with protesters in front of Parker Center.

The leaders: "Register to vote!" (Joseph Duff, NAACP) "If [the LAPD] thinks that dragging people out of their cars and beating them is justice, why don't they do it in Simi Valley?" (Rev. James Lawson)

On TV: Aerial shot of flames shooting up from a mini-mall on the corner of Vermont and Century.

DOWNTOWN

We are in front of Police Chief Daryl F. Gates's house — a.k.a. Parker Center — which is surrounded on three sides by the LAPD. But it doesn't matter: We can do anything we want. The later it gets, the angrier we get. We throw rocks. We snap a No Parking sign. We torch a parking-lot guard booth. Get that LAPD patrol car! With 25 pairs of arm and leg muscles, turn it over! Torch it! Now the Rolls Royce! Listen to the hollow thud of crowbar against windshield glass. The riot police follow us at a distance, never confronting. Trees in large round concrete planters roll down the street. Bus benches become barricades. We hold burning copies of the *LA Times* to the leaves of the palm trees that peek out above the 101 overpass. We stare in awe at the flaming palms and at the drivers down below, who slam on their brakes and attempt desperate U-turns. One car screeches to a halt in the slow lane before two burning American flags that frame a Robbie Conal "Daryl Gates" poster. We yell, "No Justice, No Peace!" and we spray-paint the walls of City Hall East and City Hall West and City Hall South and the Criminal Courts Building and the *LA Times* building. We are Revolutionary Communist Party types (manning the megaphone and spray-painting detail), we are homeless, we are barrio kids from East LA and South Central, we are bohemians from Echo Park, we are ACT-UP activists and we are journalists, a unified organism of about 300 cells on foot, on skateboards, on bikes, wearing "X" caps and Soundgarden T-shirts, moving like a big jellyfish, nudged by the waves of the LAPD.

("Fuckyouwhitemotherfuckin'pig!")

The organism mutates with each breath of smoke inhaled. We exhale fire. Phil's Coffee Shop on Spring and First goes up. Tommy's Coffee Shop at Spring and Second. The plate-glass windows at the new Mexican place on Broadway and Third are smashed — free Cokes for everyone! Trash cans through the display windows at Eagleson's Big and Tall. A wedding dress mannequin in flames at Bridal City. The unified organism starts to split up. One piece heads north on Broadway, another east on Second, another east toward Temple. People carry away cellular phones, lap-top computers, stereo receivers (Radio Shack at Second and

Broadway). We are laughing. We are screaming. Where did the LAPD go? A knife shop is looted. Suddenly, many of us are armed with switchblades and long, gleaming kitchen knives. Are we going to kill each other? Do we go on? Do we go home? What are we doing? Who is leading us? The RCP? The guy with the Soundgarden T-shirt? The homeboy from Ramona Gardens? The LAPD? Someone is stabbed at Temple and Spring. He bleeds without saying a word, crumpled in the back seat of a car. LAPD officers cordon off the area. "Y'all going to die!" yells a black man standing on a bus bench. He gesticulates, sweat streaming down his face. "I'm telling you if I don't do it, some other brother will!"

SOUTH CENTRAL

It's early Thursday morning, and many of the previous night's blazes appear to be dying out. But then a column of black smoke billows up, north on Crenshaw: a mini-mall at 29th Street. I drive toward it as fires erupt to the east. I drive east, and fires break out to the west. Any direction I point the car in, there are columns of black smoke pouring from a Trak Auto, from a Kinney shoe store, from a Thrifty, from a Boys.

The crowds gather at the intersections. Whole families watch. Tricked-out cars roll past, blasting the bass, horns honking, black-power fists shaking. The police are nowhere in sight. The fires rage unchecked. Kids on bikes ride past carrying booty: soundboards, lighting fixtures, shiny new shoes, stuffed animals, bottles of whiskey, six-packs of beer, knives, guns, shopping bags stuffed with groceries, stacks of videos. The targets of looting and arson sometimes make sense: Thrifty, Boys. "They're overpriced, and they're the white man's businesses," I am told by a black auto-body worker at La Brea and Rodeo — a man who refuses to partake in the looting. But he's more than willing to explain it: "They're hitting the insurance companies, which are the white man's, too." Even the large malls are overrun, like the Broadway at Martin Luther King and Crenshaw. Dozens of cars screech to a halt along MLK, people running in and coming out with armfuls of clothes and appliances. It is also no surprise that the Korean-

owned liquor stores, furniture warehouses and beauty-supply shops are hit: Black-Korean tension was ready to explode. "I've been waiting nine years for this day!" exults an African-American man on MLK and Muirfield as the fishmarket across the street is looted. "I owned that place until I had to sell out to the Koreans."

The shoe stores are logical, too: Shoes are a powerful status symbol, even if they're a $14.99 fake-leather pair from Payless. But the violence spreads out from the "logical" targets, begins hitting ma-and-pa stores. "Blacks are paying the price, too," a South Central resident tells me as she sits with her children on her front lawn, watching the spectacle unfold at a mini-mall across the street. "It's like a gang shoot-out. If you can't get the one you want, then you get whatever you can."

The flames that engulf the Korean-owned liquor store leap over to the black-owned restaurant. The Trak Auto store throws fire onto the roof of a Salvadoran *pupusería*. Desperate store owners spray-paint their buildings with messages to the looters and arsonists: "Serving the black community for 6 years" on the wall of a Salvadoran restaurant, "Black Owned" on a neighborhood market, "Latin Owned" on an El Pollo Loco.

The rage is doubling back upon itself, leveling everything in sight. There are persistent rumors that the Crips and the Bloods will unify and declare all-out war on the LAPD, that the Nation of Islam will set up sharpshooters on rooftops throughout South Central to greet the incoming National Guard.

There is no telling how far it will all go. "Until the jury changes its mind," says a 12-year-old black kid at Adams and Victoria, who's standing in front of a burned-out furniture store he says his family poured water on all night long in order to save the residential buildings only feet away.

• • • • • • • • • • • • • • • • • • • •

Median household net worth
for Anglos, 1991:
$31,904
Median household net worth
for non-Anglos, 1991:
$1,353
(Source: Report of the Los Angeles Community Reinvestment Committee)

PICO-UNION

The Salvadoran barrio explodes Thursday afternoon. Nobody seems to know how it started, it just did. Some say it was *los morenitos* (a racial epithet for blacks), a few groups from South Central who ventured north. Others say it was locals. Whatever the spark, by 2 p.m. crowds are looting stores from Washington to Beverly, from Western to Figueroa. Pico-Union and the surrounding neighborhoods of Westlake and Mid-Wilshire look like San Salvador at the height of a rebel offensive.

We should have expected it. This barrio's been on the edge of chaos for years, and the enmity between police and youth is almost as strong as it is in South Central. "Fuck the police!" yells a Salvadoran teenager at Vermont and Third, where Vons and Thrifty are being looted. "They diss us just as much as the blacks."

Of course, not everyone is consumed by rage, or bending back the black security gates of department stores, or throwing bricks and bottles at police cars as they race past with their sirens wailing. On TV, the aerial shots show the ribbons of dense black smoke spiralling into the sky, the crowds of "thugs" and "hooligans" — figures tiny as ants — scurrying across the streets. But on the streets there are mostly men and women and children, standing on the sidewalk, staring in shock, in tears, or screaming at reporters that their barrio is being destroyed and can't we do anything to stop it?

There is also looting borne not of greed but of fear and necessity, like the mothers and grandmothers stealing Pampers from the markets. "No, this has nothing to do with Rodney King," a young Chicana mother says. "This is about trying to get something to eat for our kids. Who knows where we're going to get food, now that everything has been destroyed? We have no choice." And there are volunteers manning the firehoses — like the blacks and Latinos and Asians fighting an inferno at a Korean-owned furniture store on Vermont and Pico. Or the Latino crew in South Central that jumped over the fence of the empty fire station across the street and grabbed hoses to save not their business (an auto-body shop completely engulfed), but the apartment building behind it — where mostly black residents live.

At four in the afternoon, flames and smoke explode everywhere in Pico-Union: Olympic, Pico, Alvarado, Seventh, Union, Washington. Neighborhood icons are destroyed. The Union Swap Meet is but one of the many decorous brick buildings (filled with mostly Korean-owned stalls) to go up, spilling enough black, acrid smoke to hide the downtown skycrapers. At Pico and Berendo, the Trotskyite Pathfinder Bookstore goes up in smoke, along with the Club Flamboyán and Lupita's Bakery. The telephone poles snap, scattering the onlookers, and the live wires spark as they swing and strike the wet twisted metal of the storefront security gates. The sun is eclipsed by the thick, roiling smoke.

KOREATOWN

"Today, I'm playing baseball," says 30-year-old mall general administrator Johann Kim, swinging his bat back and forth inside the Koreatown Plaza parking lot, behind the drawn security gates. "The baseballs are human heads."

It's the only mini-mall in Mid-Wilshire that's survived so far, he tells me. On the second floor, a crew of Korean business owners stands guard at the open windows, brandishing Uzi's, shotguns, pistols. They've been standing guard since early Thursday morning, when looters attacked another mall across the street. (It burned.) Two young Salvadorans walk by the garage. "Do you feel rich today? Do you feel rich? Come on man," Kim taunts, striking the bat against the metal gate. The kids stop,

Los Angeles: Ted Soqui

throw a hard look, but let it ride.

"We've never had any problem with blacks and Hispanics," says Kim. "We come here, put up our businesses, make some money, pay our taxes. That's how blacks and Hispanics get food stamps, welfare, the whole thing. We're doing our part."

Two black security guards who work at the mini-mall pull up to the gate. "Yo, William," Kim greets. "Whussup? Wanna play some baseball?"

The astounding Koreatown march on Saturday does not completely hide the race and class tensions. "I don't understand why blacks and Latinos always have to rob us!" says a merchant. An African-American demonstrator responds, "I don't see any signs here talking about Latasha Harlins."

The TV aerial shots give us a "positive" image of tens of thousands of mobilized citizens calling for peace. As the smoke clears, clean-up crews fan out across the city. Anglo Westsiders venture to Koreatown and even South Central, some for the first time in their lives.

At First A.M.E., the crowd of volunteers is too big — and the earnestness of liberal guilt is apparent everywhere as food

and clothing are loaded into trucks to be sped to the devastated areas. But even as the debris is swept away, the language of race continues to burn. A black man yells at the LAPD, "White devils!" But it isn't just black and white, of course. "The Hispanics..." "Los chinos [a blanket term for Asians in Spanish]..." On TV, the code words are the blanket "they," or "thugs and hooligans." The images, too, capture the gulf. White suburban LA watches from above (the aerial shots) — the black and brown are down below.

The language of race creeps into nearly every discussion. Urban League leader John Mack, sounding like a spokesperson from the English Only movement, tells *Nightline*'s Ted Koppel that Korean-Americans "are in America now," and they have to learn its ways. Korean-Americans marching for peace on Saturday carry placards protesting *Nightline*'s failure to include their voices. Latinos are eager to blame the unrest on blacks. And the city's Mexican-American leadership is virtually silent, unwilling or unable to deal with the Salvadoran problem in Pico-Union.

The strategic positions are more polarized than ever. But that hasn't stopped Tom Bradley from trying to resurrect the old multicultural myth from the ashes. Enter that master of inter-ethnic coalition-building, Peter Ueberroth, to help us sing "We Are the World" together again.

OLYMPIC & BLAINE

On Saturday afternoon, the traffic signals are still out, but civilians — Latinos, African-Americans, Anglos — have taken on traffic-cop duties at all the major intersections. Just past the La Curacao department store on Olympic, a crowd of Latino residents stands outside the remnants of a block-long apartment building. La Curacao was looted, then torched; the flames leapt from the store onto the roof of the apartment building. The top floor was completely gutted, the bottom two floors soaked with thousands of gallons of sooty water. 1301 Olympic Blvd. is a total loss — 30 families are homeless. Burnt and water-damaged TVs, stereos, appliances, clothes, are gathered in piles along the sidewalk.

"We came up to this country looking for a better life," says Andrea Toscán, a native of Guadalajara who lived in the apartment house for 11 years. "What we found was something worse."

The residents complain that the Red Cross promised them assistance yesterday, but failed to show up. The building's owner has assured everyone that insurance will fully cover the loss, and that they can move into a new building as soon as she can build it. But when will that be?

"When we saw La Curacao go up," says César Luisi of Guatemala, "we did everything we could, but we couldn't get the sprinklers to work. We tried the firehoses in the hallways, but they were so old that they broke apart. By that time, it was too late to save anything."

A group of residents walks through the darkened hallways, where cascades of water still pour through the ceiling and down the walls. People are salvaging what they can — perhaps all they will walk away with are kitchen utensils. A grandmother picks through the soggy mush of burnt carpet, looking for the pennies she'd saved.

This is what's left: ruins. Was it an

Los Angeles: Ted Soqui

insurrection, a rebellion, the beginning of a revolution? A directionless rage? A purposeful rage that lost direction? Among the many casualties is the myth of multicultural LA. It is dead because it never really lived — you can't celebrate cultural diversity when the member groups are rent by economic abuse. The image of Anglos, Latinos, Asians and African-Americans joining together in a few clean-up crews will soon fade. In the mixed neighborhoods of Pico-Union, Watts, South Central and Mid-Wilshire, the ethnic groups will eye each other warily. The whites will fear the inner-city more than ever, peering in from above now and then, praying that next time the violence doesn't go any farther north than Pico-Union. Everywhere, the rage will turn against the city's leadership, the politicos, even against the activists and spiritual guides.

Now do you see how bad it is out here? We're capable of anything, that's how bad it is...

On the night of April 29, an organism tens of thousands strong was born of rage

• •

*Largest racial group
in poverty in LA, 1969:
Anglo
Largest racial group
in poverty in LA, 1991:
Latino*

(Source: *LA Weekly* 12/30/88)

and smashed through a paper-thin wall of authority. It moved with purpose and on impulse; it split apart many times over, killing others and itself; it sought justice and carried out its sentence with fire. For now, it is still.

What's left is a gutted building at the corner of Olympic and Blaine. Staring out through a singed window onto Olympic, we watch a fleet of LAPD motorcycle cops cruise by. Two parallel lines of white helmets and Harley-Davidsons. A sudden screech and *bang* — two of the cycles collide, turn over and trigger a chain reaction. Cycles behind them crash, and now, all over the street, cops lie on the pavement. Imagining snipers, they jump up, draw their guns. A few minutes later, along Blaine Street, an impromptu soccer match begins. There are the usual shouts, laughs and curses. The ball bounces up and down the street. Suddenly, everyone has stopped their salvage work and it's just another Saturday afternoon. A man moves in for the goal, kicks the ball as hard as he can. But it shoots up high alongside the building and falls into a dumpster filled with charred, soggy debris. ■

Rubén Martínez is co-host of KCET-TV's public affairs program Life & Times. *He is also a senior editor at the* LA Weekly, *where a version of this story first appeared.*

Riot Chronology

Wednesday, 2 p.m.

While waiting for the Rodney King beating trial verdict to be announced, Dee, 51, and her brother Ty, 46, are killing time. They are watching one of their two video tapes, *Cabin in the Sky*, the 1930s all-black film featuring Ethel Waters, Lena Horne, Butterfly McQueen and other black stars of the era.

At 3 p.m., Dee clicks off the VCR and turns the television set to Channel 11. "I can't believe it," Dee gasps as the first verdict is announced. "Ain't that some shit," Ty blurts out as the second verdict comes down. "Can you believe this?" Dee asks her brother. "They found Koon not guilty of filing false fucking reports. Those racist motherfuckers." As the four officers accept hugs and kisses from their friends, families and attorneys, Dee turns and says, "You know what's going to happen, don't you?" *(Dennis Schatzman)*

Wednesday, 5:30 p.m.

Downtown at Parker Center, a small but steadily growing crowd of protestors begins to jam the area directly in front of LAPD Headquarters. The crowd chants what will soon become familiar refrains: "No justice, no peace" and "Gates must go." Barring access to the walkway and lawn area leading to the police department's front door, a line of helmeted LAPD officers clad in riot gear stands in stony silence across from the protestors.

Wearing a beret, T-shirt and jeans, African-American activist Michael Zinzun hustles up and down the line of marchers, exhorting people to keep moving. Himself a victim of police brutality and illegal spying, this leader of the Coalition Against Police Abuse says, "We are not going to allow the LAPD and the city to take away our rights, or roll back the gains our community has made in this city. Blacks are not surprised that an all-white jury let these cops off. We expected it. Our com-mittee started making plans with other groups for this demonstration three days ago. Now you see the results. We are black, white and Hispanic, and we are all outraged at these verdicts and the fact that Daryl Gates is still Chief."

Asked about the already-occuring incidents of violence against non-blacks triggered by the King verdict, Zinzun shakes his head. "This community has got to realize that an unstable black community means an unstable LA." *(Jim Crogan)*

Wednesday, 7 p.m.

In front of the jammed First African Methodist Episcopal Church parking lot in South Central, hundreds of people, mostly African-Americans with a sprinkling of young whites and Latinos, mill around outside. Inside, the meeting room is filled to capacity and people spill out into the entrance ways and church foyer. All attention is focused on a steady stream of religious and political leaders, including the mayor, City Council representatives and local legislators, who condemn the "not guilty" verdicts. The speakers also plead with people to keep their protests non-violent.

The crowd's response is lukewarm at best. "Free at last. Free at last. Thank God, we're free at last," mocks a suited man in front of me. "Same old, same old," says another. "We're not talking about peace no more. We want some *justice*," says a third. *(Jim Crogan)*

Wednesday, 7:30

Approximately 200 lesbians and gays and their supporters, alerted by fax and word-of-mouth, meet at the corner of San Vicente and Santa Monica boulevards in West Hollywood. The crowd carries signs saying "Queers of All Colors Unite" and "Stop LAPD Racism." Chanting "Guilty as hell!" the marchers, including West Hollywood Mayor Paul Koretz, walk east to La Cienega, then north to Sunset Boulevard, where they hold the middle of the street and reach the LA city limit with no opposition from the county sheriffs. At Sunset and Wilcox, they are blocked by the LAPD. After a brief sit-in and some negoti-ation, the march proceeds up the sidewalk and back onto the street. The protestors continue to Mann's Chinese Theater before they are stopped by police in riot gear. The crowd walks back to West Hollywood without incident. *(Robin Podolsky)*

Wednesday, 8 p.m.

Under cover of darkness, the crowd at Parker Center has grown larger and more confrontational. The police line has also extended, with female officers now assum-ing the point position in front of the LAPD's front door. Behind the police line, sergeants and officers continue to move back and forth, issuing orders to "tighten up the line and stay alert."

The composition of the crowd has likewise changed. Gone are the older pro-testers and representatives of well-known local leftist and solidarity organizations. In their place stands a younger, increasingly integrated crowd.

All along the line, individual police officers are being challenged by members of the crowd. "You should be out here with us throwing stones. You can't hide your color behind that uniform. You take that off and you're just another nigger to the LAPD," screams an enraged black youth to an implacable black cop. Down the line, another white protester zeroes in on an overweight Latino cop. Stepping menacingly close, he keeps yelling, "You're not only a pig, you're a fat pig. You think you're bad. Let's see how bad you are." The Latino officer swings his baton into his tormentor's stomach, shoves him back-ward and very calmly says, "Get in my face one more time and you'll find out exactly how bad I am." *(Jim Crogan)*

Wednesday, 8:30 p.m.

The crowd, which has been throwing aluminum cans and wads of paper at the police line, adds bottles and eggs to its fusillade. Suddenly a cheer goes up as a protester rushes forward with a U.S. flag which is lit, thrown in front of the police and stomped on by some of the crowd. A second protester rushes forward with the Confederate Stars and Bars, which is likewise lit and thrown in the air. The chanting crowd surges forward to a group of female officers. For the first time the officers look fearful and take a step forward, swinging their batons back to defend against the expected assault. A black demonstrator steps forward and screams at the mostly white officers, "Welcome to South Central, motherfuckers, how do you like it so far?" *(Jim Crogan)*

Wednesday, 8:50 p.m.

The first arrests finally occur at Parker Center as two demonstrators attempt to cross the police line at different points. A third protester, a black youth who had been particularly vocal, is picked off by the police and ushered back into Parker Center. Suddenly leaders in the crowd direct demonstrators to a kiosk in the parking lot near the left flank of the LAPD line. Protesters grab a stool from inside the kiosk and begin smashing windows. Someone produces gasoline and a match and the kiosk is soon fully engulfed by flames. Standing back by the police line, a white cop wipes egg from the side of his face and uniform, and says, "I guess they thought I was hungry. Maybe I should thank them for the delivery.

"It's gonna get a lot worse," he continues. "I'm a motorcycle cop and they told us not to even consider riding on the streets. I expect full-scale riots by the end of the week." What did he think of the verdict? "People don't realize what you go through out there on the streets. Nobody knows how they'll react until they're in that situation." *(Jim Crogan)*

Wednesday, midnight

Baby Saye walks past onlookers and other looters with three six-roll packs of two-ply Charmin toilet paper. "I know what you're thinking but basically fuck you," says Baby Saye, 26, who describes herself as a life-long welfare recipient. "I've been wiping my ass and my children's asses with that scratchy shit all my life because I can't afford the good shit. Now I got Charmin, just like those white jurors. So there!" *(Dennis Schatzman)*

Thursday, 12:30 a.m.

"Hey reporter, hey reporter," a woman, noting a reporter's press credentials, calls out. "Here's something you ain't got," she says as she pulls out a crumpled *Daily News* article from her back jeans pocket. "I've got the names of those people on the jury. I kept this because I knew I was going to need it." Unfolding the article, the woman, who won't give her name, points to the names as others look on. "Dorothy Bailey," the woman starts, "Alice Debord, Thomas Gorton, Henry King, Retta Kossow, Virginia Loya, Gerald Miler, Christopher Morgan, Amelia Pigeon, Charles Sheehan, Kevin Siminski and Anna Whiting. If I had some money, I'd put a contract on these white bastards," she threatens. "This is all their fault." *(Dennis Schatzman)*

Thursday, 7 a.m.

By the time I arrive at the shopping center on Venice and Western at 7 a.m. on Thursday, J.J. Newberry's department store is a gutted, charred shell. As I roll in, four police cars, each filled with five cops in riot gear, pull out, followed by two fire engines.

Down at the Sav-on, the looting has already started. People stream through the store's broken front door. Many are Latino, perhaps 70 percent, reflecting the population of this neighborhood bordering the heart of South Central. One guy, looking like John Belushi at his most bloated, walks out with his fingers around the necks of four gallons of Burgundy, the pockets of his red nylon shorts bulging with pints of whiskey. A Greek chorus of eight black men in their fifties and sixties, sounding much like Sweet Dick Willie and the corner men in *Do the Right Thing*, stands about 20 feet from the doorway. "Help yourself, help yourself," they shout as a big-bellied Latino wearing a "Fuck You" T-shirt wheels out a shopping cart filled to the brim with AA batteries and Ramses condoms.

The first flash of anger comes from a balding black man in a gray ski jacket and glasses. Earlier, four black teenagers had run into the store, each carrying empty suitcases. Now they have come out laughing, suitcases bulging. "I got a calculator," says one; "I got some ice cream," says another. The man in the ski jacket walks up to the tallest of the kids, and says, "Man, all the shit you take, it's gonna come back on you. It's real stupid shit you're doin'. Leave it and *respect* yourself." For a moment the teen looks uncertain, until his friend in a Miami Heat cap says, "Man, if you feel like you need this, then *take* it." "Take it?" says the man, "and give up your respect?" "Fuck respect," replies Miami Heat. "They didn't give *us* no respect."

As they stroll away, two black women call out: "No shame, no shame." Meanwhile, the chorus gives its view. "All the people of color that was injured," says one man, "they took 'em over to Daniel Freeman.... But that white fireman that got shot, they took over to Cedars Sinai. You see what I'm saying?" "And Westwood, Westwood," says another. "They were down there *en masse*. Stuff was happening since three o'clock down in South Central and they did not go down there — *not once*."

"That's right," says a third man. "Let them niggers destroy their *own* neighborhood."

As they talk, a dark, angry-looking man of about 30 drives up in a beat-up white Mazda, scowls and starts yelling: "Fuck 'em, take everything, fuck 'em, take everything." Then a wiry-looking black kid, maybe 19, starts doing the Ali shuffle around me, chanting, "You in the wrong neighborhood, man, you in the wrong neighborhood." The guy in the Mazda walks over and says two words: "Get going." I try not to move too fast as I head for my car. *(Joe Domanick)*

Thursday, 8 a.m.

I drive south on Normandie into South Central. By 29th Street I can see smoke framing the background of the steeple of the Abundant Life Christian

Los Angeles: Ted Soqui

Church on Jefferson and Normandie — coming from Frankie and Anne's Beauty Salon on 39th Street. The four other small stores next to Frankie and Anne's have already burned to the ground, and straight down Normandie, as far as I can see, stores are ablaze. On the street corners black men mill about, many holding 40-ounce cans of Olde English or bottles of Bud. Every corner brings another store burning or an already smoldering, looted hulk.

I cut down a side street, and at 55th and Normandie I spot an elderly Korean woman with a garden hose watering down the blackened embers of her grocery store.

"Three time fire department come. I don't know what happen....I lose everything," she tells me. Her son comes over. "All they [the fire department] could do," he says, "is wet the roof down and let it burn, they had to go to another place..."

Just then a black woman with braided hair walks across the street, comes up, stops and says: "My store, my store, what have they done to my store?...I shopped here everyday. These people were wonderful. Now there's no place to shop. I mean I need milk. I have two grandchildren to look after. Where am I gonna shop? The Valley?"

I leave, cutting down another side-street past neat bungalows and craftsmen cottages with their well-landscaped front yards. Everything is remarkably still and calm, seemingly as far from the madness of Normandie as a street in Beverly Hills. Of course, it's only 8:20 in the morning.

I get out of my car and approach two black women, Lisa, heavy-set and wearing a T-shirt with an old lady in a rocking chair that says, "I've still got it but nobody wants to have it," and Brenda, thin and wearing burgundy sweats. "Yesterday evening," Lisa says, "the Crips and the Bloods tied their rags together and said they was united. That it was now a black thing. The Crips drove up in cars. And the Bloods, you know, thought they was fixin' to bust them, and the Crips said no, and they just started huggin' each other sayin' they wanted to unite."

"That's right," says Brenda, "they said it was over for gang-banging...." Is this a Blood neighborhood?" I ask. "It was," says Lisa. "Now we united," says Brenda. "When we took that walk down there by 60th and over by Florence, we united.... They wanted to get these Korean stores out of the neighborhoods, I mean they let Due off for killin' a black girl, and then these police...."

I leave. Three black men in their thirties stand with a beautiful young African-American woman holding an infant. I ask them about the gangs. "They tied their rags together," says Cecil, tall and light-skinned. "The red and the blue," adds Kenny, a balding man of 37. "And they held up the power sign." "Now they all be wearing black rags."

"And I'll tell you," says Cecil, "the shit was *organized*....You know what I'm talkin' about. There was generals and soldiers, and when they started burning down that liquor store they sent some of them out to direct traffic, and some others had brought tools." "Uh huh," says Kenny. "And the Koreans, well, you know they gonna pay." *(Joe Domanick)*

Thursday, 1:30 p.m.

At 52nd Street and Figueroa, I stop near the burned-out ruins of the T&Y Market. In front, three African-American boys, Michael, Martin and A.G., ages 10, 9 and 7, play near the edge of the market's parking lot. The ruined store is still smoking badly.

"Why did they do it?" I ask. "They burned it up 'cause of Rodney King," says Martin. "They wanted to kill the police." "The police didn't own this store, did they?" I continue. "No," says Michael, "Mexicans owned this store and there was a Mexican policeman who beat up Rodney King and so they burned up the Mexican's store." "I liked this store," another boy says. "The people were nice to us." *(Jim Crogan)*

Thursday, 1:45 p.m.

As I finish talking to the boys, Jerry, shirtless and wearing jeans, and his brother Aaron, wearing a multicolored beret, T-shirt and jeans, approach and demand to know if I'm from the media. Both men appear to be in their late twenties, perhaps early thirties. Yes, I say, and ask if they want to talk. "It wasn't just the Rodney King verdict," says Aaron. "It's the whole thing, the shooting of Latasha Harlins and the lack of jail time for that Korean woman. The Koreans treat us bad," he continues. "You go into their stores and they treat you like, 'Give me your money and get the fuck out of here.' That's not right. They treat us like dogs."

Neither Jerry or Aaron say they know who burned the market. Nor did they engage in any looting. "That's not how we live," they say. Both brothers say they watched the market burn and the police and firemen never came to stop the fire or the looting. "Last night," adds Aaron, "I got my weapons and stayed on guard in my house. If anyone had come into my yard — and I don't care if they were black, white, Asian or fudge ripple — I would have shot them dead. So I don't think a lot of this violence here is racially motivated. The anger is mostly against the cops. They pull you over, humiliate you, call you nigger, beat you and nothing ever happens to them."

Jerry says he believes people have lost compassion for each other. "I try and tell the kids I know to be cool, but they imitate what they see —" "I think," interrupts Aaron, "it's the endtimes. I think it's Revelations and the end of the world." *(Jim Crogan)*

Thursday, 4:10 p.m.

At the intersection of Alvarado and Pico, the corner swap meet is engulfed in flames, thick black clouds of smoke from the nearby body and paint shop darkening the sky. Five fire trucks and many fireman fight the blaze, their efforts interrupted by explosions of thinner and paint cans. This was my neighborhood. I grew up a block away, and I never thought — not even in 1965 — that anything like this would occur in the quiet side of my relatively calm neighborhood.

While most of the media focus on the blazing structures, a small drama unfolds nearby. The site is the Payless Shoe Source, right behind a Mexican bakery. A lone woman faces a frenzied mob intent on looting her store. She's running from side to side, chasing people who are throwing rocks, cans, anything they can get their hands on. The glass behind her holds, but the steel curtain protecting the outside of the store is giving way as 10 people pull.

Suddenly a young man carrying a huge cement tire-stopper like a battering ram runs toward the plate glass. It must weigh 40 pounds. The screaming woman sees him and runs to intercept, knowing full well that if the glass is shattered it will be impossible to contain the mob. She catches him and wrestles the cement block from him, the crowd momentarily transfixed by the courage of this woman. I think I hear clapping from behind me. But just as suddenly, two police cruisers pull in; four cops chase the mob away. *(Tony Miramontes)*

Thursday, 5:30 p.m.

Sirens blaring, 10 sheriffs' cars lead the first contingent of National Guardsmen west on Vernon to the intersection of Figueroa. They turn right on Figueroa and head into the Ralph's lot. This is the first detachment of guardsmen deployed during the riots. In full battle-dress and armed with M-16s, 85 guardsmen have arrived at the site. One white guardsman, 22-year-old William Weber, asks me if I'm scared. "Yes, but I try not to dwell on it," I say. Weber says, "I've got two bulletproof vests on and all this gear, plus an M-16, and I sure *am* scared. I just graduated from Guard school in Alabama and now I'm here. We didn't get much notice. I'm from LA and I got about two hours' notice before I had to report to Los Alamitos. My mom was crying. She was really scared for me. I didn't get to talk to my girlfriend before I left, so that will have to wait for awhile," he says.

"My friends made fun of me 'cause they were all going to Germany, but I'm here where the action is." Weber says he wants to be a cop and feels the Guard would help him in that area. He pulls an Instamatic camera from his pocket and says, "Say, can you take a picture of me?" *(Jim Crogan)*

Thursday, 6 p.m.

During the last few hours, heavy traffic escaping the city has been general throughout Silver Lake, one of the few shallow valleys leading north out of the basin. Hyperion Avenue, under smoke, is gridlocked. Outside of the neighborhood karate studio, a half-dozen men in robes are lined up along the sidewalk, arms folded, waiting for looters now six blocks away. Zig-zagging up a hill overlooking the west, I find a single vacant lot to watch from. Arsonists have now reached Hollywood, and there is so much smoke above the city that the blue Dianetics building blends into its grey surroundings. Soon carloads of families discover our lot. They come in Jeep Cherokees, Range Rovers. They wear khaki shorts and Izod shirts and in their hands are mixed drinks.

Someone suggests a barbecue, to laughter. One father videotapes his toddler son, complete with zooming special effects that end on the burning city. Men with binoculars point and speak authoritatively; their wives tell jokes about lost shopping opportunities. *(Dave Gardetto)*

Friday, 1:30 p.m.

Members of the Church of Scientology spent Thursday night surrounding their property and the property of others along Hollywood Boulevard and Vermont. Early Friday many joined the Hollywood Beautification Team, organized through the City Attorney's office to help clean up the neighborhood. "We have a lot of property...over on Hollywood and Ivar," says Shirley Young, a church member. "There's also a senior citizen's home back there. We had a human chain around them. Today we all joined as a community group to really try to do something."

In the hot afternoon, Church members, along with approximately 50 others, walk the boulevard wearing yellow T-shirts, sweeping up debris. Unfortunately, a passer-by hears the word "Scientology" and begins looking for a fight. "They should have burned Scientology. They should have trashed the church!" he yells. A fistfight breaks out between the man and a church member. Five LAPD officers patrolling the street break it up without making arrests. *(Paul Malcolm)*

Friday, 8 p.m.

After almost two and a half days of violence, an eerie calm descends on parts of South Central. LAPD Commander Mike Bostic, the LAPD's use-of-force expert who testified against the four officers at the King trial, is at the ABC Market at the intersection of Vernon and Vermont. Bostic has taken charge of the sector bounded by Jefferson and Slauson, Western and the Harbor Freeway. "Yes, I'm the real LAPD use-of-force expert, not the pretend one the defense brought forward to testify," he says. Responding to the verdict, a very affable and open Bostic says he was "dumbfounded" that no guilty pleas were returned by the Simi Valley jury. "The jury said afterwards, 'Yeah we heard Bostic and we agree it was excessive, we just didn't think it was criminal.'"

"What's the difference?" I ask. "It has to do with intent," says Bostic. "The jury gave the police officers every benefit of the doubt. They figured there's a sergeant there and he's directing the takedown and these guys are just following orders. But it's clear that to me that they overstepped their bounds and violated department policy on the use of force. Everybody at one time or another can get pushed to the limit on the street. But normally there's someone there to reach over and put their hand on you and say, 'That's it. That's enough.' Clearly that didn't happen here."

Bostic says his reception from fellow officers after his testimony has been great. "They've been very supportive, and I'm still receiving fan mail from all over the world," he says with a laugh. "We've also taught one class on the use of force and they listen much closer now." *(Jim Crogan)*

Saturday, 3 a.m.

As three of us walk past the coffee counter to our table at the Denny's in Simi Valley, locals are discussing civil defense. The violence will never reach their quiet suburban town nestled in the rocky hills, they decide. The 118 West is the only way into their town, and "the niggers are too stupid to figure it out."

Two men in the booth must hear our reaction to their quipping, because they begin a loud litany of racist jokes and taunts. Angrily, we ask them to stop.

"C'mon," they respond, "We're all white here." The words that follow prompt the manager to ask us to stop using profanity. This is, she reminds us, a family restaurant. *(Paul Malcolm)*

Saturday, noon

We park around the corner from the burned-out mini-mall at Second and Vermont, but even there the water running down the gutter is almost over the curb. Looting has left a kind of high-tide mark: the shards of a cassette box, a tangle of audiotape, a dozen CD packages (only the

cardboard), three strawberry jello salads in lidded plastic dishes and a pair of worn — but not that worn — Reeboks. Below them, flattened by the rushing water, lie the remains of a Nike box.

At the mall, 30 or 40 people are using shovels to knock stucco loose from fallen walls. The occasional intact sheets of plywood are saved to board up windows elsewhere. The remaining chicken wire, charred beams and bent metal are pitched back into the blackened shell.

Conversation clings to the practical: "Excuse me" or "Watch out for those nails." Wire-cutters are the tool everyone wishes they'd thought to bring. When we leave, the sidewalk and parking lot are clear of debris, and the litter barrel has been restored to its place in front of the gutted shops.

On our way back to the car we dump the Reeboks and the jello salads into our last garbage bag. An elderly Latino couple passes with sacks of groceries. Their shell-shocked look deepens as they take in what we were doing. Such a damned silly, fruitless, liberal gesture. But they seem pleased all the same. *(Ariel Swartley)*

Saturday, 3 p.m.

Near the corner of 61st and Hoover, across the street from John Muir School, is what remains of a burned-out mini-mart which had mostly non-black and Asian-owned stores. Next to a Korean-owned nail-and-beauty-supply shop are traces of a small public library that served the area. Black, charred and smoking books still line the scorched shelves. Ashen remnants of books, tapes and magazines cover the floor.

Hoover Street, the scene of some of the heaviest looting, burning and violence in South Central, now retains an uneasy calm. A group of children walks up the street past the school, including four black girls and one Mexican boy. Shayla, a 13-year-old, is in 7th grade at John Muir. "We would always go in and read. It was our only place," she says. "I like the *Cat in the Hat* books the best."

Shayla says she saw the fire but didn't know who set it. "It was really scary. I feel really sad about the library." *(Jim Crogan)*

Sunday, 1:00 a.m.

Michael Moore, KCRW's late-night hip-hop DJ, turns the mike over to a man named Brother JC. The flames, Brother says, are a good thing. "We have been more unified in the last four days than we have been in the last 30 years....To the brothers and sisters out there: Don't be hardened that a few businesses were burnt down. It was nothing but urban renewal. We're cleaning up what was dirty, so we can build what is clean. We don't need liquor stores no way, brother, we got too many of them. We got too many churches, brother....We better start putting away canned goods, and putting away water, so next time this situation happens, we won't be crying about it like babies, we'll stand up like strong black men and women." *(RJ Smith)*

Sunday, 11 a.m.

During packed services at South Central's Unity Fellowship Church, Rev. Carl Bean tells the lesbian and gay congregation, "I hate violence. But I'm *not* sorry the reaction to the verdict happened. It's become too comfortable to hate a Jew, a gay, a Latino, a woman, a black person. As gays of color, we know the way the 'isms' — and the denial America has about them — are tearing our country apart. The violence on the streets is about state violence that was not prosecuted for many years. I say, 'See the links, America.' That means, 'Gay America,' too." After Bean's service, dozens of African-American, Latino, Asian and Anglo queers arrive at Bean's Church, wielding brooms to help in the clean-up effort in South Central.

"Shunned by straight blacks and rejected by white gays, I have felt like the child of a mixed marriage," says Steven Corbin, a novelist and co-chair of the people-of-color caucus at ACT-UP/LA, as he tearfully sweeps up burned debris. "But with my heart breaking, every ounce of my identity as a black queer is about putting this city together." *(Doug Sadownick)* ∎

Excerpted from the LA Weekly.

Hello USA, This is LA

What it was like on the day it was a bad day to be anybody in LA

by Frank Chin

There were signs the times were freaking out. All over LA, wherever I drove, from Echo Park, Silver Lake to Hollywood to downtown and J-Town and Chinatown, I saw magpies harassing hawks all over the sky. There were other signs, of good times. There was an oriole, bright yellow and stark black on the wings and throat in our weird tree's flowering red fingers the morning of the day my friend the TV went crazy with bad bad news.

I picked up Sam from the school bus a little before three. He buckled himself in the back seat and we were on our way to Chinatown for our usual after-school noodles when the news of the verdict acquitting the cops who'd beaten Rodney King came between country songs and an appropriately remote broadcast from Hawaii, hyping travel on the LA FM country-music station. "It's a bad day to be a cop or a black man," I said.

My seven-year-old son knew Rodney King was the black man he'd seen beaten by LA cops on TV, last March just after we

were back home from a trip up and down Interstate 5 to Seattle, through the Gulf war and back down a road bristling with a new, more blatant white racism. Skinheads in Portland. A resort restaurant in Northern California saying "We're closed" when they were full of white people stuffing all manner of breakfasts in their faces. And home to see Rodney King shot twice with a stun gun and beaten and beaten and beaten.

Between then and now, black dislike grew for Koreans in little mom-and-pop groceries and liquor stores. The Koreans spoke with guttural accents and seemed to blacks to be rude, surly and contemptuous. The Korean groceries and liquor stores had all been broken into or robbed. Mom and pop had the same prejudice about blacks as the white Americans who'd taught it to them. It might have helped if the blacks understood Korean manners and how Korean culture had been toughened by a long history of being kicked around by the Chinese and the Japanese, and how it had to endure a war-time society riddled with vicious spies. In Korea, being inquisitive

about your neighbors and their personal lives is not necessarily a friendly gesture.

The tension broke when a Korean grocer shot a black teenage girl in the back and killed her. The grocer believed the girl was stealing a bottle of orange juice. The store's security camera, which recorded the whole event on videotape, showed the girl approaching the counter with money in her open hand as the grocer raged and screamed at her. The grocer was found guilty of voluntary manslaughter and given a suspended sentence. Blacks were outraged and are even now demanding the recall of the judge who let a Korean woman kill a black teenager without jail time.

In response to the anger, the Korean mom-and-pop grocers stopped making change and throwing it at their customers. They learned to smile and make Ozzie-and-Harriet Hollywood TV-commercial small talk. I found it a little disconcerting: smiling and small talk as a Korean martial art. The effort the Korean mom-and-pop stores were making to get along with the surrounding community was obvious all over LA. No doubt about it, they were willing to work at getting along, and the standard of getting along was hard-style Disneyland.

After our noodles in Chinatown we drove home past Dodger Stadium, saw a hawk flap its wings over a line of palm trees and saw it was being run off by a pair of nagging magpies, saw the same thing across the street from our house across our view of the HOLLYWOOD sign, and turned on our friend the TV set and saw it was a bad day to be anybody in LA.

Korean mom-and-pops and generic LA mini-malls seemed to be looter- and pyro-bait. On the English-language LA channels, some newspeople disconnected major sections of their brains. The pretty faces and trained voices who thought they could do the news till the cows came home didn't see that the cows *were* home. One reporter had no idea the guns she was describing in the hands of people were real guns. When the police shoved her out of the way, she reacted not to the gunfire, but to the cop's rude shove.

Back in the newsroom, a million-dollar anchorman asked a pie-eyed, panic-stricken ninny chattering his teeth in the mike if most of the looters didn't look like "illegal aliens." The pretty face frozen on hold grabbed the anchorman's question like a lifesaver and said, "Yes, the looters look like most of them are illegal aliens." To these fools, *I* would look like an illegal alien. If Barbara Bush should be pushing a shopping cart, *she'*d look like an illegal alien.

Reporting on the looting and burning of Korean stores, now working into Koreatown proper, the reporters for the English-language news ran from pompous to melodramatic to panic-stricken. It wasn't until the newscopter saw the wave of looters charge in and out of Fedco, a huge warehouse discount store for government and state employees, that the newsies lost complete control of their emotions. Mr. Purple Prose of the news choppers gave up the morally loaded philosophical lingo and said it all, his voice going up and down out of control in amazement and moral outrage, "They're looting Fedco!" as if Fedco were a church or an orphanage.

My neighbors weren't among the looters. College-educated. Liberal. Mixed marriages. Middle-class. Still, they acted strange. As the smoke from the fires stuffed the air with the smell of burning rubber and electrical insulation and feathery black leaves of the ash fell on our houses and grass, I saw some neighbors come out of their house with a portable TV, turn it on and get into their outdoor Jacuzzi — to what? Work off the tension of the day? Others started barbecuing in their backyards at sunset and invited friends, as if the curfew didn't include them, and the gunfire we heard clearly, a block or a mile away we couldn't tell, wouldn't come any closer, and the smoke from burning LA would not flavor their meat.

The verdict from Simi Valley told us all: In LA there is no law. The looters didn't read the news in the paper. They got it off the TV and the radio, their best friends, their storytellers. The looters were the children of the children who never had a childhood. Kids of kids who grew up alone, who never had a story told them by a live body, who grew up with TV as their storyteller. The black, white, Asian and Latino kids and families out looting together were just acting like society on their TV acts when there is no law. Had they had a sense of myth that began with a live storyteller telling stories their people have valued through history, and if not those, then stories any people value — Greek myths, Bible stories, Br'er Rabbit, Hans Christian Andersen, the Peach Boy, the Boy born of Lotus — more people might have looked on themselves as more than the moral equivalent of consumer goods and stayed away from the mob.

Then on TV there was a fake Spanish California Mission P-style mini-mall, with a guard from a private Korean security outfit on the roof with an Uzi, a jumpsuit, flak jacket, baseball cap and dark glasses. The call had gone out on the channel that aired Korean programming for all good men to come to the aid of their Koreatown at the mini-mall. They showed up with shotguns, pistols of all kinds, Uzis and AK-47s. The Alamo in Koreatown was a mini-mall. In the race war that's started, are we all going to choose up sides and appear at the appropriate mini-mall to man the barricades?

The combined TV of LA, with its two Spanish-language channels and hours of Chinese, Japanese, Korean, Vietnamese, Farsi and on and on programming and visions of the action on the streets was a vision of LA beyond *Blade Runner*, and not real, I thought. It's all grotesque exaggeration. And it's impossible to choose up sides. The racially and culturally specific parts of towns — the barrios, Chinatown, Li'l Tokyo, whites, Jews, Christians and even the dreamers and movie stars of LA — are all too interwoven in each other's business and loyalties to simply drop everything and Alamo-up at our mini-mall, behind barricades of rice sacks and shopping carts. We cannot blast and shoot each other into oneness. But we can agree on a common standard and language of civility. People seemed to agree the fire department was a good thing. It was a start: Whole civilizations have been started with less.

Then George Bush declared war on LA, sounding as frustrated and pained as Alberto Fujimori ruling by mandate in Peru. This Sunday night, as Sam is down to sleep to be up early off to school in the morning, martial law seems to have worked. I drive to and from Chinatown along deserted streets in broad daylight. I am the only customer this restaurant has had in the last two days. They and their Latino kitchen helpers don't know whether to set the tables or stack them up. On the way back, I hear on the radio news of a huge peace rally in Koreatown. People are praying for forgiveness of the looters and peace in LA. Whole families show up. Others stop and join. Estimates range from 30,000 to 100,000. It seems like good news, as I drive past stuff from the looting binge appearing for sale at yard sales.

This is the America where reading is only good for reading signs and price tags. There is no story, no myth, no history, no art. Only TV. And now that the U.S. Marines and the Army have had a taste of treating American streets like Panama and Grenada, I wonder if they can go home again. ■

Frank Chin's most recent book was titled Donald Duk. *This story first appeared in the* Seattle Weekly.

For there are those who live in darkness,
And those who live in light,
Those in brightness you see,
Those in darkness, out of sight.
— Bertolt Brecht

Los Angeles: Cynthia Wiggins

Some People Don't Count

by Marc Cooper and Greg Goldin

Panama, Iraq, now Los Angeles. True, as one Marine put it, "It's not as cut and dried here as in Desert Storm — you don't know who your enemy is." But the 10,000 troops, shipped in mostly after the upheaval was over, found plenty to do. Machine-gun-toting detachments of the National Guard sealed off the basketball courts and bike and skate paths of Venice Beach. Platoons of soldiers secured their positions under the burned-out palm trees of the Civic Center. Some 45 miles from the epicenter of the disturbances, desert-camouflaged armor stood sentinel over a string of shopping malls as white suburbanites went binge-buying, stocking up on food, treats and videos before the dusk-to-dawn curfew fell again. At the boutique markets — the Gelson's and Pavilions — polished Jags and buffed-out Range Rovers shared parking space with Humvees and APCs as the patrons weathered two-hour checkout lines. Soldiers also kept the freeways open as those who could afford it raced away, booking every $350-a-night resort room on the white-sands beaches of Santa Barbara, Laguna and Dana Point over their cellular phones.

Another 1,000 Marines roared into the heart of LA's black ghetto, past still-smoldering fires and blocks of collapsed buildings, cautiously eyeing another set of anxious citizens lined up three and four abreast. But this was no frenzy for food or gasoline or videotapes. All that was long gone, either looted or incinerated. South Central residents endured hours under the smoke-filtered sun from the moment the curfew lifted to deep into the afternoon, to pick up their welfare and Social Security checks from a paralyzed Post Office — in

the vain hope that, if you got there early enough, there might be time to head north for supplies and beat it back before night-fall.

South Central certainly did not greet the soldiers with confetti and yellow ribbons. But given the Hobson's choice of being policed either by the black-uniformed LAPD, with its "super sniper squads" and battering rams under the command of Chief Daryl F. Gates, or by the winter soldiers temporarily dispatched by Mayor Tom Bradley and Governor Pete Wilson, well...there was hardly a contest.

After all, it was Chief Gates and his free-swinging clubbers who got LA into this mess in the first place. The not-guilty verdict in the Rodney King case not only launched the phosphorous flare signaling that it is completely legal to beat the stuffing out of black men, and that justice is a word reserved for whites only, but also ignited 27 years of boundless fury and frustration bottled up since the last uprising.

By early Sunday morning, the tally was 10,000 businesses laid waste, 58 corpses at the morgue, 9,500 people arrested and a

price tag approaching a billion dollars. A small, multiracial detail of civilians, armed with brooms and dustpans and led by actor Eddie Olmos, was busy sweeping the street. With the official media and bewildered political leaders latching onto this operation as "just what the city needed" and "the beginning of the healing process," reality was disappearing from the spotlight, threatening to turn this exercise of civic goodwill into one more ritual of collective denial.

What looks to the television cameras like so many mounds of rubble is, in reality, a mosaic of anger over decades of LAPD brutality, of agony over a court system that sends a black man to jail for shooting a dog while freeing a Korean shopkeeper who shot a black teenager, of frustration over an economy that no longer provides a real living, of discontent with a welfare system that punishes. The growing heap being carted to the city dump contains the recognition by blacks, Latinos and disenfranchised whites that they are not merely discriminated against, they are abandoned, written off as "losers."

"The people who were responding

42

with such violence today are not people for whom the problem is just Daryl Gates," said one black activist. "The problem is the notion that some people count and some don't."

At the height of the looting and rioting, it was difficult to escape the conclusion that the turmoil most benefitted one man: Chief Daryl Gates. In the week before the Rodney King verdict, Gates — alone among city officials and public leaders — predicted widespread violence should officers Timothy Wind, Laurence Powell, Theodore Briseno and Stacey Koon walk free. The chief triumphantly declared that he had set aside a million dollars to pay overtime for putting down an uprising. But when the uprising began, Gates appeared to be in hiding.

The shock wave that emanated from the Simi Valley Courthouse became deadly at approximately 5 p.m. Wednesday. At the intersection of Florence and Normandie avenues, practically dead center in South Central LA, what began as bottle and rock-throwing soon turned to the looting of a liquor store and a small neighborhood market by perhaps two dozen people. As television news helicopters arrived, the situation turned ugly. Live, unedited, on every station along the dial, a macabre, public reenactment of the Rodney King beating was broadcast. This time, however, it was whites being pummeled by a crowd of blacks — just as Gates had warned. For an hour or more, the audience of electronic onlookers watched three motorists being clobbered with fists and rocks. Back at the anchor desks, the talking heads confidently intoned at first, "I'm sure the police are on the way." Later, it became a panicky wail: "Where are the police? Where are the police?"

By the time the last victim, ill-fated truck driver Reginald Denny, rolled his 18-wheeler smack into the middle of the deadly mayhem, TV news crews were practically frantic. Pleading for a police presence, they narrated an attempted murder. One man yanked Denny from his cab, two others kicked and stomped him as he lay helpless on the asphalt. Finally a third

man grabbed the fire extinguisher from his truck and crashed it down upon Denny's skull. While he lay on the ground, another man came up to him and slowly went through his pockets, fleeing with Denny's wallet. It was a pitiful, wrenching picture, and the whole city was watching.

Ironically, Chief Daryl Gates, the one man in a position to halt what up to then appeared to be an isolated incident, was on his way to a fundraiser in opposition to Proposition F — the June charter amendment written after the King beating to reform the LAPD. "There are going to be situations where people are without assistance," Gates said as he was leaving the cushy Brentwood fundraiser. "That's just the facts of life."

The man who said he'd never let it happen in his town, who had fattened the public purse with a million dollars in anticipation of a general insurrection, declared no tactical alert, issued no orders to block off the streets leading to and from Normandie and Florence, offered no police escorts to ambulances and fire trucks. (In fact, it was Mayor Bradley who finally ordered police to the scene, and on May 4th the Police Commission announced an official inquiry into the delay.) The garrulous Chief, usually given to incendiary remarks and decisive action, was silent. "Daryl Gates was in a position to allow the black community to go up in flames," an aide to black state Senator Diane Watson said, "and he did."

Even after Governor Wilson granted Mayor Bradley's request for National Guard militia, Gates took a day and a half to deploy the first 500 citizen-soldiers out of a complement of 6,000.

It was vintage Daryl Gates. What other police department would allow its cops to beat an innocent man to within an inch of his life, leaving him emotionally riven and allegedly brain-damaged, and 14 months later sit idly by as three other innocents were nearly beaten to death? Gates's message was loud and clear: Now you see what it is like when you don't want an effective police department, a force that cracks heads. The boss of LA's Police Protective League quickly seconded Gates,

wagging his finger at complacent liberals: This is what you get when you have a police department that is "understaffed and undermanned."

Gates's inflammatory omissions were hardly improvised. From the very moment KTLA News aired amateur photographer George Holliday's video of Rodney King's assault, Gates has successfully stared down Mayor Bradley and his liberal allies. The Chief's seeming omnipotence stems not only from his limitless arrogance but from the policy of appeasement pursued by the Bradley coalition of downtown businessmen, black community leaders and Westside liberals — the key supporters of the Christopher Commission reforms. Like a Latin American colonel to whom democratically elected leaders are always kowtowing, Gates can usually count upon his opponents to temporize and backpeddle for fear that they may arouse the pro-police constituency to action. Hemmed in by antiquated local ordinances insulating Gates behind civil-service protections, the Bradley establishment has been unwilling to tap into the anger of its natural constituency, the black and Latino communities. Like their national counterparts in the Democratic Party, Bradley and his handpicked police commissioners, as well as his allies on the City Council, prefer to appease conservative swing voters in the San Fernando Valley rather than mobilize the mass of unregistered and potentially volatile voters at the bottom of LA's food chain.

"We didn't want to offend Daryl Gates," Meir Westreich, a civil rights attorney and author of the police reforms appearing on the June ballot, said. "We felt we had to tiptoe around." The conciliatory stance, designed to nudge Gates aside, was a failure from its inception. In March of last year, at Bradley's insistence and with the blessings of the City Attorney, the Police Commission suspended Gates. Within days, the City Council — angered by the commission's newfound independence — overruled them, with five of Gates's erstwhile liberal opponents providing the swing votes. It was a flip-flopping fiasco, only to be compounded later, in July, when Gates made a written promise to leave the department by April of 1992.

By late summer, the Christopher Commission gave the official stamp to the public's dismal rating of the LAPD as a brutal, racist, autocratic occupying force. Still, Gates persevered, despite his promise to resign. And, once again, the City Council, the mayor and the Police Commission acquiesced, insisting that Gates would be gone by April, when a new police chief would be on board and the reform initiative would be before voters.

And so the charade went, right up to the eve of the riots. One week before chaos brought the months-long waffling to a cold, sobering halt, Police Commission President Stanley Sheinbaum and Chief Gates got into a shouting match. Gates announced he was making promotions and changes among the top echelon at Parker Center — a direct slap in the face of chief-designate Willie Williams, the black police commissioner of Philadelphia. Sheinbaum — the gruff, seventyish, left-liberal rain-maker, financier of *Ramparts* magazine and former head of the ACLU Foundation — was unequivocal. Gates would make no such appointments. By Tuesday, 24 hours before LA went up in flames, the Bradley minions wimped out one last time. Gates could make his staffing changes — thereby prolonging his paramilitary legacy — so long as the commission "oversaw" the new appointments. Once again, the Chief snickered as his opponents backed down.

"Had the City Council swing votes put Gates out the door last year," Westreich concluded, "I don't think this city would have reacted with this level of anger."

Then, too, there is the possibility that Gates may stay on beyond June 30. He has not yet formally submitted his retirement, in writing, to city officials. "Until he does that," Meyer Westrich says, "it is a joke."

The whole process of reform, according to one black political insider, depends upon Daryl Gates. In the darkest scenario yet, chief-designate Willie Williams will be dragged down by the rioting. "He will be put into a position that will be construed as compromising his commitment to the department from the standpoint of the police. And he will be attacked, anonymously at first, by police on the line. Then he'll be attacked by the Police Protective League. Then he'll be attacked by Daryl Gates. And then they'll all say, the department gives him a vote of 'no confidence.' Even if Gates cannot ultimately win, he can just fuck the situation up more."

To Michael Zinzun, LA's leading crusader against police abuse (and recipient of a $1.2-million settlement against local police, who punched his eye out), whether Daryl Gates stays or goes has little meaning beyond the purely symbolic. Genuine reform of the LAPD isn't even on the agenda.

"Unless we have police accountability, we won't be able to effectively get community support to weed out the racist elements in the police department who will still be there even when Gates is gone," he says. "Without an independent investigator, without an independent prosecutor with subpoena power, without direct community participation in the disciplinary proceedings, I think we'll fail just as quickly as we have where blacks have replaced whites in the other institutions in LA, from the mayor to the City Council to the Police Commission."

The South Central convulsion snapped the confines of the 1965 Watts riots, spilling out of the traditional borders of the black ghetto, edging northward and westward, into Downtown and Hollywood, threatening the outskirts of Beverly Hills and leapfrogging the Santa Monica Mountains into the Spanish-speaking areas of the once all-white San Fernando Valley.

Like a computer-generated map pinwheeling off the screen, the geographical outlines of the violence accurately redrew the boundaries of underclass Los Angeles. While the torched-out shopping districts on Hollywood Boulevard still draw camera-laden tourists from Osaka and Oshkosh, the tattered wooden-frame homes up and along the residential side streets were long ago ceded to the burgeoning numbers of casually employed Latinos who populate city street corners selling oranges, peanuts or a few hours of their physical labor to passing motorists. Looking at the TV charts of looting and arson incidents, there must have been some thousands of white people who finally realized that in this hypersegregated town, it is they who now live in a ghetto — a white ghetto — surrounded by a Third-World city.

While the columns of smoke towered into the skies and the human and property casualty tolls mounted, it became clear that this was a rebellion not only against the white establishment, but also against its black counterpart. After Watts, the city's disenfranchised were told that their redemption resided in electing to office a progressive generation of politicians that could pass on concrete benefits to the grass roots. The 1973 election of Tom Bradley, supported by a coalition of white liberals and supposedly progressive business interests, seemingly vindicated the rioters of 1965. Yet after two decades of a liberal administration headed by a black mayor, Los Angeles's African-American community now lags farther behind other minority groups and sees its already tenuous economic standing being further eroded.

Tom Bradley as mayor did nothing to palliate the effects of GM, Goodyear, Firestone and Bethlehem Steel all pulling out of South Central LA in the last 20 years, leaving behind only minimum-wage service jobs, if any. It was Bradley who choked off spending programs for inner-city youth recreation, allocating in 1987 only $30,000 for recreational equipment for 150 centers that supposedly serve tens of thousands of ghetto children. This while black youth unemployment hovers at 50 percent.

In those early hellacious hours, as the first fires were sprouting, Mayor Bradley and the city's black leadership huddled with a roiling crowd of 2,500 in the pre-eminent First A.M.E. Church. That first night's meeting collapsed into chaos and outrage. Bradley and several other black politicians and clergy were left literally talking to themselves as the agitated audience moved into the street and melted into the whirlwind of violence sweeping around them. The car of liberal Councilman Zev Yaroslavsky — one of Chief Gates's earliest critics — went up in flames. So did the office of young black Councilman Mark Ridley-Thomas, a former executive director of the Southern Christian Leadership Conference of Greater Los Angeles and one of the original leaders — going back some 13 years — of a militant but unsuccessful campaign to place the LAPD under a civilian review board. By the morning light, other symbols of black advance had been reduced to ashes. The Crenshaw shopping district, heart of LA's black middle class and the only significant commercial district in South Central, had burned to the ground.

A yawning abyss had opened between the new urban poor (not to mention the growing underclass) and an aging black leadership forged in struggle some 30 years ago. "There is an incredible lack of respect for black elected officials," the newly appointed head of the SCLC, Joe Hicks, said. "With all of the flip-flops over the last year from the mayor's office and from the city, people just felt locked out of the political process. They have little respect for the institutions in their own community, and little respect for others' and their own lives."

As the violence spun out of control and took on increasing tones of self-destruction, another meeting at the First A.M.E. Church was called for the next morning — a closed-door conclave of the 50 top black leaders in the city. Another failure. "That second meeting demonstrated that people just plain didn't know what to do," a young activist who attended said. "It showed that the traditional leadership are comfortable with certain formulas and don't know how to go beyond them....The impulse was to keep the peace, to postpone any action. To put out the line that the people out there rioting do not represent the rest of us. I felt that saying that was to play into the hands of the racists."

And many of those racist hands were tightly gripped around the city's media microphones. With the black leadership refusing for the most part to legitimize if not condone the social explosion, the electronic media took over spin control. This was, after all, ratings sweeps week, where the scheduled reports on pregnant lesbian nuns, on sexy Mexican soap-opera stars and white men who will only sleep with black women were rudely preempted by the searing flash of reality. But no problem, the unfolding urban violence was immediately and deftly repackaged, reshaped and made suitable for maximum ratings impact.

Given open-ended air time, the TV "news" departments turned the uprising into one continuous, 24-hour-a-day drive-by shooting, all Live from Copter Five. The chauffeur-driven, $600,000-a-year local anchors, whose only contact with South Central is from inside their locked cars en route to Palm Springs, were now wringing their hands about the "innocent victims" of the violence, cowering with their families in those "nice little well-kept houses," as Channel 7's Ann Martin put it. "Creeps" is how her partner Paul Moyers described those defying police in the streets. "Hooligans," ruled Channel 2. "Thugs, criminals and gang-bangers," said Channel 4. Look out for the Crips and Bloods gangs, was the drumbeat on Channel 5. "You're going to have to control your language if you're going to be on television," Channel 7 reporter Art Rascon scolded an angry young man who had just blurted out "fuck" a number of times on camera.

By the second day of violence, Channel 7 field reporter Linda Mour was sitting on the news set being interviewed live about her experience reporting on looters. "Did you get the impression that a lot of those people were illegal aliens?" asked anchor Harold Greene.

"Yes," Mour flatly replied.

This tendentious media spin, so comforting to every racist in the signal area, also set off the panic alarms among the few black leaders willing to take a bolder stand than their peers. U.S. Congresswoman Maxine Waters fought the battle on the national airwaves of CNN and ABC, hotly defending the rage of her constituents. On the local level, state Senator Diane Watson made a tour of the LA television news shows Thursday night and one by one took on the anchors — and their prejudices.

If the reaction registered in Watson's office is any measure, this televised orgy of

Los Angeles: Ted Soqui

vilification and criminalization of the poor, this ruthless disparaging of the real anger and frustration of tens of thousands of people in this city, was an accurate rendering of the prevailing attitude among a big chunk of white LA. They had retreated from their offices and cafés as the plebes were having a whack at it, but their able and perfumed representatives still controlled the airwaves and were giving strident voice to their private thoughts. "Once Diane went public, the calls just came pouring in here," one of her aides said. "Those who called from the community were grateful and supportive and saying it was about time someone talked back to the media. But the calls from outside her district, from the Anglos, they're mostly hate calls. They say 'Diane Watson is a reverse bigot and it's her constituents that are burning the city down, you fucking nigger.'"

Out of the confusion and inertia that hamstrung the city's black leadership, a new activist force was emerging in the heat of events. Gay black organizations seemed to be the only ones willing once again to hoist the banners of aggressive protest. Phill Wilson, the 36-year-old director of the city's AIDS office and leader of the Black Gay and Lesbian Leadership Forum, attended the same closed-door meeting at the A.M.E. Church that four dozen other activists had on the second day of rioting. Unwilling to call for a blanket social peace, he proposed an ambitious series of public political protests. His call went unheeded — a partial explanation for why the Korean community was able quickly to pull 30,000 people into a street march, whereas organized black political presence was nil.

"It's not an accident that black lesbians and gays are now taking the initiative where others won't," Wilson said. "We are like those people back in the '50s. We are the ones now who have nothing to lose. My simple existence, as a gay man, in many states is in itself a violation of the law. So when we talk today of following the law or not, sometimes the law we choose to follow is the law of survival. And sometimes surviving means breaking the rules."

As the median skin hue darkened in Los Angeles in the 1970s, developers bulldozed stand after stand of California live oak, pushing the white suburban envelope to the very edge of the county line and beyond through the Santa Susana Pass. Succeeding lumps of flesh-colored townhomes (all with identical faux-Mexican tile roofs) festered into the metastasizing melanoma known today as Simi Valley. A hundred thousand souls, drawn by "good schools" (read all-white) and relatively low housing costs, set up camp just across the Los Angeles County line, separated from South Central and the Rodney Kings of this world by two mountain ranges and 60 miles of freeway. Before the high-publicity police trial of the last six weeks, Simi's only claim to notoriety was serving as home to the Ronald Reagan Presidential Library.

It was a stroke of genius, then, when the LAPD defense lawyers managed to change the venue of the police-beating trial to this somnolent 'burb. What a laugh they must have had together when Judge Stanley Weisberg acceded to their request, agreeing that adverse, saturation media in Los Angeles had made a fair trial there impossible. No matter that Simi was part of the same LA media market. Judge Weisberg, legal sources say, found the one-hour daily commute from his Beverly Hills home the most attractive and convenient of the options available.

Of the 8,300 officers on the LAPD, a staggering 2,000 of them live in Simi. Then there's the untold number of LA and Ventura County sheriffs out there, coaching Little League and fixing Sunday barbecues. Like some sort of local Huey Long, presiding over and micro-managing the entire Conejo Valley, which includes Simi and the neighboring town of Moorpark (whose mayor was forced to resign in 1987 after using the word "nigger" twice in a newspaper interview), is state Senator Ed Davis, Daryl Gates's immediate predecessor as police chief (who will always be fondly remembered as the man who suggested that any captured airplane hijacker should be tried on the spot and then hanged "at the airport").

The fateful decision made by the Simi Valley jury is destined to be more than an asterisk when the history of this period is written. The sensibilities that underlie that verdict will surface again, in the months to come, when the "solutions" to the uprising are proffered. The tsk-tsking about the destruction of South LA has led many to delude themselves that something good must come of this, that such a wrenching *cri de coeur* from the LA underclass just cannot go unheeded.

But these are the '90s, not the '60s. That message was unabashedly transmitted when Mayor Bradley named utility *ubermensch* Peter Ueberroth as head of the commission to rebuild Los Angeles. This Prophet of Profit immediately warned there would be "no handouts" and that it would be not the state or federal government, God forbid, but the private sector that would reconstruct the ghetto.

But it is that same private sector that has, under Bradley's stewardship, systematically retreated from, abandoned and ultimately strangled South Central Los Angeles. In 1992, 12 years into the Reagan Revolution, are we to believe these entrepreneurs will experience a moral conversion? All this while Republican Governor Pete Wilson, who had the audacity in the midst of the unrest to quote Martin Luther King, Jr., and Thurgood Marshall, will quickly return next week to his preferred political cause, a ballot initiative aimed at a 25 percent cut in welfare. "We are operating in a political atmosphere marked by a myth of scarcity," says Phill Wilson, "so that even people of goodwill believe that the only way for them to survive is to contribute to a poorer community's destruction."

Indeed, LA's most insightful social historian, Mike Davis, author of *City of Quartz*, warns that our immediate future is more likely to be determined by the mean, myopic, empty spirit of places like Simi Valley than by the fleeting compassion symbolized by the multiracial clean-up of the riot zone. "The riot in the inner-city will be probably be followed by a second, even more devastating 'riot' in the suburbs," Davis wrote as the rage about the Simi Valley verdict burst around him. "The suburbanites won't burn Korean liquor stores or stone Parker Center. They will simply tighten the fiscal vise around the central city — where they will never again venture — and let it bleed. T..ey will organize death-penalty parties and victory parades for the LAPD and the National Guard (Operation Urban Storm?). And Daryl F. Gates's book will top best-seller lists in [the white suburbs of] West Hills and South Pasadena." Perhaps Davis's grim vision was shaded by the death and destruction. But while the Watts outburst of 1965 seemed to some a dress rehearsal for revolution, its 1992 encore was but a rumbling, tectonic shift, an adjustment along the seemingly bottomless fault line of day-to-day despair.

Once the wrenching was over, Los Angeles was back to business as usual. According to KFWB radio, Sergeant Stacey Koon, acquitted for supervising the beating of Rodney King, had got himself an agent and was negotiating a movie deal. ■

• •

51 percent of those arrested at the peak of the rioting were Latino, 36 percent black. The largest group was young Latino men ages 18 to 24, who accounted for 30 percent of those arrested. The analysis was made of 5,633 adult arrests on felony and misdemeanor charges. The population make-up of Los Angeles according to census figures is 39 percent Latino, 37 percent white and 13 percent black.

(Source: Rand Corporation computer analysis)

Marc Cooper and Greg Goldin write frequently for the Village Voice, *where a version of this story first appeared.*

Los Angeles: Virginia Lee Hunter

Streets of Fire

by Lynell George

Drinks are on the LAPD...
— Found voices, Harvard and Adams,
8:15 p.m., Wednesday, April 29, 1992

By midnight, no one phoning long distance bothers with hello. Instead, they just ask: "Is it as crazy as it looks?" I want to say, "It started long before all this…." Long before this afternoon's bewildering decision left me less astonished than strangely numb. Long before George Halliday ran tape capturing Rodney King's struggle and submission. Long before Latasha Harlins, Eula Love and Marquette Frye became cautionary symbols. Long before Watts shouted its existence into the sky in '65, sending up searchlights in the form of flames.

Go home, stay home. Lock your doors.
— KFWB 980 AM, Thursday, April 30, 1992

I've already seen the look. Driving though the Silver Lake hills to avoid Sunset Boulevard's panicked snarl, I climb along the incline. People are out jogging and walking their dogs, even though fires have moved closer, are no longer a distant TV hell. The higher I climb, the more I see residents take note of my car's make and color; they mentally record the license number, but most importantly, my unfamiliar deep-brown face, any distinguishing marks. They look at me as if they will at any moment join together to form a human barricade if I make a wrong or abrupt move. Later, across town, a blond man in the next lane looks over LA pick-up casual, then quickly raises his smoked-glass window.

The same video feeds that have inspired their terror have fueled my own curiosity. For hours I've been transfixed, watching childhood landmarks swallowed up in the surprisingly liquid images of billowing smoke and flames — stores and streets, memories, futures. I'm watching my old neighborhood blister, turn to embers, rendered entirely foreign. I hear fear in the voices of my relatives and friends who've been trying to track the course of the flames, follow the trajectory of anger.

"If you've got your ass out here you might get shot," one seen-it-all onlooker tells me. We're standing near the corner of Walton and Jefferson looking at the remains of a corner mom-and-pop still smoldering, a single red flicker looking like some eerie twist on an eternal flame. "Brothers getting busy." He backs it up recounting a staggering list of the display of firearms he's seen the past week, from shotguns to .357 Magnums to Uzis. "They shut everything down early last night. I went down on Arlington, everybody started hitting the pawnshops. It was kids, old women, not just like criminals, like they've been sayin' on TV. It's like a free-for-all.

Get it while you can. Let's roll and see what's poppin'."

"The message was there, but the method was wrong," offers one of the playground prophets chillin' at Denker Park. "We've inconvenienced ourselves now," he says, looking into the sulfur-tinted sky. Fires rage around us, sirens scream, puddles of water left by pump trucks look more like polluted lakes. "Folks are gonna start getting real hungry down here. RTD shut down, people don't have cars."

"It's sad to me 'cause I grew up here and now they're burning it down," says the office manager from a Century City law firm. He has his hair cut into a neat, close fade and is still wearing his pink shirt and paisley tie with a square knot and pager clipped to his belt. "I had to drive over and check on my relatives," he explains "I don't agree with the looting but I understand the frustration."

"I'll put it in two words," a woman strolling by, looking at my notebook tells me: "fucked up." She wants to make sure that I've underlined the words, that they stand out somehow from all the rest on the page. "Two words: '*fucked up*.' We hurt our folks the most. *We* deal with that. People scared to open up their shops today. Scared to walk out on the street." As the burned-out buildings multiply and look more abstract as they collapse upon themselves, the stories become more tragic. Like the little boy who's decided not to leave the cement backyard behind his house because "I don't want to get caught by no police. I don't want to have to go through that." There is Francis, bewildered, who stands in front of the Church of God and Prophecy on Western, watching his electronics business smolder: "What do I feel now? Upset. Angry. We as black people have been told that we could achieve anything if we put our minds to it. Now, because of a couple of days, it's going to take 20 or 30 years before we can achieve anything again. People here complain about South Africa. It is no better here." ∎

Lynell George is a staff writer for the LA Weekly, *where a version of this story first appeared. She is also a contributor to the book* Sex, Death and God in LA.

An armored Humvee truck — the type U.S. troops used to repel Saddam Hussein's Republican Guard — braked suddenly in front of two young black men walking casually past a fire-bombed gas station in South Central LA. "If y'all run, y'all gonna be two fucked-up niggas, man," the battle-ready black MP shouted as an LAPD squad car mounted the sidewalk to cut off the men, who sprinted when a huge machine gun was aimed at them. One of the men is a suspected arsonist who, for his own safety, prefers to be called the Angel of Death. The slower of the two was caught and treated like a prisoner of war. "No, we don't need the motherfucking blindfold today," a white LAPD officer told the MP.

"Let him go," the MP said. "We don't need him. We want the fire starter." Later, the Angel of Death said in an interview that he'd watched the detainment of his "blood" from a secret "hole in a wall." The Angel of Death has seven fingers, five on the left hand and two on the right. He carried a battered black Bible stained with the blood of his 22-year-old brother who was ambushed in a drive-by shooting last year. And he packed an altered .357 Magnum, its nozzle painted red, black and green.

On the eve of the Rodney King verdict, Bigfinger Blood, a reputed leader of the Rolling 20s Bloods, one of West Los Angeles's most brutal street gangs, gave the Angel perhaps the most important assignment of his life. He was to deliver a warning to some black store owners: Read the 12th chapter and the seventh and 12th verses in the book of Exodus and prepare for the end of the world. Now the Angel

Los Angeles: Ted Soqui

When the Word is Given

by Peter Noel

whipped out his Magnum and pointed to those chapters, which recall the deliverance of Israel from Egypt. The Angel read the scriptures with a tremor in his voice: "And they shall take of the blood and strike it on the two side posts of the houses. For I will pass through the land of Egypt this night, and I will smite all the firstborn in the land of Egypt, both man and beast; and against all the gods of Egypt I will execute judgment: I am the Lord."

As was foretold, the merchants who heeded the gangstas' no second warning and posted advisories that their businesses were black-owned were, for the most part,

spared. But the pillage and carnage that left LA smoldering in ruins could not have been accomplished without the cooperation of rival gang-bangers who apparently called a truce before the King verdict came down. About 72 hours earlier, Tecate, a member of the Mara Salva-Trucha, a Salvadoran gang, met the Angel of Death on a city bus. They talked about stockpiling an arsenal of urban smart bombs — Molotov cocktails created from St. Ides, Corona and Olde English 40-ounce bottles. The message was passed from gangsta to gangsta on the tops of buses. Anyone who saw the ID number on a certain bus knew how many smart bombs were available. One expert gang watcher identified the PJs, Imperial Courts and the Bounty Hunters, three of the most powerful gangs in Watts, as instigators of the retribution. But there were also Chicano gangs involved — the 18th Street Diamond gang, the Easy Riders and the Crazy Riders. They all fought side-by-side in skirmishes with police and Korean businessmen. "The Rolling 20s Bloods were ready to send out a message," recalls one merchant whose pest-control company and typing service remained intact. "And they were not concerned about the police."

LA's blacks are divided about the meaning of the riot. Most agree that the King verdict, coming on top of the suspended sentence given to a Korean store owner last year for the shooting death of 15-year-old Latasha Harlins, a black girl, was too much to bear. But once the looting started, politics had little to do with it. As one looter explained, "We wanted shit and we took shit." Still, there was a sense among many looters that they were fol-

among many looters that they were following a pattern of sorts. "We were burning out the Koreans. When they come to clean up their places, we told them don't build it again. Black folks gonna buy it: We don't need y'all liquor stores. All y'all doing is selling us liquor. Your place is burned down already. Why don't you just move out? Sell us the store." T and his crew of gang-bangers bombed Koreatown on the first night of the riots. "The black man can't get a $100,000 loan but the Korean can come into the neighborhood and buy us out, sky-high sales. Gus, a white man, had his hardware store. He know we needed it. Know we need it. But he sell it to a Buddha-head. The Buddha-head stop renting stuff to us to farm, to cut our stuff with. I'm glad we burned that down."

On a dusty Watts street bounded by rows of dilapidated wood-frame homes, four teenagers leaned against a corrugated chain-link fence. Twin, a 19-year-old gang-banger, was wearing the voguish red-and-black down coat with the LA Lakers insignia, a red Chicago Bulls T-shirt with matching hat, blacktops, red corduroy pants and a cheap watch. He "got it all from the white man on the first night of looting." The Bloods and the Crips were right by my side," he recalls. "It wasn't no gang-banging thing. It was no Bloods against Crips, just people grabbing shit that supposed to get took."

"They were calling us niggas, 'You, niggas, get outta here!' " Carla, also 19, recalls. "Everybody thought, well, crackers calling us niggas and stuff, we really start going crazy. It was lame and serious. Then they put the guns to our heads and we went outta there."

James Galipeau, a deputy probation officer with the Metropolitan Specialized Gang Unit, has been working with LA's street gangs for the past 27 years. He doubts that any of the major gangs ordered violence and specific attacks on Koreans. "This was anarchy," Galipeau insists. "People just saw these stores open. They thought that they could loot with impunity, and they did." Galipeau has a proposal before the LA County Board of Supervisors to stop the plague of gang violence. He intends to hire six OGs (original gangstas) and give each of them $2,000

monthly along with medical and dental plans.

"Then we are gonna go out into the streets and make peace between the Van Ness Gangsta Bloods, the Rolling 60 Crips, and the Eight-Trey Gangsta Crips, three of the worst gangs in LA. The police won't help us. They wear helmets, flak jackets, ride in cars with bulletproof windows, shotguns. They are looked upon as an occupying force in the ghetto."

As fire trucks race through the almost deserted streets of South Central LA under heavy police escort, a lanky well-dressed man scampers onto the sidewalk. He is Edward Jackson, a retired LA county sheriff turned community activist, and he is holding aloft a box covered in gruesome autopsy photographs of blacks and Latinos killed by the LAPD during the past 20 years. He is eager to bare his Rue Morgue of photos to a reporter. "This here is Anthony Reeves," he says, "killed April 20, 1977, shot to the head, no crime was committed, justifiable homicide. Of course you remember Eula Love, murdered January 3, 1979, in her front yard in front of her daughters by two officers, justifiable homicide. Larry Morris, murdered by the police in 1980, not in the commission of a crime. Then this here is David Angel Ortiz, shot in the back in 1991, the county also called his death a justifiable homicide."

Jackson rips out another page in his dossier. He has a collection of more than 90 photos — his own book of the dead. But before he can show them all, something catches his eye, and he disappears into the dust, the smoke and the ruins.

"The LA riot was not just a promiscuous kind of riot," says Gerald Horne, chair of the Black Studies Department at the University of California-Santa Barbara, and author of the upcoming book, *The Fire This Time: The Watts Uprising and The Meaning of The 1960s.* "If it was promiscuous, houses and churches would have burned down. In 1965, as in 1992, the places that went up in flames were not residences or schools and libraries but mostly outposts of major corporations like Boys Market and Thrifty....It took 15,000 troops to subdue Watts and South Central Los Angeles in 1965, which is more than it took to subdue the Dominican Republic."

A candidate for the U.S. Senate,

Horne says LA's blacks are barely holding on to their territory because of their combustible relationships with the people of Koreatown. "California right now is about 30 percent Hispanic, about 15 percent Asian and about 8 percent black," he points out. "It's not like New York where blacks are the largest so-called minority. The blacks feel that they are being pushed out. And certainly in terms of the political economy of California there is not much room for unskilled labor."

Added to the black community's shrinking turf is the psychological and physical torture it must endure from the LAPD. "The curfew zone in 1965 was 45 square miles, longer than the island of Manhattan and larger than the city of San Francisco," Horne explains. "The LAPD is one-third the size of the NYPD. So part of the theory many lawyers put forward is that the LAPD is so brutal that they operate on the premise that you beat one slave and you keep the whole plantation in line. This is to say that their ranks and minds are stretched so thin that they treat suspects brutally and the message gets out not to commit any crimes. That compensates for the fact that they have to cover such a big city."

Jean swallowed her tears as the LA riots came home to the starving residents of a gray concrete jungle ingloriously referred to as Nickerson Gardens, the largest housing project in Los Angeles. She had been on her feet for 12 hours passing out meal tickets to tenants in 110,000 apartments that have been without electricity and water for three days. As the curfew hour neared Friday evening, Jean gave up all hope of persuading the LAPD to provide a truck driver with an escort. "We need to get the food in here, but they don't want to give our driver any protection," says Jean, who paid the driver $20 of her own money to haul the food. "Why can't they help our community? We have not thrown a brick at anything, anybody." ∎

Peter Noel is a staff investigative reporter for the Village Voice, *where a version of this story first appeared.*

Los Angeles: Ted Soqui

Where the Fuck Were the Cops?
Without Bob Vernon, Daryl Gates Flounders

by Joe Domanick

Reginald Denny lies on his knees and elbows outside the big-rig truck he'd been driving, getting kicked by two or three blacks while another walks up, raises his arms above his head, takes careful aim and hurls what looks like the base of a lamp directly onto Denny's head. Up steps another, and, as Denny rises slightly, his assailant casually kicks him in the back before proceeding repeatedly to beat his head in with a metal object.

Then he splits, replaced by a third thug who will render the *coup de gràce*: Walking up to Denny's right, and standing not more than a foot away, he fires a rock into his temple before raising his leg in triumph, pointing disdainfully at Denny, and dancing away.

The message is clear: If you're white,

we are your worst nightmare. It was a scene as ugly and powerful in its racial and class implications as any we've seen since Powell and Wind whaled away on Rodney King. And compelling. You change channels to see what else is going on, but you keep going back and Denny's still there. Back and forth you go. This can't be live — I was sure I saw him half an hour ago. He must have been picked up. Then you turn and with the rest of LA — the rest of the nation — ask the question that was asked everywhere for the next 36 hours: Where the fuck are the cops?

The definitive answer to that question won't come until the inevitable commission is appointed, but already some facts — as well as lots of speculation — are beginning to surface.

At the center of the mystery is the

mind of Daryl Gates — and here, much of the speculation has broken down into two theories: the vindication theory and the Führer bunker theory. The first, raised by people like former San José Chief of Police Joseph McNamara and state Senator Diane Watson (D-Los Angeles), is that Gates may simply have let the rioting get out of control to suit his own political purposes and vindicate his tough style of policing. As McNamara put it: "'See,' Gates can say, 'we were right all along — what we've been doing is what has to be done [to keep order].'" The second theory holds that Gates is so angry at being forced out of office that he wants, like Hitler in the final days, to bring it all down with him.

The facts, however, point to answers slightly less bizarre: the traditional arrogance of both Gates and his department, a lack of preparation and sheer incompetence. The chief's own explanations for the 36-hour debacle were his usual mix of rambling contradictions minus his overweening propensity to blame others — this time, he merely refused to accept any blame. Sunday, on *Meet the Press*, he said that one of the reasons the department was so unprepared was that "No one knew when the verdict was going to come out." No one, that is, except every person in the LA Basin with a radio or TV turned on — the court having announced that morning that verdicts on all the counts save one would be read at three in the afternoon. Then at a

on the scene

press conference the day after the rioting started, he explained the department's failure to rescue people pulled from their cars by saying his troops had all been tied up fighting fires. But when a reporter pointed out this had happened *before* the fires had been set, Gates backtracked, saying he didn't want his troops to appear too aggressive or provocative.

The underlying message had now become: All you critics out there have handcuffed me. The explanation provided by Commander Ron Banks, the officer in charge of the riot area at the time the motorists were being pulled out of their cars at Florence and Normandie, was, if slightly less insulting, far more startling: "Our units that responded initially were assaulted," Banks told the *LA Times.* "Windows were broken out of their police cars. Several received minor injuries....We were not going to go back and be taken hostage or incur more injuries until we had sufficient personnel." An amazing statement that only someone truly unconscious could have made. As Joseph McNamara told me, "I can understand firefighters not wanting to go into an area where people are shooting at them. But the police? That's their job, that's what they're getting paid for. It's unthinkable for them to say they didn't want to risk their lives to save others." Nobody, in any case, had shot at the police when they'd gone to the intersection. Nor were there any reports of gun-packing men on PCP. Nor had any large crowds yet gathered or large numbers of fires been set.

But the LAPD leadership in South Central, like Daryl Gates downtown, seemed paralyzed as well as unprepared. "If they had been even minimally ready," says LAPD Detective Zvonko G. (Bill) Pavelic, "they'd at least have sent their undercover men to assess the situation — see if there were any snipers, how large the crowd was, that sort of thing, and then stopped and rerouted traffic so innocent people weren't driving into harm's way." Nor, as McNamara and others have pointed out, were there groups of police stationed on reserve — out of sight so that their presence wouldn't provoke tensions,

but who could move quickly to protect people, make arrests and quickly take the ringleaders out of circulation — a now standard policy in riot control.

So what went wrong? Why was the LAPD so unprepared, so leaderless, so rudderless? First, Gates, like most of us, was caught short by the not-guilty verdicts (although it didn't take a cultural anthropologist to know that, given the conservative nature of the community and jury, not-guilty verdicts were a distinct possibility). Far worse, according to sources in the LAPD, Gates didn't realize that an acquittal would so outrage people. "I don't think he understood the ramifications of acquittals," says one high-ranking LAPD official, "because he was so sympathetic to acquittals."

So, despite the escalating violence and arson, Gates left his post at what turned out to be the most crucial hours in the city's history — and, in a highly charged political atmosphere where other high-ranking LAPD officials were not about to go out on a limb and make a decision, he went to a political fundraiser to defeat the Christopher Commission reform initiative. He's also changed his story about how long he remained at the fundraiser: In the early days of the riot, he said he stayed for 20 minutes; on *Meet the Press,* he said 10 minutes, which he later reduced to five. According to the *LA Times,* which obtained a tape of Gates's speech, the chief was at the Brentwood gathering for half an hour.

There is also the matter of contingency plans. Although the LAPD claims that several options were outlined to deal with the verdict's aftermath, one LAPD official told me, "To my knowledge there never was a contingency plan. The Police Commission was never able to get Gates to tell them what it was. It was nonexistent." If there was a plan, why wasn't it implemented? The fact that the verdicts were to be rendered was known by at least 10 o'clock that morning, yet the majority of the department's 1,000 detectives — who work between six a.m. and two in the afternoon and live outside the city — were permitted to go home as usual. And, when the rioting started, where was the tough, elite Metro Squad? Where were the narcs? Where were the CRASH gang units and the hundreds of officers who work at

Parker Center? And what priority in Daryl Gates's heart prompted him to leave so many officers in safe areas of the Valley and elsewhere?

What of the Anti-Terrorist Division (headed by Gates's brother, Captain Steven Gates), so busy little more than a decade ago spying on the department's critics? Where was the intelligence? If they didn't know not-guilty verdicts would involve unrest, why didn't they? And, if there was a plan, why didn't the LAPD know how to deploy the National Guard more quickly? That the County Sheriff's Department had a deployment plan is one reason why 1,500 of the first 2,000 Guardsmen were assigned to help the sheriffs.

The traditional arrogance of the LAPD as well as the vanity of the chief also impeded calling for assistance. "This department has never reached out to others like the Sheriff's Department, the Santa Monica PD or the Highway Patrol — the attitude has always been, 'We are the LAPD, the best, why should we?'" says an LAPD source. "So the sheriff was offering assistance for 12 hours and there was no response to it." And just as Gates had initially opposed the calling up of the Guard because it was an admission that his much-vaunted police department needed help, so too did he not want federal troops. It would be a blot on the city's reputation. Besides, he told KNBC's Linda Douglass, he didn't want to be taking orders from a general.

But perhaps the biggest reason for the department's disastrous response was that Gates himself, the king of modern high-tech policing, the father of SWAT, had to direct the LAPD during the riot. "Gates hasn't run that department in an operational sense for five or six years," a high-ranking LAPD source told me. "That was Bob Vernon's job." (This was the same Robert Vernon who had written a devastating critique of the inefficiency and failures of the department's war on gangs.) Vernon had retired from the department just a week earlier. As this observer sees it, the riot was dumped in Gates's lap and he couldn't handle it. ■

Joe Domanick is a contributing writer to the LA Weekly, *where a version of this story first appeared.*

Los Angeles: Virginia Lee Hunter

Riot Homecoming *by Elston Carr*

I t is 9:30 p.m. Wednesday. I drive south on the nearly empty Harbor Freeway. Plumes of smoke snake into the sky in the east and west from Slauson Avenue on out to Florence Boulevard. I am in what the racist, entertainment-oriented media vaguely refer to as South Central Los Angeles: code for where most of the black people are, code for the non-white dumping ground — the Third-World region of a dubiously First-World city; a place that only gets attention when the trouble there threatens other parts of the city.

This place is not a point on the map to me, a gray area to avoid, a trying distance to blur through on the 110 Freeway behind rolled-up windows on the way to the airport or Lakers, Clippers and Kings games. I lived here from age eight to 22. My family still lives here. They called earlier to tell me they were all right and I shouldn't come, but I did anyway.

I exit the freeway at Florence. Wayne's used-car lot and the mini-mall on the southwest corner of Florence and Figueroa are in flames. There is a blue-and-white Bronco near the exit. The windshield is shattered. I don't see a driver. I move east on Florence. Police officers drive by in helmets and riot gear looking as bewildered as I feel. I sit here at Florence and Main looking south to what I suspect is another grocery store in flames.

It is different being here, different from seeing it on television or flying over it in a helicopter. I begin to shiver and cry. How do I explain this...people looking out at buildings burning? A teenager with the number 16 stenciled on the back of a maroon jersey walks by proudly, like a man, toward the flames at the corner of Florence and Figueroa — his chest out and shoulders back, his fists clenched, his arms tensed. Moving south on Main from Florence: At Main and 79th there are more people at the corners. Liquor stores are burning on both sides of the street. I feel the heat inside the car. Another liquor store has been looted. More people gather, Latino and black. It is 10:30. Three squad cars turn on Manchester and Main heading east. Another fire burns near the ABC Market at Manchester and Hoover. More squad cars. A spray-painted sign on a market reads, "Black Owned." That store

hasn't been touched. I pass Pep Boys on Manchester. Adults and teenagers pass through broken windows with carts and hands full of goods. Men and boys ride bicycles with car tires precariously balanced on their handlebars. People look out from windows nearby. Police stand at the corner of Broadway and Manchester with shotguns pointed into the air. No one obeys stop signs, and traffic lights are out. An auto-insurance place burns at Manchester and Vermont near the sign pointing to Reverend Price's Faith Dome. I turn right on Vermont through a section just south of a short strip of Korean mini-swap meets, all of them on fire.

I drive north on Vermont and turn left on Florence. The ABC at that corner is being looted. My 22-year-old brother just got a job there doing floor work. He and my parents live nearby on 71st Street, a block away from Florence and Normandie.

I decide not to stop there; I want to see more.

I move north on Normandie. No one is in sight. The liquor store near 69th burns. I used to buy the newspaper there. I cross Gage. The liquor store and laundry between 62nd and Gage burn. We used to live on 62nd. My mother did laundry there. I bought candy from that liquor store. Near 59th, Kwong's, the medium-size Korean-owned market, is in flames. Only an apparently new chain-link fence remains where the north side of the store used to be. At least two generations of people in the area have stopped at Kwong's. I move through smoke from fires on both sides of 39th and Normandie. We lived there, two blocks away from the Coliseum, after we moved from 62nd. The market and liquor store will be rubble in the morning.

Later that evening, I watch the television news turn South Central Los Angeles into another Desert Storm bonanza. This time around, the specter of doom is conjured with buzz words of white paranoia: barbaric, violent, brutal and senseless. The video of the white truck driver being beaten at Florence and Normandie is shown repeatedly. They interview the "good black people" who helped the trucker. At First A.M.E., our man, Mayor Tom Bradley, dances the black-folk boogie with other Christian pacifiers; they call for calm after the city has already had a seizure. (Later, we would see Tom do the Westside-and-Valley shuffle when he named Peter Ueberroth — that homeboy from the 'hood — to clean things up.)

South Central has been home, but at times not a pleasant one. It is a home with probably as many liquor stores per capita as anywhere else in the world. Liquor, the poor man's psychiatrist. Home is where the media say there is a major drug problem among blacks, never mind that white USC students and others venture into the neighborhoods to buy drugs. Home is where you can pay three times as much as you would on the Westside for a bottle of apple juice, where the meat and vegetables are not as fresh. It is where certain grocers keep milk on the shelves until it spoils and try to convince you it's all right to drink it. Home is where cops have kicked ass and

will continue to kick ass.

These wonderful images of home make me hate white people when they fake sympathy, say stupid things and act surprised that this all happened. "Yes, it does indeed mean something — something unspeakable — to be in a white country," says James Baldwin in *The Fire Next Time*. "You very soon without knowing it, give up all hope of communion. Black people, mainly, look down or look up but do not look at each other, not at you, and white people mainly look away."

And despite their protests to the contrary, the LAPD loves the media. They want this "revolution" televised. The highly selective images of African-Americans as "savages" (in the words of one TV anchor) will later justify institutional abuse and brutality. The cameras have not shown nearly as much footage of whites, Jews and Latinos participating in burning and looting all around the city.

Thursday and Friday at the school where I work, I hear some racist and paranoid shit. I bite my tongue a lot and come close to choking an idiot with the brains of a snowman. He explains the "riots" in Los Angeles by pointing out that the black family is matriarchal and that black men are lazy. Had I put my foot on his neck and pulled his tongue out, I would have lived up to his expectations. A black student tells me that his family had received calls at home saying, "Niggers, get out; we're coming to get you."

On Thursday there are long lines at the bank machines in South Pasadena. I'm the only black person in sight. And I feel real warm and cozy next to my Anglo brothers and sisters as they withdraw hundreds of dollars at a time. When I get to the Chevron on Hillhurst and Franklin, the owner looks me up and down before he

• • • • • • • • • • • • • • • •

Ratio of residents to stores in LA County, 1990:
203 to 1

Ratio of residents to stores in South Central LA, 1990:
415 to 1

(Source: Claritas Corp.)

decides to sell me two one-gallon containers of gas. I'm buying them for my father's car, since they've stopped selling gas in and around their neighborhood. When I deliver the gas to my parents, they have no electricity. I don't stay long because the curfew will take effect.

On Friday, my mother calls me at work. She's upset. My father's boss chewed him out for leaving work early on Thursday in order to get home before the curfew. My father cursed him out and almost walked off his job.

Later that day, Rodney King makes his orchestrated appearance. It's painful to watch him — emasculated. Once again his image is manipulated. The law rules.

As Wanda Coleman put it, "The law, a tool of the empowered in America, is a means of furthering and maintaining the oppression of a pseudo-slave class, including poor whites."

I leave work early on Friday. I check on my parents. They still have no electricity. I leave before dark and stop at the Vons to the north of the Santa Monica Freeway on National. The lines are long. People are hoarding food. The butter-croissant bin is empty. A blond woman with dreadlocks pushes a cart loaded with soups. She looks nervous. Another woman turns the corner with a quart of Dreyers vanilla ice cream and a box of Eskimo Pies. She mentions to someone in passing that she just had to stock up on food. As she disappears, I think about the worlds I move between. To survive, to work, I have to at least acknowledge that white people exist. Most whites do not have to acknowledge my existence, even when I am in their presence. "I could also see that the intransigence and ignorance of the white world might make vengeance inevitable," Baldwin says. "A vengeance that does not really depend on, and cannot really be executed by, any person or organization, and cannot be prevented by any police force or army: historical vengeance, a cosmic vengeance based on the law that we recognize when we say, 'Whatever goes up, must come down.'" ■

Elston Carr contributes regularly to the LA Weekly, *where a version of this story first appeared.*

Atlanta: Michael Harrelson/Creative Loafing

A New Civil Rights Militancy Threatens the Nonviolent Legacy

by Robert Morris and Michael Harrelson

Race riots are not supposed to happen in Atlanta. With some notable exceptions, its distinction as the birthplace of the Civil Rights movement and its history of racial tolerance, going back to Mayor Willie Hartsfield and before, always seemed to rule out the vicious cycle of violence and hatred that linger with the mention of cities like Little Rock, Birmingham and Selma.

But the city too busy to hate, the proud Olympic city where Martin Luther King, Jr., was born and is buried, took its place in the larger, more uncertain global village of the '90s in the two days of violence that erupted last week over the Rodney King verdict in Los Angeles. Old civil-rights traditions seemed lost in the 36 hour melée, replaced instead by hostility and violence reminiscent of the turbulent '60s and '70s. As frightening as it was fascinating, it added up to a militant black intellectual movement, courtesy of the power of mass communication.

What began April 30 as a peaceful protest against an inexplicable jury verdict emerged as bitter, burning passion on the streets of Morehouse College Friday as hundreds of students traded bricks for tear gas with Georgia Bureau of Investigation agents, state troopers and Atlanta riot police. In the window-smashing, Caucasian-bashing romp down Peachtree Street, in the emotional shift from getting along to getting even, the mood of race relations shifted suddenly and dramatically. And black leaders who had helped lead the South out of the dark days of segregation now faced a frightening new challenge from people young enough to be their grandchildren.

"They're blaming nonviolence for not having produced, rather than the twisted political system," said Joseph Lowery, president of the Southern Christian Leadership Conference. "There is some intensity of hatred [for whites] that I was not aware of. But the [King] verdict violated all black males and gave a license to [beat them] with impunity."

Lowery was among black leaders

who met with President Bush last week and urged the president to move immediately to prosecute the four Los Angeles police officers. When Bush tried to stall for time, Lowery says he became insistent: "[Bush] talked like he had to get the cabinet to look it over and I said: 'There's nothing to look at and nothing to update.'"

Surveying the downtown damage Thursday night after the first wave of violence, other black leaders sympathized with the outrage, but pulled no punches in placing responsibility for the riots. Ashen-faced Fulton County Commission Chairman Michael Lomax put it at the doorsteps of the students, who he said had made their intentions clear to Atlanta Mayor Maynard Jackson earlier in the evening at Morehouse College.

"He said books and ballots," said Lomax. "They added: 'bullets.'" Lomax held out no guarantees about the future safety of downtown. "It's very difficult to control [the students] and very difficult for black officials, whom they see as part of the system, to control them."

Instead, Lomax hinted at the need for a broader solution, drawing comparisons to the race riots he witnessed growing up in California during the 1960s. "This is much more socially hostile to the white people who have allowed this [Rodney King] injustice to occur," said Lomax. "It's very clearly a message to white America."

As wicked as the first day turned out to be, it only foreshadowed the confrontation that ensued between students and police on Friday. Contrary to word from faculty leaders that an afternoon student rally would not result in another episode of wilding downtown, students found themselves overwhelmed by an atmosphere that grew increasingly volatile as the afternoon wore on.

At first, the crowd was peaceful, marching through the campus in a cat-and-mouse game, dodging walls of police attempting to keep them on campus. The march took a turn for the worse when Atlanta City Councilman C.T. Martin was unable to persuade students to return to campus rather than turn toward the John Hopo

Housing Project. "This way! This way!" Martin shouted, waving his arms wildly.

As the students weaved in and out of the alleys and sidewalks of the project, mothers grabbed for their children and older brothers shouted for siblings to go home. As rocks began to fly, so did night sticks. One young man's forehead was cracked open, and a young female student was lying handcuffed, face down and unconscious. The more the students saw the willingness of police to get tough, the more they were persuaded to use force.

There were two attempts made by police to overtake the students with tear gas and force, and twice the police were repelled. Inside the university buildings, school officials and employees tried to calm and attend to students who were gagging from the tear gas.

The efforts by a few students, civil-rights leaders and university faculty members to calm the crowd were drowned out. "This is crazy," said James Orange, former member of the SCLC and currently

Atlanta: Michael Harrelson/Creative Loafing

a coordinator for the AFL-CIO, who could barely be heard over the mayhem. "We are the educated elite," one student protested. Others were more imaginative: "Let's make their worst nightmare their reality," one student urged.

"[The police] say they are going to shoot you," said a student who had worked with school officials to arrange the rally. "You are risking your life if you go out there."

When police fired gas a second time, glass bottles rained down from the windows of Joseph Brawley Hall and several police officers and a photographer fell to the ground, wounded.

By late afternoon, Police Chief Eldrin Bell had surrounded a four-square-block area of the university and felt comfortable pulling his troops back off the frontline to Northside Drive and sending Lowery in to bring calm. There were many heated exchanges between Lowery's gathering of SCLC representatives, whose tenets of non-violence did not hold weight with the students. Sporadic acts of violence and destruction continued in front of Lowery before he was forced to hustle out of the area, gagging from the tear gas.

The students seemed to respond more favorably to an older spokesman, who told them how to react when told to practice peace. "If anyone tells you to be non-violent, you tell 'em to shut up and bust them upside the head," the man urged.

But throughout the day, the attempts to rationalize the use of violence came across as empty rhetoric. Some leaders spoke of "struggling for the liberation" and wanting to make their community ethnically pure. Others seemed to believe that random violence had somehow endeared them to the world. As one student boasted, "This is a rebirth of the student activism from the 1960s." ∎

Robert Morris is an Atlanta-based freelance writer. Michael Harrelson is news editor of the Atlanta-based Creative Loafing, *where a version of this story first appeared.*

same verdict: different location

Atlanta: Michael Harrelson/Creative Loafing

Smoke and mirrors

by Robert Morris

Pacing between opposing front lines — burning cars, tear gas and angry students on the one side and a wall of 600 retreating police officers on the other — the 70-year-old civil-rights veteran Rev. Joseph Lowery refused to listen to the university president, who pleaded, "Joe, don't go any further, it's not safe."

Thirty-five years ago, in an effort to distance themselves from a more conserva-tive church leader-ship, Lowery and Dr. Martin Luther King, Jr., founded the SCLC to organize students in protest. Last week, after downtown Atlanta was ransacked and police officers, reporters and white workers were pelted, beaten and stomped, Lowery was in the unusual position of asking students from Atlanta University Complex, the nation's largest educational institution for blacks, not to march. The students threw the advice in his face, showing him first-hand that they were not interested in his slow road to change.

When we approached a burn-ing police car and a Korean-owned liquor store that was being ransacked, a core of students shifted in and out of a pall of smoke. Lowery tried to explain that the police were wrong for trying to overtake the campus and that the students were wrong for resorting to violence. "That's not going to work any-more," said one student.

Another student approached and ges-ticulated wildly at me with one hand and held the other behind his back. "Why did you come here when you knew what was going to happen?"

"I came back with Dr. Lowery," I began to tell the student, whom I had walked beside earlier in the day. "Leave! Get out of here!" the student said, and Lowery looked at me with sad eyes while his aide, the Rev. Randall Osborne, pointed at me and said, so that the students could hear him: "You aren't with us."

I took two steps back, looked to Lowery, the student standing beside him and then to the police barricade that had withdrawn two blocks.

"You got to get out of here," the stu-dent protested. I turned to walk away, and had taken about 10 steps when he hurled a double quart-sized bottle at my head from point-blank range, snapping my body for-ward as I stumbled, dazed, reeling from foot to foot and trying to stop the blood coming from my skull with an open note-book. A colleague later told me that the student standing next to Lowery who had thrown the bottle laughed while others chimed in, "How does it feel?" and "You got it, white devil."

Images of Rodney King and the white trucker from Los Angeles who were sav-agely beaten raced in my head along with images from a year ago, when I had walked with Dr. Lowery on Dr. King's birthday through pouring rain to protest the Gulf war. The thin veneer of racial har-mony that city officials had painted to attract business and the 1996 Olympics, the image that most members of the media faithfully reproduced and wanted to believe, was shattered. In the two-day melée, at least 25 journalists, mostly pho-tographers, were bludgeoned with bottles and bricks, jumped or stomped, suffering broken ribs and other internal injuries. All told, more than 75 people were admitted to the area's four hospitals.

As each of us returned to the camp of ambulances bleeding or bruised Friday afternoon, it was hard to believe that the violence had spread here, to the cradle of civil rights — and even harder to accept that we, the mostly white and mostly liber-al press, had been branded as the enemy.

"I'm on your side," I pleaded to one student after getting shoved and called "white devil" earlier in the day. He looked at me in complete disbelief and shouted, "How can you be?" ∎

Robert Morris's articles have appeared in the Village Voice, Boston Phoenix *and* Atlanta Constitution. *This story first appeared in* Creative Loafing.

f ever there was a community where the four cops who beat Rodney King could be judged by a jury of their peers, Simi Valley is the place. Just over the Santa Susana Pass, on LA County's northwest border, Simi Valley (population 100,000) is home to no less than 2,000 LAPD, Sheriff's Department and other law-enforcement personnel who make the daily commute over the rolling hills along Freeway 118 to Parker Center and dozens of other police stations around Los Angeles County.

Judge Stanley Weisberg's decision to move the King beating case to Simi Valley rather than Alameda County is called even further into question when the number of documented instances of racism in that part of Ventura County is considered. For this reason, John Hatcher, president of the Ventura County chapter of the NAACP, who has been prodding county officials to implement equal-opportunity or affirmative-action policies in at least some of the county's school curriculums, was not surprised by what the jury found. "When it happened, I said, 'I told you so.' I knew it was going to happen," Hatcher said.

In 1986, the issue of racism captured headlines in daily newspapers covering Simi Valley and its neighboring city, Moorpark. In November of that year, one of a handful of black families living in Moorpark complained to local Sheriff's officials about an act of vandalism in which the word "nigger" was scratched into the roof of a car owned by a black Moorpark high-school student. The case was eventually resolved with the arrest of two teenagers, but not before other racial attacks were exposed to the press. One

Photo of Rodney King by Ted Soqui

Policeville: Why People Who Know West Ventura County Weren't Surprised by the Verdict

by Kevin Uhrich

family regularly received threatening late night phone calls. Another had threatening notes attached to its front doors, warning family members to go back to Los Angeles. One black woman who worked for Tandon Corporation's satellite office in Moorpark was told by a gas-station attendant that he didn't serve blacks.

People living in the two communities were outraged, not so much by the various incidents but by the fact they were getting attention in the local newspapers. Although the furor quickly died down, less than

five months later the former mayor of Moorpark, 69-year-old Texas businessman Bud Ferguson, used the term "nigger" twice in an interview.

It soon became apparent that officials like Ferguson regularly used not only the word "nigger" but also "wetback" and "*taco frijoles*" when referring to members of the region's Mexican community. And they didn't use such terms in smoky private backrooms. They said them publicly. Interestingly enough, the reporters covering Moorpark didn't question the veracity of the quotes when

they started appearing frequently in a local newspaper. They wondered why they were reported at all.

"Why did you quote him? He talks like that all the time," several reporters who cover Moorpark lamented.

At that point, there was no doubt that an institutionalized if not organized racist element existed in eastern Ventura County, not only at the highest levels of local government but also among the journalists who covered those cities. In Simi Valley, if only by virtue of its size compared to

same verdict: different location

Moorpark (pop. 30,000), incidents of racism were isolated and subtle, but no less hurtful to the people at whom the attacks were aimed.

"To make us responsible for this is unfair," insists Simi Valley Mayor Greg Stratton, who said he was surprised at the jury's verdict. Since the verdict was handed down last week, city officials have received bomb threats at the courthouse and at the Ronald Reagan Presidential Library on Madera Road, near Thousand Oaks.

"We have to get the focus off of us and onto the jury. What we have to ask ourselves is, what did the jury see that we didn't?"

The question actually is, what did Stratton, Hatcher and others know about eastern Ventura County that Reiner and White possibly did not? Could Reiner or the lead prosecutor in the case, Los Angeles Deputy DA Terry White, not have known about these incidents?

White has acknowledged he faced an uphill battle when the case was moved to Ventura County. Of some 300 prospective jurors, all had ties to the Southern California law-enforcement community. The 27 who did not were excluded by the defense. The prosecution was further hamstrung by the application of a provision of Proposition 115, under which the judge, and not the opposing lawyers, questioned prospective jurors.

Wayne Lee, editor-publisher of the *Enterprise*, the newspaper that broke most of the racism stories during the latter part of the '80s, called the jury's verdict "depressing." Simi Valley, Lee said, is a law-and-order town and will probably remain one for the foreseeable future. Of course there have been cases of police excess, some of which have been argued in federal court. But most of those cases have involved white people, Lee said.

Over the years, Simi Valley's counterculture — young people with little more to do than drive their cars fast, drink beer, dance and piss off the cops — has developed through the help of music. Several local night spots have sprung up, with local talent headlining.

Culture Shock, Share the Power is a racially mixed, loosely organized coalition largely of musicians intent on reversing the social stigma that has been hung on Simi Valley since the King verdicts. The group will be holding a clothes and food drive for LA residents who were victimized in the looting and rioting.

But despite their effort to minimize the impact of being labeled a racist community, coalition members rapper Kenny Law, 26, and Lynn Greaves, 33, have discovered the local police do not seem to be keen on interracial relationships. Greaves is white, Law is black. Greaves said she has been pulled over at least eight times by Simi Valley cops in the past two months for no apparent reason. Law says the same thing. Both believe they are being harassed for no other reason than the fact they are dating. Still, Law tries to look at the positive.

"In Simi Valley," he says, "everyone is trying to pull together right now." ∎

Kevin Uhrich is a staff writer for the Pasadena Star News. A version of this story first appeared in the Los Angeles Reader.

Black and Blue: The Oakland Cop Who Would Be King

by Pearl Stewart

While the verdict in the Rodney King case reverberated throughout the nation, San Francisco East Bay resident Derrick Norfleet became physically ill. Not only did he identify with King as an African-American man, but he also understood the excruciating pain and humiliation King suffered at the hands of his attackers.

Norfleet, too, recalls being bludgeoned by cops — not in LA, but in Oakland. Two years ago, he was intentionally struck by a patrol car driven by an Oakland police officer. He says the officer and two other policemen, none of whom was black, leapt from their cars and pounded him with their fists and kicked him and hammered him with a flashlight. Like King, Norfleet claims he was attacked because of his race. But when the pummeling ended and the three officers turned Norfleet's limp body over, they gazed into the face of a fellow cop.

Officer Derrick Norfleet was working undercover in East Oakland, and he must have delivered a first-class performance buying crack from local drug dealers. But when he volunteered for undercover work, Norfleet didn't realize that his acting ability would provoke such a violent response. He didn't know then what his fellow officers were capable of.

These days, Norfleet is wiser and $60,000 richer, after winning a lawsuit last August against the Oakland Police Department, which employs him. He's back in uniform, though he says his undercover days are over. Given his experiences, Norfleet had a special interest in the Rodney King case, and he felt an even deeper agony than the rest of us when the Simi Valley jury found King's assailants not guilty.

In his own civil suit, Norfleet says, he faced a similar problem with the jury in U.S. District Court in San Francisco. His award came only against the officer who knocked him to the ground with the patrol car. "The jury basically found that the beating they inflicted on me was OK," he says, "but that one guy went too far when he ran me down with the car." The jury of six people in his case included one African-American; the others were Hispanic, white and Filipino.

Once he decided to file suit, Norfleet found out that being a "fellow" police officer didn't help. After filing his initial claim, Norfleet says he was subjected to various forms of harassment, including racist graffiti and threatening notes. He says a commanding officer told him he would have no future in the department if he didn't withdraw the lawsuit.

Shortly before the case went to trial, one incident nearly devastated him. "A black guy driving a car identical to mine —

incomprehensible the repeated thrashing that Rodney King suffered at the hands of LAPD officers, Norfleet has been a first-hand witness to the pent-up fear and hatred many white cops feel toward black men. When white cops get together, their conversations often reinforce stereotypes about black men, he says. "Basically, they don't understand black culture and what they don't understand, they fear."

Norfleet believes the situation will improve only if sensitivity training is provided to officers. In his seven years with the Oakland Police Department, Norfleet hasn't heard of any classes to teach officers about Oakland's numerous ethnic groups

low officers. "Even in my case, those guys lied and they brought in outside people to lie," he says. "I know for a fact that if I hadn't also been a police officer, I wouldn't have had a chance in that courtroom."

One would hope, in the wake of the King verdict and the rage in its aftermath, that the training Norfleet urges and the breaking of the code of silence may finally take place. But Norfleet believes that's unlikely. "People of color have been at the bottom of the totem pole for a long time, and [King's] case isn't going to change that right away," he says. In fact, Norfleet worries that the verdict may lead to more "recklessness" on the part of some police officers and more skepticism from the community toward the police.

Norfleet's attorney, John Burris, agrees. Burris, who has handled dozens of cases in which citizens have charged East Bay police with misconduct, fears that fewer people — of any race — will now choose to file complaints against police. "People are asking themselves, if the beating inflicted upon King wasn't police misconduct, then my twisted arm or bruised shoulder won't mean very much." Several witnesses in cases Burris has pending have called him to say they're no longer willing to testify against officers. They're afraid, and in light of the King verdicts they doubt their testimony will help.

San Francisco: Maggie Hallahan

a 1988 pearl white 300 2X — was shot to death while driving on the freeway," Norfleet recalls. "Somebody drove alongside him and shot up his car." The victim turned out to be an Alameda firefighter about the same size as Norfleet. The shooting remained a mystery, but Norfleet is convinced he was the target.

From his unique vantage point as both cop and cop-victim, Norfleet has special insights about the King case and other incidents of brutality involving law-enforcement officers. Although many of us found

and their respective cultures. "I was appalled that even after the Rodney King beating happened and people saw the tape over and over, there was no special training [in Oakland] for officers so that they could avoid similar incidents."

Norfleet views the "code of silence" among cops as a big part of the problem. In some cases, he says, the code is nothing more than an excuse for covering up criminal activity involving fel-

But Burris thinks the King case served an important purpose. "In many ways the case performed the same function as the Clarence Thomas hearings," he says. "It raised the consciousness of the nation to the fact that a problem exists." When millions of women watched the all-male Senate Judiciary Committee mercilessly grill Anita Hill, it became vividly apparent that something was wrong. As a result, the gender makeup on Capitol Hill is likely to change as soon as this election year.

Even though the hearings were bizarre and unpleasant for many African-Americans to view because they pitted a black man against a black woman, many of us were enlightened by the painful proceedings. We learned that justice doesn't always prevail. Similarly, the grim events of the days following the King verdict have been edifying for those who may have had the misguided notion that the nation was moving toward racial harmony.

According to Burris, whose current police brutality caseload numbers 30, "Very few cases of police misconduct are ever prosecuted [on criminal charges]." He calls a case like King's "highly unusual." District attorneys are reluctant to prosecute, Burris says, because criminal cases against police are very difficult to win. Civil lawsuits against the police, on the other hand, are frequently successful. In 80 to 85 percent of the cases he sees, the plaintiffs win damages or settle out of court. For the most part, Burris's clients are blacks and Hispanics.

One of Burris's clients is Darrell Hampton, the popular black West Oakland recreation director who claims he was thrust to the ground and beaten by two white cops in front of several young children. Hampton was charged with resisting arrest and possession of a deadly weapon — a pool cue. The charges against Hampton were later dropped, but he has sued the police department for $6 million. Burris is also representing rap artist Tupac Shakur of Digital Underground, who alleges he was beaten by two Oakland patrol cops after he jaywalked across the street. He has filed a $10-million claim against the Oakland PD.

Burris says the King case provides insight into how some police departments "condone over-aggressiveness." Burris points out that most officers who are found guilty of misconduct remain on the police force and often are promoted. If they do leave, they are usually hired by another police department. "Unfortunately, overly aggressive cops are often considered good cops by the leadership of the police departments," Burris says.

Oakland's seven-member Citizen's Complaint Board, appointed by the mayor, has not done much to change this. Those with complaints can take their grievances before the board, but in most instances the officers are cleared of charges brought against them. From the board's inception in September, 1980, to December, 1990, a total of 719 complaints were filed; 202 of those resulted in hearings, and 39 complaints — or 20 percent — were sustained, according to hearing officer Larry Carroll.

Only one of the complaints was sustained between 1986 and 1990. Carroll says one reason for that is that more officers began showing up for the hearings after 1985. Their presence is not required, but in recent years the department has been encouraging them to attend. "When the officers appear at the hearings, it often boils down to credibility," he says. "When you get three officers saying one thing and the citizens saying another, the board, whose seven members are appointed by the mayor, usually goes along with the officers."

Many of us have wondered: What might have happened if black cops had beaten a white person that badly, with the incident captured on videotape. Is there any way those men would be walking the streets today? Would they even be alive?

What if Derrick Norfleet had run down a white suspect in his patrol car, and then he and other black cops had pounded and kicked the white man, who turned out to be a fellow officer? Those black officers wouldn't be allowed to work in animal control, let alone remain on the police force. But all three cops who beat Norfleet are still working as police officers — one in Oakland, one in Berkeley and one in Pleasant Hill.

In fact, the officer now stationed in Berkeley, Mike Cafalu, was recently brought before the Berkeley Police Review Commission on charges of improper detention of a black teenager. The charges were sustained in early February. Cefalu was the officer driving the car that struck Norfleet.

The Rodney King verdict was just a continuation of the injustices Derrick Norfleet, Tupac Shakur and countless others have experienced. No video cameras were around when they were attacked — but it turned out the camera didn't make a difference anyway. ∎

Pearl Stewart is a columnist for the East Bay Express *in Berkeley, California, where a version of this story first appeared.*

Panic in New York

by L.A. Kauffman

Shootings at Saks Fifth Avenue. Widespread looting at Macy's. Fires at Lord & Taylor. The 113th precinct under siege. Grand Central Station shut down. Angry black mobs swarming through all five boroughs, beating any whites they encounter.

This was the massive city-wide riot that hit New York City in the wake of the Rodney King verdict — the phantom riot, that is, produced by New York's collective subconscious in a binge of panicked rumor-mongering. For one afternoon, two days after the decision was announced, New Yorkers let down their infamous guard and revealed the depth of fear and mistrust wrought by a decade of racially inflected economic polarization.

Nothing happened, of course — not at Saks, not at Macy's and not at Lord & Taylor. The only losses sustained on Friday were business losses after each of the three landmark Manhattan stores opted to close early because of concern about a planned demonstration to protest police brutality.

Though there was some violence during the march that followed the peaceful late afternoon rally at Times Square, it was relatively undramatic: flying bottles, a few smashed windows, an upturned car or two. No significant looting was reported in New York City. No fires. No shootings. No deaths.

In the end, the social fact of the panic proved more significant than the journalistic facts of actual injuries (40 or so), arrests (131) or damage (several dozen store windows). Midtown was a mess all

New York: Gerard Gaskin

same verdict: different location

New York's phantom riot was born of guilty knowledge — among those privileged enough to have a job and a home — that the yuppie boom of the 1980s led quite directly to increased poverty for this city's African-American and Latino populations. For every trendy new boutique or restaurant that opened in SoHo or the Upper West Side, it seemed that 100 more people were added to the homeless population. As property values and rents skyrocketed in the 1980s orgy of real-estate speculation, the lines of class and race became virtually identical. And now, as the recession is putting those same boutiques out of business, the desperate and accelerating crisis outside New York's tony neighborhoods — above 125th Street and across the bridges and tunnels — is, in Stuart Hall's phrase, "only policed, never addressed."

By Saturday afternoon, the stores had mostly reopened, the broken windows had been replaced and New York's pose had returned. Few would admit to having taken part in the panic: What was sweat on Friday had turned into swagger by Saturday. A street vendor bragged that he had kept his wares displayed until the crowd was just a hundred yards away. A cab driver laughed at what good business he had done the day before by picking up those to afraid to walk or take the subway.

But in the street and in the subways, you could see people jump every time they heard a loud noise. For the events in LA made it impossible for anyone in New York to ignore the simmering discontent of the castaways of Reagan, Bush and Trump — victims of an economic beating less graphic than, but just as brutal and deliberate as, the physical beating of Rodney King. ∎

L.A. Kauffman's stories have appeared in The Nation, *the* Village Voice *and* Mother Jones. *She is currently writing a book about radical politics since the 1960s. This story first appeared in* SF Weekly.

afternoon as offices sent worried workers home hours early to escape the imagined Great Black Threat.

The city's biggest mob scene occurred at Penn Station, where thousands of frightened commuters fought to catch the next train to Long Island. A white friend of mine, chatting and smoking a cigarette on 42nd Street while waiting for the rally to begin, was repeatedly approached by other whites who warned her to leave the area as fast as she could. The sidewalks were filled with animated conversations as New Yorkers broke one of their biggest taboos — talking with strangers — in order to share their fear. "Do you think it's safe?" a woman asked as I walked along the street. "Everyone should get home as soon as they can," announced another woman in one of the few shops that remained open by mid-afternoon.

It wasn't only whites who gave in to the hysteria. An Asian friend made plans to go over to Times Square, but joked that he had donned ACT–UP and Queer Nation buttons to show which side he was on. A Latina worried about her children's light complexions. "My two young boys look really white," she said. "I hope they'll be OK." Black and Latina secretaries at a well-known Wall Street law firm gratefully accepted cab fare from their employer and

hurried out of Manhattan.

By 4:30 pm, when the protest was to begin, Times Square — and everything else downtown — was eerily deserted. It looked more like a wintry Sunday morning than a sunny Friday afternoon. As the multiracial crowd marched down Seventh Avenue, the most striking thing was how the city sounded. The usual cacophony of rush-hour traffic was replaced by the constant rattle of rapidly closing windows and gates a block or so ahead of the march, punctuated only by the screams of police sirens and the echoes of the protesters' chants. It wasn't until the march reached the West Village that anyone other than the protesters and the police could be seen on the streets: Wide-eyed café patrons sat behind lowered metal gates, nervously sipping their $4.00 cappuccinos.

The hysteria that overtook New York spread so quickly because all the terrifying rumors seemed eminently plausible to so many people. It wasn't just that the stories of lootings and beatings all around town fed into longstanding racist images of black lawlessness, though they all too obviously and grotesquely did just that. The store closings and rushed exits revealed more, even, than the growing paranoia of a city that seems to be caught in an unending spiral of decay.

New York: Gerard Gaskin

New York's Lost Weekend *by Brian Palmer*

At dusk on Thursday evening, I joined 15 young African-American men on the corner of 125th Street and St. Nicholas Avenue. Bricks and bottles lay at their feet. Most of the shops on Harlem's busiest strip were shuttered. Some of the brothers half-listened to a black transit cop, who told them to be smart and stay cool, but also to watch their backs. Some of his white colleagues are nervous, the officer said. Then he disappeared into the subway.

A Transit Police bus rolled up to the light, and the young men jeered and shouted at the white driver. Something could have happened, but the crowd was small and there were too few cops in sight to provide a focal point for their anger. The light changed and the bus rolled on.

New York last weekend was nothing like LA. There were no fires, little looting and no one shot to death. But there were intimations of what the city might have been like: a Korean woman crying as men rushed to bring crates of vegetables inside and close the gates in response to chants of "Shut it down"; a *Newsday* reporter hit by someone with a two-by-four. All around the city, there were rallies and some disturbances, colored by rage, fear, nihilism, reason and opportunism. The crowd, mostly made up of high-school and college students, was changeable, spirited, even militant, but also weirdly playful.

Friday morning, hundreds of high-school students walked out of class and swarmed through Times Square and then lower Manhattan, surging through the streets past the few Wall Streeters who hadn't yet hit the commuter lines. Cries of outrage mixed with teen babble. Marchers recited the Pledge of Allegiance, punctuated with a hearty "Bullshit." At the World Trade Center, black, white, Asian and Latino kids posed for photographers and each other.

"That was the first time I ever marched for something," said a girl named Marnie. "It was fun." More than a few people felt that way. The King verdict had given them a permission slip to break the social order, or at least bend it. "I was ready to wreck shit," a young brother with Ray-Bans perched on his forehead and droopy pants hanging off his waist told a friend. His tone was more macho-blasé than enraged.

Friday afternoon at around 3:30, a demonstration stepped off from the Harlem State Office Building, led by Omowale Clay of the December 12 Movement, the miltant African-American group that brought us the Days of Outrage. For hours, several hundred marchers wandered through Harlem, Yorkville and East Harlem, halting periodically to hear Clay stress the need for discipline. "You are the heart and soul of the Black and Latino nation," Clay told the racially mixed crowd. "You are also the main target. Some of our young brothers don't want to understand that the movement for our liberation didn't start the other night. To beat these pigs, i isn't enough to have heart. You have to have a plan." ■

Brian Palmer contributes to the Village Voice, *where this story first appeared.*

Seattle's Little Big Riot

by Eric Scigliano

Seattle's days of grief and nights of rage began in imitation of the much larger riots that ravaged Los Angeles: As ever, fashion travelled up the coast, passing through San Francisco to Seattle. But the Seattle outbreaks took on their own distinctive character. A range of groups as diverse as the modern city itself — from neighborhood activists to clergy to campus anarchists to street thugs — seized the frenzied moment and claimed Rodney King as their patron martyr.

For young revelers and cruisers, Thursday night downtown is always the warm-up for the weekend. So it was with the raw revelry that started around midnight last Thursday, the evening of the day the King verdict was announced.

The authorities breathed deeply and imagined that the violence might pass by Seattle. Then, shortly before midnight, about 50 youths gathered in an unannounced protest rally in front of the McDonald's at Third Pike, a favorite hangout for street kids and gang-bangers near the center of Seattle's downtown "Blade." They carried placards and shouted what would become the weekend's main refrain: "No peace without justice!" Street people swelled the march, and police dogged it closely. As tempers rose, a police car ran onto the sidewalk and over a marcher's foot, and the crowd scattered. Small, fluid bands rampaged through the dark streets, brawling, smashing and grabbing from store windows, lighting dumpster fires and turning over cars.

As the sun rose Friday morning, Seattle Mayor Norm Rice convened the city's political, business and civil-rights establishments for two hours behind closed doors. They strategized on how to contain the outrage and nurture it into a force for reform. It was classic Rice-style coalition-building, of a strictly insider sort.

Rice and a dozen of the various leaders appeared later at a peace rally held at Martin Luther King, Jr., Park, a site that should have been movingly appropriate, but in fact seemed ironic. King's assassination in 1968 touched off the last great wave of national riots, and a skeptical gallery of African-American men who listened to the rally saw a different, dispiriting symbolism in the choice of Martin Luther King, Jr., Park. The unfinished, ill-designed park represented all the broken and deferred promises they held against the Rice administration, as well as the half-hearted tokenism with which the mainstream deals with black America, when it deals with it at all. One bystander lamented the deeply symbolic setting of the park — in the gentrifying area around the Interstate 90 lid, "next to all these $100,000 white homes, instead of where people could really use the inspiration, in the [Central District] or by Holly Park."

A few members of the mostly white audience grew restive, demanding practical measures *now*. The dean of Seattle's African-American clergy, Rev. Sam McKinney, compared the Rodney King verdict to the 1857 Dred Scott Decision, which denied citizenship to the descendants of slaves. He recalled marching to Selma, Alabama, with Martin Luther King 27 years ago. McKinney noted that "The majority of young African-American men are caught up in a justice system that's out to destroy them." Then he asked, rhetorically, "Where do we go from here?" Jesse Wineberry, Washington state's sole African-American legislator, sounded a familiar refrain about "George Bush hitting the snooze button of denial for poor people for 20 years in government."

From the back of the audience, an angry voice shouted, "I'm sick and tired of all the talk." Linzy Burton, a stocky, clean-cut black man wearing a movie T-shirt emblazoned "Living Large: A Comedy" unleashed his rage. "Like Jesse said, it's been 20 years. All that diplomatic stuff is dead. It's time to take it to the street! If it takes bloodshed, fine!"

Wineberry and several ministers tried to calm Burton down. "I need more brothers like you," said Wineberry, "but I need you *outside* of jail."

Burton, who grew up in Seattle, saw his father and brother "beaten, spit on, stepped on, pressed down in the mud" by police. He is a vivid example of the economic downspin of blue-collar America, which hits minority workers first and hardest. After attending college for three years, he worked for four years as a warehouse manager. But he was beaten out for another warehouse job after what he considered a great interview. "A white boy who came in dirty, stinking, in torn jeans and dirty sneakers," got the job.

Burton planned to go downtown Friday night to join the action. But to achieve what? "I would get a sense of relief of all this anger that's built up," he snarled. "It's like a powder keg in my chest. Sure it's going to be people killed. But it will have to do something. There's no chance of change till you hit white America right in their homes!"

Some whites who had seen the gruesome reports of random interracial attacks in Los Angeles were reluctant to attend the rally Friday afternoon at the Federal Building. By that time, many downtown stores and offices had been evacuated. But race-related attacks, and even outward racial tension among individuals, were rare in the Seattle melée. Looting was also relatively light, in marked contrast to the

same verdict: different location

Seattle: Saul Bromberge

grab-and-dash shopping bazaars of the Los Angeles and earlier Miami riots. Even when they smashed the windows of Musicland on Third Avenue, rioters grabbed only a few tapes and left the costlier CDs. Mostly, they were after "action." At times the riot-zone streets seemed filled with sightseers bumping into one another's cameras. Video and still cameras were ubiquitous, and the vandals ignored them.

But the Seattle riot wasn't limited to thrill-seeking under cover of outrage. The Simi Valley verdict was the occasion for a venting of real anger. The rage was directed not at individuals — looters of all races and ilks shared a weird camaraderie — but at perceived common enemies: authority and wealth in general, and the police in particular.

Nor were the rampages novel to Seattle. At least twice last summer, black youths confronted the Seattle Police Department in numbers comparable to those of any single demonstration following the Rodney King verdict. In one case, according to police reports, some 40 officers in riot gear were driven back by more than 200 kids who threw bottles, rocked squad cars, stormed for a mile up to 23rd and Cherry and looted a mini-mart there. Perhaps because those riots happened on weekends and in minority neighborhoods, neither one made the daily papers.

Friday, at the Federal Building, as the speakers decried the Simi Valley verdict and racism and other ills, one rakish neo-Yippie who somehow recalled Walter Huston as Scratch in *The Devil and Daniel Webster* murmured, "When the sun goes down, we'll take this town!" to his companions. As the rally dispersed, he rushed out onto Second Avenue waving and yelling, "You've got to stay *in* the street." A hard core of 100 to 200 agreed and marched up Madison toward Capitol Hill.

There they attacked the precinct house harder than before, breaking some windows. Vandals ran across Pine to smash into the state liquor store. Police, complete with cavalry, arrested some protesters and drove the rest toward downtown, where young "gang-bangers" who hang around the downtown streets were already roaming and breaking windows, as they had on the previous night.

The police operation to stop the rioting was impressive, inexorable — and futile. The downtown police battalion stopped at the border of its precinct, Boren Street. East Precinct deployment was either insufficient or unprepared to contain the rioters, whose tempers had been inflamed by the long prodding and pushing.

Released, the group scattered into more flammable, densely populated and hard-to-patrol Capitol Hill, where they did the week's worst damage. They smashed windows and overturned cars. They torched one apartment house and seriously damaged an adjacent one at Summit and John. And they ignited a spectacular blaze, complete with a fuel-tank explosion, in a vacant building near Pike and 14th. Suburban fire trucks were called in to fight the 30 or so fires, all ignited in response to a suburban jury's verdict on a distant city's police practices.

Thus the little big riot — in the end, still a suitably subdued, Seattle sort of riot — subsided. The slow-motion turmoil of everyday urban life resumed. As I walked back to my office, a man approached me. He was black and looked around 30, older than the rampagers whom he'd avoided all night. He asked me for a buck for food, which I gave him, but he wanted more — though not more cash. On this bleak street corner at three in the morning, the stranger asked me for a job. As though he were being interviewed, he told me his story: He was from East Texas, he was a licensed nurse, he could talk the way white people want you to talk.

"In East Texas, people will say straight out, 'I hate you, nigger,'" he said. "You know where they're coming from. In Seattle, they're so nice, they smile and say 'How are you today?' and toss your application in the wastebasket." ∎

Eric Scigliano is senior editor of the Seattle Weekly, *where a version of this story first appeared.*

The Emergency That Wasn't

by Vince Bielski and George Cothran

Angry as a wounded bull, a man jumped the railing separating the politicians from the people in the San Francisco Board of Supervisors chambers and charged toward the supervisors screaming, "We have constitutional rights, you motherfuckers." The board had called a special Saturday session to consider lifting the one-day-old state of emergency in the wake of the downtown riots, which had given police extraordinary powers to arrest anyone for almost any reason. It took four police officers to drag the man from the chambers. It was the single violent incident on the Saturday following the Rodney King verdict, but the angry protester spoke for many who were outraged about events in the Mission District the night before.

Friday evening, a massive police sweep through a peaceful "speak out" on Mission and 24th streets had resulted in the arrests of 400 people. Bystanders, local residents and journalists were all caught up in the sweep. Authorities refused to release most of those arrested for almost 36 hours, to prevent them from taking part in further demonstrations.

Mayor Frank Jordan and Police Chief Richard Hongisto showed no concern about violating people's constitutional rights. When Supervisor Jim Gonzáles asked Hongisto about reports of police arresting neighborhood residents who were waiting for a bus, Hongisto smiled and said, "As the old saying goes, anything is possible."

The mayor and his top cop insisted that the state of emergency continue, on the grounds that Friday night's mass arrests prevented more rioting from breaking out. Hongisto even used the uproar from protesters in the packed Board of Supervisors chambers to argue for martial law. "There's a potential for violence right here in City Hall," he told the supervisors.

Hongisto's argument assumed that protesters were planning a repeat of Thursday night's rampage through San Francisco's downtown. The supervisors, however, weren't convinced and shot down the request by a 7-1 vote. There were no incidents of violence on Saturday night, or during the remainder of the weekend. The mayor and police chief were proven wrong.

"We didn't imagine it would be abused the way it was," said Supervisor Terence Hallinan of the state-of-emergency declaration he had approved the day before. "That's why we revoked it." Legal observers can't recall the last time the city has used state-of-emergency powers to make mass arrests. They fear the possibility of a repeat performance. "The scariest part is the precedent this sets," said the ACLU's John Crew, an expert on police practices. "On the theory that there *might* be unrest, officials now have a standard that could be applied to any protest."

But Jordan and Hongisto's tactics caused much more damage than a brief suspension of constitutional rights. Just the declaration of a state of emergency sent shivers through a jittery city. Could LA be happening here? It was evident all day Friday that fear had taken over San Francisco. Store owners throughout the city closed early; many boarded up windows and doors. By Friday evening, San Francisco was a ghost town.

While television news left the impression that the protests following the King verdict on Thursday constituted one big riot, much of the action was non-violent and political. Protesters began early in the day, led primarily by students from San Francisco State University and City College who belong to Roots Against War, the African Student Alliance, *La Raza* and other groups. They marched without inci-

dent through the Mission and Fillmore districts, collecting others on the way to the State Building for a rally.

From the State Building, as some 1,500 protesters headed down McAllister Street, things turned ugly. A handful of people began breaking car windows at about the same time the police blew through the crowd on motorcycles and arrived on foot in riot gear. The heavy police presence clearly helped instigate the rioting that followed.

The vast majority of the protesters weren't violent, but they seemed to sympathize with those who were, particularly young blacks who chose to attack and loot commercial outlets, the locales America holds most sacred. Most protesters just stood around chanting slogans like "No justice, no peace," while the more adventurous followed behind the small bands of looters as they hit several stores. Mixed up in the fury were bystanders like R.J. Omania, a 58-year-old unemployed engineer. "This whole fucking thing starts at the top, in Washington," he said. "Just look at the condition this country is in."

The Limited was one of the clothing stores hit by looters. Its well-lit windows attracted a group of African-American youngsters, who smashed the glass before spending what seemed like five minutes emptying entire clothes racks. Elementary-school-age kids were among those who filled their arms with goods.

From across the street, a 24-year-old African-American student from UC Berkeley offered his opinion. "This is wrong. I can't condone it," he said. "But this society lives by the sword, and it will die by the sword. It's not right to go into other people's stores, but how else can they get their frustrations out? You can only listen to politicians talk for so long."

Thursday night, the police far outnumbered the looters, but made little effort

same verdict: different location

to arrest them. More than once, cops marched or drove in single-file lines, passing by looters, apparently afraid that making arrests would agitate onlookers and spark more violence. Instead, the police spent most of their time dispersing the non-violent protesters.

Few observers questioned the need for a strong police effort Thursday night to quell the window-breaking and looting in the Market Street area. But Jordan's request for emergency powers on Friday (which the board approved) and Saturday raises a serious question: Was the state of emergency necessary, or were political motives fueling Jordan's heavy-handed crackdown?

All indications show that the state of emergency was called not because it was needed, but because Jordan was desperate to repair his faltering mayoralty. The rebellion gave Jordan a tailor-made opportunity to overcome his image as a bumbling, indecisive leader. His swift call for a curfew Thursday night made Jordan, for a few hours, the perfect picture of the effective leader — calm, forceful and decisive. But on Friday, he continued to milk the previous night's protests. The state of emergency was declared Friday afternoon, long after the violence had ended.

The state-of-emergency declaration gave the police extraordinary new power to "take all steps necessary to cause the dispersal and prevent the continuation of any gatherings of people anywhere in San Francisco whenever the peace officer on the scene has reason to believe that the gathering endangers or is likely to endanger persons and property." That is, the police were free to arrest people *before* they engaged in any illegal activity.

The emergency order required the police to issue dispersal orders and give people time to leave before arresting them. But the only dispersal orders given Friday evening were at 24th Street. Hundreds of people several blocks away never heard the order before they were nabbed. The only violence of the evening came when protesters lobbed three bottles that crashed at the feet of cops on 24th Street before the crowd scattered.

About 30 minutes later, helmeted, baton-toting officers began sandwiching more than 100 protesters, onlookers, passersby and journalists a block away. The cops ignored pleas from many people to let them leave before arresting them. By now, this part of the Mission District had been transformed into a police state. Anyone walking in the area could be arrested — and many were. The police told one group to move toward Valencia Street, and as they did other cops arrested them. Many people waiting for buses and coming out of shops got caught up in the sweep and were carted off to jail as well. "One older Latina woman started crying," said a photographer on the scene. "They arrested her, too."

Bay Times reporter Tim Kingston, who was wearing his police department press pass, was one of many media personnel who were arrested. Kingston said he heard a cop say, "'We know him from last night.' The Police targeted me because they know me as a reporter who has been at many demonstrations," Kingston said. "It's an outrageous violation of my First Amendment rights."

There is something ironic about the position recently appointed Police Chief Hongisto found himself in on Friday. As a candidate for mayor last year, Hongisto proudly boasted of being a "card-carrying member of the ACLU." Now he was in direct conflict with the same organization. Not only was he threatening San Francisco's constitutional rights, but he added a bizarre racial twist by implying that it was whites who lead minorities into battle. "Yesterday, you had sophisticated Caucasian students and political organizers who organized demonstrations, got a lot of poor people involved who were angry about their status in life and their situation, and involved them in the looting and destroying of downtown," he said. "And we're not going to let it happen."

To Hongisto, the state of emergency was apparently necessary to avert a revolution in San Francisco — a revolution that, by all accounts, had already fizzled to a small gathering resembling a college lecture far more than it did a social rebellion. ■

Vince Bielski is the news editor and George Cothran is a political reporter for SF Weekly, *where a version of this story first appeared.*

San Francisco Police Chief Pays the Price

by Jonathan Nack

Since the Rodney King verdict, San Francisco has seen an explosion of protests, one night of looting, a three-day state of emergency, mass arrests, police brutality and even the seizure of thousands of copies of a newspaper. Mayor Frank Jordan has been locked in a face-off with a defiant Board of Supervisors, while Police Chief Richard Hongisto, who was fired, is under criminal investigation.

San Francisco's unrest is the result of unorthodox police tactics. The police arrested more than 1,000 non-violent protesters and non-participating bystanders, and treated them with considerable brutality.

Though none of the demonstrations drew anywhere near the 100,000 people who protested the Gulf war here, the level of confrontation was much higher. The 380 people arrested May 1, and the almost 600 arrested May 8, experienced baton beatings, hours in tight handcuffs and stays in jail as long as 36 hours. Reporter Katharine Fong, who was arrested in the police sweep May 1, witnessed a police officer kick a gay man with AIDS in the back after he asked for medicine to treat his bronchitis. "Here's your medicine," the cop allegedly said.

On May 15, the Police Commission voted unanimously — after an all-night emergency session — to fire Hongisto. The commission was responding to charges that the chief had ordered police officers to confiscate at least 2,000 copies of the *San Francisco Bay Times* newspaper from news racks. The newspaper, which serves the lesbian and gay community, featured a cover photo of Hongisto's head superimposed on a body in police uniform, with a nightstick in a phallic position and a headline reading, "Dick's Cool New Tool: Martial Law." Hongisto is currently the subject of an investigation by the San Francisco County District Attorney. A civil suit by the *Bay Times* is also expected.

The day before accusations regarding the newspapers surfaced, Hongisto had gone before the Board of Supervisors with the mayor's support, calling for a month-long moratorium on all demonstrations. The board rejected the proposal 7-1. Supervisor Angela Alioto commented that such a breach of people's constitutional rights "is completely unacceptable."

Five supervisors lent their names to a May 17 "Justice for Rodney King! Defend the Right to Protest!" demonstration. "Why should we need permits to exercise our First Amendment rights?" asked Supervisor Terrance Hallinan at the protest, which drew about 3,500 people. "Why do we need permits to say the Rodney King verdict stinks?"

Nevertheless, Jordan has steadfastly supported the police's recent insistence on permits for all protests, and at a May 15 press conference he said that the police chief had made "major positive contributions to the SFPD" during his six-week tenure. The next day, the mayor said he

San Francisco: Maggie Hallahan

was committed to finding another government job for Hongisto. There was speculation he might be named parking commissioner, with a $95,000 per year salary.

Ironically, Hongisto had maintained a liberal reputation for more than a decade, and his appointment as police chief had been part of a now-shattered quid pro quo. Though Jordan's core conservative constituency has supported his get-tough policies, it probably represents only a quarter of the city's voters.

"The protesters were the driving force behind the whole drama — they knew it and are feeling their power," José Gato of Roots Against War, a group of young activists of color that sponsored earlier demonstrations, said. "The uprising in the streets has forced [the supervisors] to take a stand. The people led them, and not vice versa."

Despite the controversy, protests continue to proliferate here. On May 15,

Queer Nation organized a demonstration in honor of Malcom X's birthday. That night, an annual candlelight march in memory of people who have died of AIDS drew 10,000. The annual march to commemorate Harvey Milk — the city's first openly gay supervisor, assassinated in 1978 — was scheduled for May 20, Milk's birthday. The march's agenda was broadened to include demands to stop police harassment and brutality, as well as institutionalized racism, sexism and homophobia.

Coalitions that came together during the Gulf war have been reinvigorated. Anti-racist activists have been joined by people active in anti-war, international solidarity and gay-liberation movements. First Amendment issues have also brought progressive and liberal political, labor and religious leaders into alliance with the protesters. There are strains on these alliances, however. Many who have been protesting since the verdict expressed skepticism of the supervisors, who initially voted to support the state of emergency. Others, such as Judy Rohrer of the Pledge of Resistance, which has supported all the protests, worried that the supervisors' endorsement "could be problematic in setting up a dualism between good demonstrators and bad demonstrators."

The issue of march permits and police response is sure to come up again. Jordan hasn't backed off. Jordan's working agreements with the liberal establishment, key to his election last November, have been ruptured, but it's too soon to predict the outcome of this political crisis. ■

Jonathan Nack is the San Francisco Bay Area bureau chief for the Guardian News Weekly, *where a version of this story first appeared.*

Las Vegas

by Mike Davis

Seattle: Sandra Hoover

Las Vegas's frenzied Memorial Day weekend was winding down with the promise of a big storm. As raindrops the size of silver dollars intermittently splattered the sidewalks outside, weary casino tellers counted a quarter-billion dollars in holiday revenue. Across the Mojave, 50,000 homebound revelers were strung out almost bumper to bumper, from Ivanpah Dry Lake to the outskirts of LA, 250 miles away.

In a small park in the northwest part of town, several hundred Crips and Bloods, ignoring the storm warnings, were merrily barbecuing pork ribs and passing around 40-ounce bottles of beer. Earlier in the day, dozens of formerly hostile sets with names like Anybody's Murders (ABM), Donna Street Crips and North Town Bloods had joined at a nearby cemetery to mark a gang truce and place flowers on the graves of their homeboys (there were 27 local gang-related deaths in 1991). Now these erstwhile enemies and their girlfriends were swapping jokes and new rap lyrics.

But gatherings of six or more people, however amiable, have been banned since May 17 by Sheriff's order throughout Las Vegas's black Westside, as well as in the neighboring blue-collar suburb of North Las Vegas. To enforce this extraordinary edict, Metro Police pulled up in front of Valley View Park in three V-100 armored personnel carriers. When defiant picnickers refused to disperse, the cops opened up with tear gas and concussion grenades.

The Las Vegas "riots" had resumed for the fourth weekend in a row since the Rodney King verdict ignited a tinder box of black grievances.

West Las Vegas (population 20,000) is the antipode to the pleasure domes of downtown and the Strip. Grit without glitter, it has no hotels, casinos, supermarkets, banks or even a regular bus service. Yet, like South Central LA, it scarcely resembles the frost-belt stereotype of a ghetto. Its detached homes lack the verdant, Astro turf-like lawns and backyard swimming pools of the white neighborhoods, but they appear to be lovingly tended, with groves of shade trees to protect against the blast-furnace desert heat. Even the spartan public-housing units in Gerson Park have a tidy ambience that belies their poverty.

The destruction in Las Vegas, seemingly less systematic than in LA — also less extensive: $6 million in damage compared with about $1 billion — was somewhat less spontaneous as well. Everyone agrees that rioting did not begin until about 7:30 on the evening of April 30th, after police used tear gas to turn back several hundred young blacks trying to march from the Westside to downtown. From that point the stories dramatically diverge: the local newspapers' version, almost totally reliant on police reports, versus the street-level perspective of young African-Americans like D., a 20-year-old member of the Valley View Gangster Crips, whom I went looking for the day after the Memorial Day picnic.

According to Metro Police Lieutenant Steve Franks (who would shoot a teenager during the second weekend of disturbances), "Our intelligence was that if that group had reached downtown, they were ready to set fire to the hotels. Had it not been for our officers, this town would have gone up in flames." D. says, "This is total bullshit. We were only trying to demonstrate against the Rodney King verdict and apartheid right here in Las Vegas. The police just wanted an excuse to attack us."

Having broken up the march, the police cordoned off most of West Las Vegas and drew weapons on anyone who approached the barricades. Hundreds of young people, meanwhile, had regrouped near the Gerson Park projects, where the local Kingsmen Gang was hosting an impromptu party for the various Crip and Blood sets who had agreed the previous day — apparently influenced by news from LA — to stop fighting. According to D., a Metro squad car drove straight into the festive crowd. "People went crazy. They started throwing rocks and bottles; then one of the homies opened up with his [gun]." The angry crowd burned down a nearby office of the Pardon and Parole Board, while other groups attacked stores and gas stations with Molotov cocktails.

Lieutenant Franks claimed that snipers "hid in trees and rooftops, and used human targets when they came out in the open to fire....These yellow-bellied rats stood with young children around them and then opened fire on police cars." Another police spokesman claimed that gang members tried to kidnap an infant from a white family living on a predominantly black street. I found no one who could confirm either of these lurid stories, which the city's two daily papers disseminated uncritically to a horrified white public.

At the same time, the media, as in Los Angeles, studiously avoided any reference to police misconduct during the disturbances. D., however, has vivid recollections. "Me and my friends left after the shooting started,"

same verdict: different location

he said. "Our car was pulled over a few blocks later. When we asked what we had done wrong, a big redneck cop said, 'The rules have changed, nigger' and hit me in the face with his pistol. I was held five days in jail for 'obstructions.' The cops threw away my ID and health card, so I lost my job at Carl's Junior."

D. got out of jail just in time to witness the renewal of violence on Sunday, May 10. Once again kids gathered near Gerson Park to play softball and party. Metro Police brought up an armored personnel carrier and began shooting wooden bullets at the crowd. The following weekend was a virtual rerun.

D. thinks these now ritual confrontations will only grow more violent during the summer. Like other black youth with whom I spoke, he believes that Clark County Sheriff John Moran "will do anything, however extreme, to break up the [gang] unification process." Indeed, D. warned me that Las Vegas is on the verge of what he calls "an underground holocaust."

Although Las Vegas's mythographers (most recently Warren Beatty in *Bugsy*) typically elide race, black entertainers and laborers played decisive roles in the transformation of a sleepy desert railroad town into a $14-billion-a-year tourist oasis. But the sensational rise of the modern casino economy went hand in hand with the degradation of black rights. Glitter Gulch was built by Jim Crow.

As exiled LA gamblers began to buy up the old Fremont Street casinos in downtown Las Vegas in the late 1930s, local black residents were barred from the blackjack tables and slot machines. When Tom Hull opened his El Rancho in 1941 — the Strip's pioneer casino and resort hotel — restrictive covenants were being used to force black families across the Union Pacific tracks into West Las Vegas, a wasteland without paved roads, utilities or fire protection. By the time Meyer Lansky's gunmen ruined Bugsy Siegel's good looks in 1947, segregation in Las Vegas was virtually total. Blacks could wash dishes, make beds, even entertain, like Lena Horne and Sammy Davis, Jr., but they could not

Seattle: Sandra Hoover

work as dealers or bartenders, stay in a hotel, live in a white neighborhood or go to a white school.

An all-white police department, with a national reputation for brutality, enforced the color line in a town that African-Americans began to call Mississippi West. When in 1944 black GIs guarding nearby Boulder Dam tried to defy the racist rules that kept them out of downtown bars and casinos, they were attacked by police. A quarter-century later, in October 1969, heavy-handed police tactics, together with disgust over continuing job discrimination, again ignited a riot. For nearly a year afterward, Clark County's only partially integrated schools were rocked by battles between white and black students.

While racism was building the premier city of the Silver State, racial turmoil was tarnishing its image. The major hotels and their complicit union reluctantly signed a consent decree in 1971 guaranteeing open employment. In the same year the Nevada legislature passed a long-delayed fair housing law. Clark County schools followed a year later with an integration scheme that overrode white resistance to busing. After 30 years of wandering in the wilderness, black Las Vegans thought they could see equality ahead.

Like so much else in the desert, this has turned out to be a cruel mirage. Although token integration is the rule, the

majority of blacks are locked out of Las Vegas's boom economy. In recent years, as the rest of the Sunbelt has slipped into recession, Clark County's population has increased at warp speed (1,000 new residents per week), and Nevada, the "most fortunate state in the nation," according to the local AFL-CIO, has repeatedly led in job creation. Employment on the strip has soared with construction of mega-hotels, like the 5,000-room M-G-M Grand, the biggest in the world, while the so-called South Nevada Industrial Revolution has seduced dozens of high-tech computer and military aerospace firms from California.

But only a handful of black families have found their way into affluent new-growth suburbs like Winchester and Green Valley. Blacks remain vastly underrepresented in the higher-paying hotel jobs and construction trades. Although minorities make up 20 percent of Nevada's labor force (25 percent in Clark County) they hold only 14 percent of public-sector jobs. And the explosion in the city's Latino population and a huge influx of jobless whites from nearby states have severely crimped traditional black employment in the low-wage service industries.

For too many native sons like D., the recent boom has been an embittering "prisoners' dilemma," offering equally futureless choices between menial labor and the underground economy. As in Los

Angeles, the shortfall between the spectacle of profligate consumption and the reality of ghetto life has been made up by street gangs and rock cocaine. The first Crip set, transplanted from Watts, took root in Gerson Park in 1978-79; now an estimated 4,000 Crips and Bloods (together with 3,000 Latin and Asian gang members) are locked in a grim twilight struggle with police a few dozen blocks from the Liberace Museum and Caesar's Palace.

Chan Kendrick is a scraggy, angular Southerner who headed the Virginia ACLU for many years before moving to Las Vegas to run the organization's Nevada chapter. He makes no bones about which area is morally farthest below the Mason-Dixon line: "Police abuse here is worse than anywhere in the contemporary urban South. In an average month I get more complaints about police misconduct in Las Vegas than I received altogether during twelve years in Richmond."

According to Kendrick and other critics, the Metro Las Vegas Police Force, headed by Sheriff Moran (whom a local reporter described as being "as accessible as the King of Nepal") is little more than a mean guard dog for the casinos and the Nevada Resort Association. Kendrick is constantly challenging the use of nuisance, loitering and vagrancy laws to keep "undesirables," especially young blacks and homeless people, off the Strip. Likewise, he fights to force the police, particularly rogue narcotics squads, to respect the constitutional constraints on search and seizure.

In one of many notorious recent incidents, in 1990 casino floorman Charles Bush was asleep when three plainclothes police, wanting to question him about the arrest of his pregnant girlfriend for prostitution, broke into his apartment without a warrant and choked him to death. The official police explanation was that Bush, surprised in his sleep, had fought with them. The strangulation was ruled "justifiable" — the 44th time in a row since 1976 that the police had been exonerated in the death of a suspect.

Despite a storm of criticism, the Clark County DA would not indict the three cops. The Nevada Attorney General's office brought them to trial for manslaughter, but the all-white jury deadlocked 11-to-1 for acquittal, and the case was dropped. The local U.S. Attorney ignored the ACLU's petition for prosecution under federal civil-rights statutes. As Kendrick points out, "The legacy of the Bush case is even more disastrous than the Rodney King verdict. It shows that the Las Vegas police are condoned, on the flimsiest of pretexts, to break into black people's homes and kill them when they resist."

For D. and his friends, meanwhile, the Bush case "is just another lynching, Las Vegas-style." They point to the hypocrisy of a new state law that doubles sentences for gang-related offenses, while local law enforcement "plays patty-cake with the Mafia on the Strip." They complain about the humiliation of being strip-searched in the street in front of girlfriends and neighbors. And they acidly contrast the feds' apathy in the Bush case with their zeal to crush "Killa" Daniel and the other ABM Crips from North Las Vegas

But their most bitter feelings are reserved for the politicians who think black Las Vegas's grievances can be swept under the rug with a few token gestures, like liberal Mayor Jan Laverty Jones's grandiloquent promise of 42 new jobs in the casinos, or Sheriff Moran's offer of "better communications" with the Westside. For D. — who feels the only people "telling the truth about radical-level reality" in America these days are rappers like Ice Cube and Chuck D. — "things are already near the ultimate edge. The time for lies is past," D. says. "We built Las Vegas for them, and without equality we will tear this motherfucker down." ∎

Mike Davis, an LA-based writer and political activist, is the author of City of Quartz: Excavating the Future in Los Angeles. *This story first appeared in* The Nation.

• • • • • • • • • • • • • • • • • • • •

I don't un-der-stand *informal*
"I have money."

thug *n Someone I don't understand.*

op-por-tun-ism *n*
*An act committed by someone
I don't understand,
who somehow got an opportunity.*

(Source: *LA Weekly*, May 8, 1992)

he week of the LA riots, Cliff and Claire Huxtable dealt with the crisis of scraping together enough tickets to son Theo's college graduation to accommodate their entire loving extended family. At the same time, the ultimate George Bush campaign commercial played out on the streets of Los Angeles.

By now we should know that the race card is the Republicans' trump, the not-so-secret combination to their lock on the Electoral College. For decades, an attack on affirmative action has been the forehand volley of their repertoire; fear of street crime has been their overhead smash. More recently, they've added some topspin in the form of African-American conservatives, who don't miss a beat exploiting the rhetoric of victimization whenever their opportunism is challenged.

But exposing radical divisions in this country has become the political pundit's correlative to the Rodney King video; say it enough, and the effect is perversely desensitizing. I'm white and as passively hung-up on this question as the next person; I've also observed over the years that change is usually effected not by hectoring the middle class, but by jerry-building a confluence of interests with it. In the clearing smoke and thickening intellectual fog of the first days of May, let's concentrate on a few less convenient truths of the LA rebellion.

One is the extent to which the neglect of urban America has split open the social fabric along lines more jagged than black vs. white. After all, the original rioters, at the Parker Center LAPD headquarters, included skinheads, Valley girls, Catholic school moralists and more than a few alienated young Asian-Americans, as well as blacks. When the torching began downtown, Los Angeles Police Chief Daryl Gates cordoned off South Central — the goal being more to keep whites out than to deter a binge of self-destruction any fool could see coming. (Another messy truth: A disproportionate share of the carnage was accounted for by the Chicano community, co-tenants of our written-off underclass, but largely invisible in the media coverage.) Only when enough

San Francisco: Maggie Hallahan

Deracinated Despair: The less convenient truths to be learned from LA

by Irvin Muchnick

death and terror had been beamed into our living rooms to shift the focus from injustice to law and order did our courageous commander-in-chief send in the National Guard, the Army and the Marines.

Who says the military isn't converting efficiently to post-Cold War reality? And if the delay was just long enough to turn the relationship of blacks and Koreans from one of tension and hostility to one of open warfare...well, you can't make an omelet without breaking eggs.

In San Francisco, where the scenario unfolded far more spontaneously, the cleavage was obviously generational, not merely racial. The same was the case along Berkeley's beleaguered Telegraph Avenue,

though that particular *mise-en-scène* has always been a unique blend of fuzzy ideologues, neighborhood activists and the homeless — political and apolitical alike.

Most telling of all was Seattle, where the disturbances were largely lily-white. The grievances there may have been inchoate, but the sense of disgust, from unlikely sources, was not. In the '80s, yups who'd play their cards right made off like bandits; even I, a royal screw-up, made $23 an hour noodling after midnight on law firm word-processors that dutifully spat out the paperwork of Wall Street's systematic rape of our economy. But in the '90s, ever-rising tuition is buying an ever-less-marketable education; real estate is

out of sight; and those $70,000 first-year assistantships just aren't there.

Hip-hop's combative cadences and romanticized violence are giving expression to an ecumenical anger that we children of rock and roll, for whom pop culture was wedded to rising expectations, can't begin to comprehend. That's the key difference between the recession-fueled riots of '92 and the Watts uprising of '65. It's also what makes the upshot of all this so much less hopeful than the aftermath of the Clarence Thomas-Anita Hill outrage, which immediately mobilized a confident, high-profile, broad-based women's movement with a good shot at winning seats in this fall's Congressional housecleaning.

By contrast, Mayor Tom Bradley's appointment of Peter Ueberroth, the dry-ice-and-mirrors *meister* of the 1984 Summer Olympics, to supervise the rebuilding of South Central comes off as some kind of sick joke. Perhaps Bradley and Ueberroth propose to restore the estimated half-million manufacturing jobs that have left South Central in the last two decades by making us feel better, by licensing riot-night memorabilia and by auctioning off network TV coverage.

The rational and emotional connections between the white working class and the plight of people of color used to be the Democrats' stock-in-trade. No more. Bill Clinton's response to one of the five most important events of recent American history has done absolutely nothing to justify the patience with him that many of us over-cautious liberals counseled. Fearful of losing Reagan Democrats rather than determined to build sensible, non-bigoted bridges to them, Clinton waited until Monday, four days after the King verdict, to travel to Los Angeles and stand among the ruins with Congresswoman Maxine Waters (who, by the way, has been one of his crucial African-American supporters). Instead of inspiring words, what we got was a call for a day of national prayer. ∎

Irvin Muchnick's work has appeared in The New York Times Magazine, Spy *and* Mother Jones. *He is a columnist for* SF Weekly, *where this article first appeared.*

making sense: commentary

Blow by Blow

by Lisa Kennedy

What becomes of a technology deferred?

For those unfamiliar with what it feels like on the receiving end, the events in LA offered the chance to find out what racism is like. Art tries to make another's point of view our own (and succeeds from time to time), but nothing in recent history has done this as dramatically as the Rodney King tape and the Simi Valley 12's audacious denial of its reality. His reality; *our* reality.

With those acquittals, for one shocking moment we all knew what it meant to feel something, to know it like the back of your hand, the bruise on your jaw, and then to have it denied. No, what you saw, experienced, suffered was really something other than what you saw, experienced, suffered. This is one of the great tactics of racism (sexism, homophobia, classism). After a while, it's enough to make you crazy. It's enough to make you angry.

Here's a newly minted joke. The Rodney King jurors have reconsidered the Zapruder film and concluded that John F. Kennedy's wounds were self-inflicted. In *JFK*, the surprise witness was another movie, a jumpy, eight-millimeter piece of history. In the Koon, Powell, Wind, Briseno trial, the star witness was 81 seconds of videotape. What happened? Here was the witness who'd come forward immediately, whose 81 seconds of testimony seemingly could not be worn down by attorneys; this witness wouldn't crack

under pressure; this witness was objective. But when the 81 seconds became hundreds upon hundreds of seconds, backward, forward, frame by frame, the witness, according to the jurors, began to tell a different story. Slowed down enough, a reflexive jerk of the leg, a movement set in motion by a "stomp" or a swat of Powell's baton, became Rodney King kicking at the cops.

Face it, if Kevin Costner had been the DA and the final argument had been scripted by Oliver Stone, those four good ole boys in blue would be in the clink. Instead, while Costner's frame-by-frame deconstruction of the snap and slump of Kennedy's head breathed life into one conspiracy theory, the defense team's manipulation of the Rodney King beating video attempted to put another to death: the one that suggests a thing called racism exists, that it is systemic.

What would be the jurors' conclusion? That JFK's wounds were self-inflicted. Or at least that Rodney King's were. And in some twisted way, of course, that is what the jury found. Fleeing at high speed, ignoring traffic signals, resisting arrest —

in light of these, force became not a legal definition but a "state of mind," as defense attorney Howard Weitzman called it. Ladies and gentlemen of the jury, you are now entering the land of projection, racial anxiety, racism: Welcome.

Of course, that land was as close as the Simi Valley 12's backyards. And during the "insurrection," as Congresswoman Maxine Waters so correctly called it, other obscene images flickered across our screens. There was the footage of people being robbed of their proper names, their dreams, their sense of individuality as they were dragged from a car or a truck and stupidly, gleefully beaten. Unhh! Take that. Unhh. This is for Rodney King. But what was especially sickening was the naiveté with which the media initially met the challenge. Not since the Thomas-Hill hearing has it been so starkly clear that not only are the nation's decision makers over-

Michael Schumann/SABA

whelmingly white and mostly male, but so are its storytellers, its reporters.

All that gee whiz, how come, omigod, omigod reporting of the first 24 hours was revolting. Maybe Peter Bart, editor not of the New York or LA *Times* or the *Washington Post*, but of *Variety*, the entertainment mag, was right: Those reporters were intoxicated with the Big Screen of it all. The helicopters cutting and swooping through the smoke in the night, like *Boyz N the Hood*. No, strike that: That's a view of the copters from the ground, from that very hotspot, South Central LA. This was like *T2*, or something not as fun, like the Gulf war.

Never has the gulf between black and white been so clear as when it became obvious that part of the reason we weren't seeing images from the ground was that the image feeders were afraid of the frenzy. There was the patronizing Greg Lamotte

on CNN doing his damnedest to win a Peter Arnett Award. There was the painfully hysterical voiceover — "Jesus, that's attempted murder!!!" — as Reginald Denny was yanked from his truck and pummeled by several manboys. A new word must be coined for the response that goes beyond ordinary empathy, a term for one's own racial terror presented as objective reportage. Maybe that term exists already: bias.

One wonders, didn't any of these reporters and anchors take in the best movies of the last few years: *Do the Right Thing* and *Boyz N the Hood*? Or did they view them as just so much ethnography? Why did Mookie throw that garbage can through Sal's window? Figure that out, or at least don't fear it, and maybe your lead-off question won't be, "Congresswoman Waters, Reverend Jackson, Representative Conyers...Why are they so *angry*?" From the get-go, it was clear that many of us were not considered part of the privileged viewing audience; for us, the answer to that question is as apparent as a city block. Then there were phrases like "When the violence started" or "When the violence stops," thrown around as if their truth value were uncontested. In South Central, the violence didn't begin with the acquittals and it doesn't end with the withdrawal of federal troops. Of the 58 dead, most were black and

Hispanic men from the nabe.

If the S&L scandal were televisual, the physical evidence as persuasive as watching citizens take freely from a supermarket, what would it look like? All of New York City burnt to the ground — block after block looted, then destroyed. Perhaps the entire state singed and smoky. White men running in suits, or why not, walking casually with sacks of dough. Fuck the color TVs, guys, we'll bumrush the networks and studios. And gosh, though we the TV audience seldom got to see it in human terms, those Gulf war videos of bombs hitting their targets proved that even if white men can't jump they can kill with the best of them. If those Brooks Brothers hoods had to, they could do the deed.

There is no denying that video has a way of grabbing us. We're in second grade and it's our nation's show-and-tell. Still, as a country we shared an extraordinary moment: The polls showed that pretty much all of us agreed that the cops were guilty of using excessive force. Less than half of whites polled, however, agreed with the following statement: The justice system is biased against African-Americans. Nearly 90 percent of blacks did. A video can show us only so much, and then we must rely on history, reporters, politicians, teachers, our own minds to tell us what is going down. Maybe TV is only as good as its viewers? In response to one juror's explanation that they had to take into account not only the 81 seconds of the Rodney King beating, but the many minutes leading up to that teeny, diminished 81 seconds, a friend said, Yeah, and the rest of us had only taken into account the last 100 years. ∎

Lisa Kennedy is the film editor for the Village Voice, *where a version of this story first appeared.*

*Yesterday was Judgment Day —
How'dja do? How'dja do?
Were you sleeping
When your nightmares and your
visions all came true?*
— Butch Hancock
and Jimmy Dale Gilmore

A few doors down the hall of this motel in Austin, Texas, a man is screaming into a telephone. What an image of impotence: raging into a plastic receiver. From my room it's just a wordless din, but when I step out to the ice machine I can hear him clearly: "Gina, tell that bastard to come to the phone. *Tell him!* Do you want me to come over there? Then you tell him. *Make him!*" When I return with my ice, my message light is on and I call down to the desk, where a young woman informs me that Lillie Kretchfield has some information and I'm to call tonight. But I've never heard of a Lillie Kretchfield. "It's for Room 327, that's your room," the desk clerk says. So it is. Ms. Kretchfield didn't mention a name, only a number; she has left her message for the wrong room. It's a normal night in America: one man screaming to someone who won't listen; one woman leaving her message in the wrong place; and on the TV, LA is burning.

Isn't someplace always burning on the TV? Isn't that what we take for granted now? Isn't that our century? One by one, country by country, each city and each generation discovers what it's like to be in the midst of a given day's flash point. Beirut, Baghdad, Sarajevo, Kabul, Belfast, Miami, Moscow, Peking, San Salvador, Johannesburg, Philadelphia, Berlin, New Delhi, Jerusalem...LA. Speaking as one whose old neighborhoods in Brooklyn and the Bronx have been destroyed in similar riots, and who has both made and received the inevitable calls to and from New York, South Florida, Oakland and now LA — riot-time seems to have become part of our shared education. No, strike the word "education"; we learn from history that little is learned. It's just "shared experience" — though it's fair to say that until the prolonged riot that is the 20th Century materializes in your presence, you are not yet truly a citizen of this age, you do not

Los Angeles: Ted Soqui

A Riot Every Day

by Michael Ventura

yet know in your bones the seriousness of the energies afoot.

Now and then the TV cuts away from the fires in LA to feature a mayor, a governor, a police chief, a fire chief, a president, a candidate, a leader, a film director — all of who, whether their names are Gates or Bush or Brown or Jackson or Singleton, say precisely what you knew they were going to say, and what each of them knew the other was going to say, and all of it is uncannily identical to what other fire chiefs, presidents, leaders and mayors have said in other decades, other cities, other languages. This does not bode well for change.

There are also interviews with people on the streets, people of all colors and ages. Consistent through their various viewpoints and levels of intelligence is the demand that their riot be viewed more seriously than they themselves viewed the riots in, say, Miami or London. Not bloody likely. Though there have been

sympathetic flash points as far off as Seattle and Tampa, other people will, for the most part, treat our riot as we've treated theirs, as a form of entertainment, fast food for thought.

We share something else with those who have made statements at every flash point, riot, flood, earthquake and war: the poignant and fierce hope, voiced by citizens and officials alike, that this event will be a "judgment day," a "defining moment," a day we can frame and point to and say, "Here something ended, and here something new began." We need to think this, we must think this, for it gives us the personal power to act. It's even true on a personal level: During such events, individuals experience moments that change them forever. It's even sort of true on a slightly larger, city-wide scale: Shifts in social forces and changes in the terrain com-

74

pel our behavior to shift and change with them — though often that sort of change doesn't go very deep.

In a still larger sense, however, there are no "defining moments" in history, not really. History behaves more like a great wave, rising and falling in vast interconnected patterns, than like a train proceeding from point to point. History behaves like a storm — wind, humidity, air pressure, terrain, solar phases, tides, a million variables, ultimately uncountable, forming a system that keeps its wholeness, its coherence, for just a short while before it changes into something else, some other pattern, some other weather. In history, one pattern of "weather" can last centuries or decades or just a few days, and the element that seems to change the pattern can be as dramatic as an assassination or as silent as the drying of a water table — but neither the drama nor the silence holds the key, for the drying of the water table could have influenced the conditions that led to the assassination, or the assassination could have changed how people perceived the meaning of the drought, which in turn changed how they did such and such...and on and on, in the wild growth that is life rather than history.

In this longing for a defining moment, in this clamor for solutions and proposals, lies the assumption that here, at the close of the 20th Century, there's something abnormal about a riot, though it's clear that the whole world is rioting in one form or another all the time, that it's all one vast riot bursting out in one flash point after another, with webs of interlocking causes and ripples of overlapping effects.

For instance, all the street actions in Peking, Moscow, Berlin and LA during the last several years have at least one cause in common: The vast amount of money spent on armaments has drastically deprived people everywhere of resources and opportunities. Yet this newspaper, as part of its solution to LA's and America's problems, will probably suggest that you support the same Democratic Party that just overwhelmingly approved President Bush's defense budget without so much as a trim. What does this mean? That hidden in most of our "solutions," no matter how well intentioned, are future riots, here and every-

where. We can't seem to get around that.

What can we do? To say that there's nothing one can really do is to be hopeless, and we don't want to be that. Yet any program, as soon as it's proposed, is revealed as limited and ineffectual. This is because the worldwide riot is happening on the same scale and plane of activity (the political and historical plane) on which the program is proposed. The behavior of our legislators has been, in effect, a kind of riot — a quiet riot, a pervasive and hysterical panic that has them going round and round in circles. Because any new legislator immediately becomes part of that riot, what we can do politically is limited. What is far less limited (and the riots themselves prove this) is how we can behave.

The TV, for instance, is at this moment displaying some strange behavior: Black, white and brown people are helping each other destroy some property. They seem to be having a lot of fun, and they display no fear or anger toward each other whatsoever. The announcer is saying that this behavior is apparently not uncommon this evening. It's a strange way to conduct what's being labeled a "race riot." It means that within this tumultuous event, where elsewhere people are dying, a few unexpected decisions, and behaviors, are being enacted. Everybody expected the instantly famous image of the truck driver being beaten; everybody expected that somebody — in this case Koreans — would be targeted; nobody expected this image of interracial rioting. If you can distance yourself from your fear of property damage, there's something new about this riot.

These people are doing something, choosing something, enacting their own program, and there's something in their behavior to watch and respect. Their solution, tonight, is their behavior. They've decided to fight their environment without fighting each other. They've demonstrated how original and generous behavior can be, even in a riot. For myself, that's where I look for hope. Perhaps this strikes so deep in me because four days ago I stood outdoors in a crowd of about 10,000 listening to Al Green in New Orleans. This was at the Jazz and Heritage Festival. At least half,

perhaps two-thirds, of Al Green's crowd was black. In this huge mixed crowd there was no forced friendliness, but neither was there fear. As usual at the New Orleans festival, there was a sense of allowing — of people gathered for the same purpose and without any other agenda. There was a minimal police presence, at the outskirts of the festival — I barely noticed them. And, standing listening to Al Green give his heart to this crowd as we gave ours to him, I realized that this was the first time in 25 years that I'd been in a huge interracial crowd without tension. Without drawing any grand conclusions, it was just refreshing to be reminded that it's possible.

Notice that both at the Al Green concert and in the case of those kids happily destroying property together, the society as it's been given to us by our government and our economics were ignored, abolished, discarded — for a brief time. The lesson I draw? My suspicion is that we must be more and more ready to find our lives at the limits of this society's conceptions. Our solutions won't come from the center and won't be condoned by the center, because the center (government, business, even what passes for culture) is in a state of perpetual riot called "history," a set of preconceptions about what "order" and "prosperity" mean that seem to be systematically destroying the well-being of all of us. The change may be in what we most fear. Metaphorically, if you like, it's not about how you stop the riot, it's about how you join the riot. Because we're all already in an enormous riot, one that, for the present, seems unstoppable.

Once more I try to call a loved one in LA. Once more the circuit's busy. Once more my gut contracts in fear. On the screen, the city I love is burning, and I find I've been listening to the circuit signal on the phone for several minutes while I try to think my way to a face in LA. Yes. It's all a question of how to get through, and can your heart reach out where the system can't? ■

Michael Ventura is the author of Shadow Dancing in the U.S.A. *and* Night Time, Losing Time. *He is also a staff writer for the* LA Weekly, *where a version of this story first appeared.*

Once Upon a Time in America

by Robert Neuwirth

Black driver, white cops. A minor traffic violation escalates into a national case. The motorist pulls away, the cops in pursuit. They chase him across the expressways at breakneck speed. Many minutes later, he pulls over. The cops jump out of their cars.

That's when the beating begins. More than 81 seconds of savage blows. The officers beat the man long after he is cowering and defenseless.

The black community, already enraged by previous incidents of violence against African-Americans, demands justice.

Initially, the police are silent. Then one officer who was on the scene breaks ranks and tells his story to the district attorney. Several cops are suspended from the force and put on trial. But the judge grants a change of trial venue because of pre-trial publicity in the city.

The case is heard by a jury with no blacks. Prosecutors argue that the evidence speaks for itself. Defense attorneys go on the attack, asserting that the officers were threatened, that the victim resisted arrest, even attacked them, and that they had to use force. Despite the gruesome details of the beating, the jury makes short work of the case, the foreman pronouncing two words after each charge: not guilty.

Hours after news of the verdict hits the streets, the city blows up. Three days of killing, looting and arson. White motorists are pulled from their cars, beaten and stabbed. Store owners arm themselves and duel with the rioters. The police department is unprepared. City firefighters won't go to the riot areas because they're afraid they'll be attacked. As a result, scores of buildings are totally destroyed. Rebuilding will cost hundreds of millions of dollars.

"The white man ain't been doing us no good," one angry resident says. "So we didn't do him no good. The white man got the jobs and we don't got no jobs. The white man got everything and we got nothing." Says another: "The only way to get the message across is to set this town on fire."

Disturbances spread to several other cities.

The mayor sets a dusk-to-dawn curfew. Schools close. Liquor stores are shut. Sales of guns are halted. The courts stay open late to process all the people arrested for rioting. The governor calls in the National Guard. Armored convoys roll through the city.

"The area resembled a stark, bombed out city in wartime," the *LA Times* reports. "Sniper fire echoed through streets of overturned and demolished cars and trucks. Entire blocks of buildings were reduced to charred rubble and twisted molten steel."

The president criticizes the demonstrators: "Violence can contribute nothing to the resolution of problems or alleviation of grievances." In an attempt to quell the outrage, he sends in the Justice Department to assess whether to bring civil-rights charges against the cops. Later, he visits the gutted neighborhoods and offers seed money for rebuilding.

The New York Times asks, "What happened to the administration's vaunted urban policies?" The editorial continues: "Neither a 'sensitive power structure' nor Federal programs have relieved chronic troubles of poor blacks. Their unemployment rate is twice that of whites; among black teenagers the rate is four times as high. Housing is scarce and run down. Tensions between the police and blacks have run deep for years....It still seems so hard for the legal system to provide equal, elementary justice to black citizens."

The *LA Times* echoes these concerns. "The black experience began in America as tragedy, and it continues as tragedy," the newspaper says. "The historic dilemma of race in America will not be resolved until blacks have an equal opportunity to claim their 'fair portion of the American dream.'"

Columnists and community leaders compare the riots to the famed uprisings of the 1960s. Little has changed since then, they say. Jesse Jackson finds a message in the ruins: "I would hope this riot is instructive — making the black and the poor visible again."

For a while, national newspapers report on racial issues. "Minority Groups Distrust of Police Found To Be on the Rise Around the Country," reports *The New York Times*. "Black Ghettos Remain Grim: Changes, Improvements Don't Reach the Poorest," announces the *Washington Post*. Within a week, the stories thin out and gradually disappear.

It happened once in America. Twelve years ago. In Miami. Arthur McDuffie, a black insurance executive, was riding home on his motorcycle on a balmy December night in 1979. Though he was driving with a suspended license, McDuffie allegedly popped a wheelie in front of some cops. They pulled off in pursuit, starting an eight-minute chase across the city's highways, at speeds faster than 100 miles per hour. McDuffie finally spun to a stop on a deserted expressway interchange. At 1:59 a.m., the cops reported to their dispatcher, "We have him." The first cop on the scene pulled his gun. "I give up," McDuffie said. Those were his last words.

That's when the beating began. The cops hit McDuffie repeatedly in the head. At 2:01 a.m., the police called for an ambulance. While waiting for it to arrive, they hastily arranged a cover story: McDuffie had an accident. They trashed McDuffie's Kawasaki in an attempt to fake a high-speed crash. Arthur McDuffie died four days later.

Four officers went to trial in far-away Tampa. They were acquitted. During the riots that followed, 18 people died, hundreds were injured and dozens of buildings burned.

Four young black men were charged with murder for beating people to death during the riots. Despite all the publicity, their cases were not moved out of the city. They were tried in Miami. Three of them were convicted. The federal civil-rights case against one of the officers who beat McDuffie failed. No one ever did time for his murder.

It happened once in America. Twelve years ago. And it happened once again this year. ∎

Journalist and playwright Robert Neuwirth is a regular contributor to the Village Voice, *where this column first appeared.*

F

ire everywhere! Across the miasma of Los Angeles the flames lift into the night and they proliferate. They rise, explosive, from my heart. Is there horror? Is there heat unbearable? And is there light where, otherwise, we could not see ourselves? Is there an unexpected/ unpredictable colossal energy alive and burning, uncontrolled, throughout America? Behold my heart of darkness as it quickens now, with rage! Behold a hundred, no! — a thousand young black men whose names you never knew/whose neighborhoods you squeezed into a place of helpless desolation/and whose music you despised/and whose backwards baseball caps and baggy jeans you sneered at/and whose mothers you denied assistance/and whose fathers you inducted in the Army or you broke to alleyways where, crumbling at the marrow of their spine, they aged in bitterness and waste. Behold them now: revengeful, furious, defiant, and, for hours on end, at least, apparently, invincible: They just keep moving! And the fires burn! And white kids and Chicanos and Chicanas join them, yes! There they stand or run beside/among these young black men who will not bow down! They will not say, "OK. I am nobody. I have nothing and you hate me and that's fine! Where should I sign, now, for service to my country? Show me how to worship at the shrine of law and order!" What happened? How come we finally woke up? Why would a jury's verdict of "Not Guilty" galvanize and rescue so many from protracted/profound passivity, suicidal torpor and fratricidal craziness? How come all of the steady, punitive, self-righteous and official attacks on poor people didn't get us going? How come presidential vetoes of civil-rights legislation and the unspeakable insult of Clarence Thomas as proposed replacement for Supreme Court Justice Thurgood Marshall didn't push us into the streets? How come the senseless and the racist throwaway of $42 billion on Operation Desert Storm didn't pack the highways with a 3,000-

Los Angeles: Ted Soqui

Burning All Illusions Tonight

by June Jordan

mile-long caravan of fired-up folk determined to evict killer lunatics from the White House and the Pentagon? How come?

We had seen the 81-second videotape of LA police attacking Rodney King. We thought we believed — that this time, and for once, the cops could not escape. Their brutality was clear. Their brutality was nauseating. The case opened and would soon be shut. We viewed the trial as a procedural nicety. We would actually live to see one important episode of equality before the law! And then the jury found for the defendants. The jury concluded that there never came a moment when they felt, as they watched four cops attack an unarmed black man, there never came a moment when they felt "enough is enough." And get this straight. And remember Rodney King was neither charged nor convicted of any crime. On the video, the jury watched police sur-

round him. They made him lie down on the street, face down to the street. They beat him. They stomped him. They shot him two times with a Taser gun that injected 50,000 volts of electricity into his nervous system with each shot. But that was not too much. That was never excessive use of force: not for that jury. Not one member of the jury was a black man or a black woman. Rodney King was denied due process according to the law. He was not judged by a jury of his peers! And what was the crime of Rodney King? He was a young black man, not yet dead, and not yet ready, and not yet willing, to die: He was black. He should have been dead. He should not have been born. Or, as defense attorneys for the police explained: Rodney King kept getting up on "all fours." He wouldn't stay down! He kept raising up his head! He kept rising and rising. He would not bow down. He never assumed "a compliant mode." And now we have Los

Angeles in flames. The mode is nowhere compliant. People of color run around, or walk, without fear. We're off our knees: Heads up. Fists in the air. And fire everywhere. I condemn and deplore the violence of poverty and the violence of hatred and the violence of absolute injustice that makes the peaceful conduct of our days impossible or cowardly. Twelve years ago when Miami police murdered Arthur MacDuffie and black people rose up, I wrote: "It was such good news. A whole lot of silence had ended at last! Misbegotten courtesies of behavior were put aside. There were no leaders. There were no meetings, no negotiations. A violated people reacted with violence. An extremity of want, an extremity of neglect...had been met, at last, with an appropriate extreme reaction....And why should victims cover for their executioners? Why should the victims cooperate and agree to discuss or write letters....But this has been the code, overwhelmingly, for the oppressed: that you keep cool and calm and explore proper channels and above all, that you remain law-abiding and orderly precisely because...it is the power of the law of the terrorist state arrayed against you to force you to beg and bleed without acceptable recourse except for dumb endurance or mute perishing....If you make and keep my life horrible then, when I can tell the truth, it will be a horrible truth, it will not sound good or look good or, God willing, feel good to you, either...." Twelve years later and I still understand that anarchy is not about nice. Still I understand that the provocation for anarchy is always and ever the destruction of every reasonable basis for hope. And tonight I understand that the Simi Valley, California, jury's verdict of not guilty feels like the destruction of any reason for hope. But I must conclude that "the good news" of the 1980 Miami uprising was politically indefensible as such because it did not lead to something big, new, human, and irreversible. Today, for example, there is another victim of state violence: Rodney King. And I believe we must take care not to become like our enemies: I do not accept that we should fall upon a stranger, outnumber him or her, and beat and possibly kill our "prey." And I believe we must take care to distinguish between our enemies and our allies, and not confuse them or forget the difference between a maniac and a (potential) comrade. And I have learned about the histories of Native Americans and Chicanos and Asian-Americans and progressive white peoples in these United States and I know that we have more in common than our genuine enemies want us to realize! And on this evening of the first day after the jury's not-guilty verdict, I attended and spoke at a rally across from the Superior Court Building, here, in Oakland. And the 500-plus Americans gathered there embodied the full racial and ethnic and class and age and sexual diversity that will give us the political and moral strength that we need for successful revolution. And, as the graffiti proclaimed on the lone wall still standing after flames gutted an LA bank, "La Revolucion es la solucion." This enormous moment belongs only to each of us. Now we can choose to free ourselves from cross-cultural ignorance and second-hand racist divisions of thought and response. We can unite in our demands for equal human rights and civil liberties. We can secure further prosecution of lawless police in LA. We can change the nature of official power. We can gain a second Bill of Rights that will deliver at least as much money to support every African-American child as we spend on the persecution and imprisonment of young black men. I am talking just for starters. Obviously, a second Bill of Rights should, and would, bring new entitlements into the life of every kind of American citizen. But these necessary, humane and irreversible and democratic gains cannot be won without political and moral unity centered on principle rather than identity. And I am writing tonight by the light of the fire everywhere. The begging body grows cold. I am beginning to smell something clean. I am beginning to sense a victory of spirit risen from the death of self-hatred. I am beginning to envision our collective turning to the long-term tasks of justice and equal rights to life, liberty and the pursuit of happiness right inside this country that has betrayed our trust, repeatedly. Behold the fire everywhere! ∎

UC-Berkeley professor June Jordan is an African-American poet and essayist. This column first appeared in the San Francisco Bay Guardian.

The Fire This Time

by Steve Perry

The LA riots have passed. I'm sitting in a café talking to Larry Blackwell, a black man who's been the city of Minneapolis's director of affirmative action for more than a decade, when the subject of Los Angeles comes up. I'm still sorting out what I think, but I offer that the most heartening thing about LA, despite all the hype about "the race riot of the century," is the multiracial character of what happened there and the response all across the country — including Minneapolis, where a march the Saturday after the LA uprising brought out a very mixed crowd of 6,000-plus. And then I hear myself saying something I didn't know I believed: LA has given me hope that in the streets and at the grassroots, America may not be as racist as its institutions. Say what?

"I think that's right," says Blackwell. And he proceeds to tell a story. A few years ago, city officials closed the north beach at Lake Calhoun. Though they had their official reasons, the perception in many quarters was that they did it simply because it was the black beach. Predictably enough, a lot of its patrons started going to the south beach — that is, the white beach. There began to be problems with police, eventually leading to a public hearing. Oddly, though, none of the neighbors who showed up for the hearing expressed any animosity or claimed any problems with the blacks who'd come down to the south beach. A few said the real problem was that police came around and harassed blacks there. "I remember feeling very surprised," Blackwell muses. "It was really the police and one councilmember who were pushing the issue. Not the community."

Los Angeles: John Goubeaux

— who happen to come in all colors.

Keeping the dialogue fixed on race is a great camouflage for problems of class, which we can't talk about openly in America. The United States is one of few industrial countries that doesn't keep health and mortality statistics by class. In 1990, a professor of health policy from Johns Hopkins University did a study that looked at U.S. mortality rates along class lines. He found that when you break things down that way, race differentials are very slight: White people who don't get decent food or health-care die at roughly the same rate as blacks who don't get decent food or health-care. He also found that no American medical journal wanted to publish his study. When he submitted it to *Lancet*, the leading British journal, it was accepted immediately.

The lesson of LA and its aftermath could be that the racism of workaday white Americans is less severe and uniform than that of institutional America. But George Bush isn't going to tell us so; if it's the case, we have to affirm it for ourselves.

It's a small story, but a hopeful one. I don't kid myself that racial harmony has triumphed while nobody was watching. But I do find myself wondering where the epicenter of race hate and division is in 1992: in the souls of people, or the practices of government and major institutions? It's a hard question, and we aren't supposed to ask it. The principal myth of American "democracy" is that the government is merely a reflection of the people — even though, more and more, the people don't vote and, when they do, the inexorable logic of money ensures that the candidates churned out by Democrats and Republicans offer them little choice.

The recent past abounds with evidence that the government fails to reflect broad American values and interests. The most notorious example may be the S&Ls, whose precarious state was well known to government insiders for at least half a decade before it was made public in 1989. In the early days of the crisis, there had been talk of making up the shortfall by forcing thrifts to pay more into the federal deposit insurance fund. The issue was ignored for so long not just because of lack of nerve or vision. Stalling on the problem until it was too big to be solved by anything short of a massive taxpayer bailout served the interest of both parties' cash patrons: the owners and financiers who were engaged in an orgy of profit and fee-taking all through the '80s.

During the Cold War, whenever rapprochement was in the air, it used to be fashionable to distinguish between the Soviet people and their corrupt, anti-democratic government. But not in America. When it comes to facing problems, we're told repeatedly that politicians are advancing as fast as "the people" will let them. Race is no exception. At least two books published in the past year rationalize the Democrats' long swing to the right by pointing to the entrenched racism of the white working-class voter (as opposed to, say, the growing incestuousness of Democrats' and Republicans' contributor lists). It's this white backlash (as opposed to, for example, the breathtaking tax give-backs to the wealthy in the 1980s tax reforms) that supposedly precludes social spending by government or frank public discussion of the problems of poor people

Racism has always depended in part on white people's faith in their own innocence — not just the right to evade consequences, but the means to do so. That faith may be approaching its breaking point. Real wages have shrunk in the U.S. virtually every year since 1973. More and more of white America finds itself chronically unable to make a decent living. No one knows what will happen next. Can it remain satisfying to blame the situation on an obviously destitute black America? If the likes of another Willie Horton were enough to answer the current hunger for clarity and meaning, would there have been such a flight from the status quo in the past year in favor of figures ranging from Ross Perot to Jerry Brown, even David Duke and Pat Buchanan — all of whom, in their own ways, are beyond the ideological pale of both parties?

It seems we'll find out. The growing air of confusion and cancelled promises that's evident now is cracking open fault lines in our history, making us ask questions we've managed to avoid. This time, we won't simply outgrow the problem. The jobs lost to automation and cheap foreign labor markets aren't coming back, and the polarization of wealth and power inside U.S. borders, which accelerated faster in the past 15 years than in any other period, amounts to a new domestic order. Despite all the promises of recovery, there is a lurking sense that the rules of the game are changing, or perhaps they've never been quite what we thought.

In the wake of Los Angeles, when people in the street frequently had more trenchant things to say about what happened than politicians and pundits, you could see the recognition soaking in. Every-day America has a much more acute sense of its problems than the words coming from politicians and the media might suggest.

Washington senses this, but doesn't understand how deep it runs. Likewise most of the media, which have grown so close to their institutional sources that they reflect little beyond that field of vision. I can't prove it and polls can't measure it, but the conversations I've been having lately make me believe that nearly everything about America is more volatile than the usual arbiters of reality would have us believe. Questions are getting asked every day, quietly and sometimes loudly about who we are, where we've been and where we go from here. And just not in an academic sense, but because there's a pit in our guts that nothing we've been taught to believe about America holds true anymore. A great deal seems to be up for grabs. In the past, the sprawling wealth and promise of this country seemed to absorb as many contradictions as America — or, more precisely, white Americans — could conceive. No more. Now we get to find out who we are — and maybe, for better or worse, to reinvent a nation. ■

Steve Perry is the editor of City Pages, Inc., *in Minneapolis, where this story first appeared.*

Crime and Reason

by Hugh Pearson

For the second time in a row, I had a completely different column planned for this space; circumstances once again forced me to pull it. By the time this appears, most of us will have gotten through our initial shock and expressed and re-expressed dismay to family and friends, and transformed our anger into smoldering embers in the aftermath of the verdict in Simi Valley, California, exonerating the four police officers in the Rodney King beating.

For the zillionth time, non-blacks will declare a commitment to eradicating racism. Some of them will really mean it, and others will think they really mean it. Still others will regard what has happened as reason to hold onto their racism. And African-Americans will play the same tune about racism we have been playing for so long already.

As we act out these rituals, few of us will admit what we're really thinking. We know that plenty of black males can give anyone the creeps, and we also know that plenty of black males are every bit as harmless as anyone else. The second kind of black males get swept aside by the feeling that it's better to be safe than sorry. So our society treats all black males as potential criminals.

We know how palpably uptight the average white American is. Many whites seem so "serious" that we wonder where they would be without blacks to show them how to enjoy life. Asians and Latinos fit somewhere in the constellation, too. But the bookends of our society — the groups that exist at opposite extremes, while everyone else falls in between — are black and white Americans.

The trial's outcome conjures memories of a debate I had one recent night on a visit to New York City. I was in a bar with a writer from the *Village Voice*. We were discussing the prosecution of rapists. I told her that as long as our criminal-justice system exists in its present state, convicting a man of rape will be a very difficult task. Our judicial system insists that a person must be found guilty of a crime beyond any reasonable doubt. And in most rapes, there are no witnesses except the victim herself, which in many cases in and of itself creates a reasonable doubt. My companion responded that a woman knows when she's being raped, and that a man knows the difference between sexual persuasion, coercion and outright force. I told her I don't doubt the truth of this. It is the criminal-justice system that requires it be proved.

The King verdict has demonstrated once again that the criminal-justice system has been exacting in another manner. The system has decided that a white defendant accused of committing a crime against an African-American hasn't really committed a crime, even though millions of witnesses have seen the crime on videotape. Black America feels raped. One of the ironies of black America feeling raped is that, whenever the nation thinks of rape, it usually envisions the crime being committed by a large, brutish black man.

The vision of a black man intent on raping the entire Los Angeles metropolitan area is responsible for the acquittal of the King defendants. One juror kept describing Rodney King as a 280-pound black man, possibly on drugs, who needed to be subdued after a high-speed chase. Such a threat was simply too much for that juror to bear. Rodney King became a potential invader in a speeding vehicle, ready to wreak mayhem on an innocent and unsuspecting populace. To her, the videotape merely showed "LA's finest" as if they were all Matt Dillon on the old TV show *Gunsmoke*, doing their best to protect the men, women and children of Dodge City from the big bad nigger.

Because we black men have spent nearly our entire existence in the eyes of the nation as big bad niggers, we often embrace that image, particularly today in the musical genre of gangster rap. Ice Cube, Ice-T and groups with names like The Poison Gang cash in on the image. They embellish it, creating variations on something that passes as African-American ethnicity, an ethnicity built largely around anger about racism.

African-Americans have been reacting to racism for so long that we barely know how to do anything else. Our minds are drunk with the irrationality of our reactions, as was evident in the looting and burning after the Rodney King verdict. The ill-conceived idea of burning down buildings in one's own neighborhood adds fuel to the racist notion that blacks cannot be assumed to have normal reasoning abilities. As a result, even non-blacks who aren't overt racists will end up with a profoundly distorted view of blacks, causing them to continue to treat African-Americans in ways that amount to racism.

The combination of this situation and the realities of a post-industrial society will continue to create a scenario that threatens to recreate Jim Crow-style segregation. The King decision is the most recent taunt, the most recent rattle of the sabre. The decision enraged black men from all walks of life, be they drunken speed-limit violators, rap artists, muggers, financial-district executives, street beggars, doctors, lawyers or professional writers.

This particular professional writer's anger isn't merely abstract. In 1989, on the way home from Manhattan to Brooklyn, I had an encounter with the New York City Transit Police in which a cop hit me in the eye and I was arrested for disorderly conduct. My crime? Merely being in the wrong place at the wrong time when the police needed someone to pick on. Eventually, I was exonerated. But the experience convinced me of one thing. It convinced me never to exonerate the police anywhere when it comes to their horrible attitudes toward African-American men. ∎

Hugh Pearson is an associate editor for the Pacific News Service and a former columnist for SF Weekly, where this column first appeared. He is currently writing a book about the legacy of the Black Panthers.

Los Angeles: Ted Soqui

Deciphering LA Smoke Signals
The word is class, not race

by Luis Rodriguez

Go ahead and kill us; we're already dead.
— Young Latino participant in the 1992 Los Angeles uprising, as quoted in *USA Today*, May 1

From Chicago, I watched the fires that consumed miles of Los Angeles and other American cities beginnning April 29 — the day a jury in Simi Valley declared four police officers innocent of using excessive force against Rodney King.

Fire for me has been a constant metaphor, the squeeze of memory against the backdrop of inner-city reality. South Central Los Angeles was once home. I was 11 years old when the 1965 Watts uprising tore through my neighborhood. In 1970, at age 16, I participated in the Chicano moratorium against the Vietnam War — the

so-called "East LA Riot" — which exploded when sheriff's officers and police attacked demonstrators, leaving at least three dead and much of Whittier Boulevard in flames.

So watching Los Angeles burn again is nothing new or surprising. Yet the spray of TV images and the reportage that followed failed to jibe with what appeared on the streets or with what I know. To me, this wasn't about blind rage. It wasn't about "race" or "crime" — America's twin fears. It wasn't even just about Rodney King. For one thing, unlike Watts in 1965, this uprising was not limited to blacks. Latinos — who make up from a third to half of South Central's population — were heavily involved. Whites and Asians from Fairfax, Westwood and parts of the San Fernando Valley also took part. In fact, Latinos seem to be the most consistent element in all communities affected during the violence. While

LA Point of View

by Manning Marable

blacks are largely absent outside of South Central, Latinos live in sizable numbers in the San Fernando Valley and even Hollywood, once almost all white. In cities across the country, all kinds of people led protests against the Rodney King verdicts, an issue most Americans agree with regardless of color.

Although "race" continues to be rammed down our throats, the issue here is class. Los Angeles's violence was the first major social response to an economic revolution that began years ago. Today, almost a quarter of the American population lives below the poverty level. The great abundance in most cities is inaccessible to many because the distribution of goods is limited to those who can afford them — not who needs them.

I saw a TV image of two mothers, black and brown, putting shoes on their children in the midst of a smoldering ruin. I don't call this "looting"; as far as I'm concerned, at a time of S&L bailouts and false check cashing, the real looters occupy the highest levels of power in America.

What's more, the violence was far from random. Mostly markets, banks and liquor stores were struck, most known for their exploitative prices and general mistreatment of African-American and Latino customers. It was not against Koreans per se, as the media suggests; it is against exploitation.

I remember Watts, 1965, but the situation has drastically changed since then. From 1965 to 1967, federal spending in Los Angeles increased from $10 million to about $5 billion. Today, Bush promises no such assistance — and California Governor Pete Wilson plans to go ahead with 25 percent cuts in the state's welfare program. The only thing left is a crackdown. U.S. immigration authorities, for example, seized 1,500 Latinos during the rioting.

The 1992 uprising came as the polarity between wealth and poverty increased everywhere, changing the temper of our times. Words like race, riot and lawlessness are inadequate in describing what we're facing here. In spite of all the armies, all the media distortions, all the code words, there will not be any peace until the great possibilities the country can offer are equally accessible for all. ■

Luis Rodriguez is a Chicago-based poet, journalist and critic. This column first appeared in the National Catholic Reporter.

For generations. California has been known for its San Andreas fault, the geological fracture beneath the earth's crust. The periodic eruptions along the fault line have been responsible for massive destruction and hundreds of deaths.

Yet far more devastating than the San Andreas fault is America's race/class fault line, the jagged division of color and income, education and privilege that slashes across the soul of this nation. The Los Angeles race uprising once again highlights the connection between race and violence in American life; it can only be understood from the point of view of the race/class fault line.

The unanticipated eruption of rage stripped away the facade of black progress in the central cities, which are boiling with the problems of poverty, drugs, gang violence, unemployment, poor schools and deteriorating public housing.

On opposing sides of the race/class fault, groups tend to perceive issues in radically different ways. The vast majority of Americans believed the innocent verdict in the King case was wrong. But while 81 percent of African-Americans stated that the criminal-justice system was clearly "biased against black people," only 36 percent of whites thought the justice system was racially biased, according to a *USA Today* poll. Sixty percent of blacks felt police brutality against minorities was excessive; only 17 percent of whites thought so.

The white media tried desperately to turn attention away from these issues, in part by arguing that the Los Angeles uprising was merely a "riot," one that was opposed by most African-Americans. Such language was also used to describe the civil unrest of the late '60s in Detroit and elsewhere to obscure both the political impulses motivating thousands of young African-Americans into the streets and the degree of concurrence for these actions among blacks who remained on the sidelines. This ignores all historical evidence about the dynamics of civil unrest. Following the Watts riots, for example,

sociologists determined that only 15 percent of residents actually participated in the arson and violence. Nonetheless, about two-thirds agreed that "the targets of the rebellion got what they deserved."

For black middle-class professionals, many of whom had come to believe the mythology about race during the Reagan-Bush era, the King verdict was like a fireball in the night. They were jolted into the realization that they, like Rodney King, could be halted by the police, brutalized, kicked and possibly killed — and that their assailants in police uniforms would probably walk way free. They were wakened by the haunting fear that their college-bound sons and brothers could be stopped for minor traffic violations, and later be found dead or dying in city streets. As Representative Floyd Flake of Brooklyn put it, "When Rodney King was on the ground getting beat, we were all on the ground getting beat."

While blacks reacted with fear and rage, whites in southern California took immediate steps to protect themselves. In the first 11 days of May, California residents purchased 20,578 guns, a 50 percent increase over the previous year. A thousand new members a day have joined the ranks of the National Rifle Association since the onset of racial unrest. Newspapers even reported instances in which suburban whites fled in panic when confronted by anyone with a black face: delivery boys, mail carriers, sanitation workers.

From the unrest, however, a fragile peace pact emerged between the Bloods and the Crips, who announced to the media that the current street violence was "a slave rebellion, like other slave rebellions in black history." Violence — including the absence of full voting and legal rights, as well as substandard wages — is the force that has perpetuated inequality of material conditions between blacks and whites throughout American history. It is behind the forced separation of slave families, rapes and whippings, the thousands of lynchings in the Jim Crow South and the murders of Martin Luther King, Jr., Medgar Evers and other civil-rights leaders. Violence by whites against blacks also continues to permeate African-American life, although it no longer manifests itself in the traditional forms of lynching or terrorism against black leaders. High rates of unemployment, the closure of businesses in black areas, the proliferation of drugs and the failure by government to provide decent housing and health care for the poor are all manifestations of institutional "violence."

One tragic outcome of this legacy is the rage directed against the Asian-American community during the Los Angeles riots, during which 1,800 Korean-owned businesses were damaged or destroyed. Black young people need to understand that it is not the Korean-American small merchant who denies capital for investment in the black community, controls the banks and financial institutions or commits police brutality against blacks and Latinos. There may be legitimate complaints between the two groups. But such misdirected anger makes a unified response to race and class oppression virtually impossible.

Although most civil-rights leaders are committed to legal forms of protest, the Los Angeles uprising is a desperate warning. If we listen carefully to young African-Americans in the streets, their dissatisfaction is with more than just the King verdict. What our young people painfully realize is that the entire "system" — the government and its politicians, the courts and the police, the corporations and the media — has written them off.

These youth recognize that Bush offered virtually no coherent policies addressing urban problems until he was confronted by massive street violence. They feel instinctively that American businesses have no intention of hiring them at real living wages, that the courts refuse to treat them as human beings, and that the politicians take their votes and ignore their needs. By taking to the streets, young African-Americans are crying out to society: "We will be heard! We will not be ignored, and we will not go away quietly." ∎

Manning Marable is a professor of political science and history at the University of Colorado-Boulder. He is the author of The Crisis of Color and Democracy *and* Black American Politics.

Los Angeles: Ted Soqui

The War of '92

by Nell Painter

Tragic and telegenic, the Rodney King beating began with and produced enough violence to shock viewers around the world.

Taken all together, the beating, the verdict and the riots may even have brought masses of Americans to consider the significance of class within race, a connection that national politics of the '80s tended to erase. We may now come to realize that, even though poverty more and more wears a dark face, issues of race are no longer merely stories in black and white.

The politics of the '80s — characterized by evasion and the willful manipulation of negative racial stereotypes — aimed at obscuring historical relationships. National leaders severed the connection between centuries' worth of oppression

and discrimination on the basis of race on the one hand, and the remedy of affirmative action on the other. It is well past time to realize that little in the Rodney King affair is new or mysterious.

The very accessibility of the images seemed to set this case apart from previous instances of police brutality. But the only part that is new is that this time a cameraman happened to catch it on video. Black people, other people of color and the poor of all races have been familiar with police brutality for generations. Police brutality is as old as time, as old as slave patrols, as old as the Pinkertons. In recent decades and with uneven success, victims have taken their cases to court. This time the evidence perfectly suited the medium of television, and an old story reached a wide audience. This time the amazement — at the beating, at the verdict — spread beyond the people who were beaten and those who were on their side. Thanks to that cameraman, a lot of Americans discovered the crime of police brutality for the first time.

Remembrance — of the long histories of officially sanctioned police brutality, of the urban disturbances that have followed in their wake and of earlier reports full of thoughtful remedies — further deepens the tragedy of the Rodney King affair. Trials of police who use too much force aren't very common, but they too, have their history, as in Liberty City, Miami, in 1980, when police were acquitted of murdering an innocent black motorcyclist.

The history of urban riots that were anti-black dates much further back than the history of burning and looting in the '60s. Nonetheless, most Americans don't know or don't remember the New York City Draft Riots of 1863, the worst urban disturbance in U.S. history. Although the Draft Riots began as a protest against conscription, more than 100 African-Americans, many of whom were children, died in the violence. The East St. Louis, Ill., riot of 1917 (which inspired Harlem Renaissance poet Claude McKay to write "If We Must Die") and the Red Summer of riots across the country in 1919 also produced far higher death tolls for blacks than whites. This pattern of white attack on non-white victims persisted into the '40s: In 1943, white mobs attacked Mexican-Americans in Los Angeles (the "zoot suit riots") and African-Americans in Detroit, although the casualties were not completely non-white.

Only in the '60s was the connection firmly established between the word "riot" and black people. African-Americans took to the streets, setting fires and looting in New York in 1964, in Watts in 1965, in Newark and Detroit in 1967 and in Washington, D.C., in 1968, as well as across the country in the aftermath of the assassination of Martin Luther King, Jr.

The Los Angeles riot, "the war of '92", seems most to resemble 1968's outbreak of grief and frustration. By the time tempers flared in Watts and Detroit and Washington, D.C., so many blacks had died — 50? 60? more? — in the pursuit of basic civil rights that support for the non-violence associated with King was wearing awfully thin. Appeals for self-defense and for black power were mounting. In 1968, King had less and less company in his insistence on non-violent protest, but his pacifism did not protect him from murder. King's assassination was shocking and infuriating. If even Martin Luther King had fallen victim to murderous white supremacy, if even *his* life was worth naught, what was the worth of any black person's life in this country?

A generation later, the acquittal of Rodney King's assailants, captured on videotape in the act of administering a savage beating to a man handcuffed on the ground, seemed shocking and infuriating. Now television coverage has rewritten for

the nation a question that people of color have asked themselves time and again in their own neighborhoods. The nation — along with the neighborhoods — wants to know: Why?

The inevitable inquiries, findings, recommendations and remedies have a history as old as the riots. The immediate causes of the disturbances of the '60s were nearly always police brutality or rumors of police brutality. The underlying causes — explained in report after report — also began to sound familiar: discrimination, poverty, unemployment, lack of governmental services.

The most eloquent of the reports, the Kerner Commission Report of 1968, is still current. But its roots lie in the 1947 report of President Harry S. Truman's Committee on Civil Rights. The report, titled *To Secure These Rights,* began by indicting lynching and police brutality — practices that proved how little America respected the value of black life.

An inclusive report that touches on most of the themes that reappeared in the civil-rights movement of the '50s and '60s, *To Secure These Rights* is well worth reading today, if only to remind us how long remedies have been recognized and agreed upon — and how long the political will has not been sufficient to sustain fundamental reform. Today's remedies will be familiar from 1947 and 1968, but because South Central Los Angeles has changed over time, some answers must change also.

One great lesson of the '60s that came out of the civil-rights movement and the war on poverty was the importance of

• • • • • • • • • • • • • • • • • •

Status of Job Training Partnership Act, 1988:

South Central received $49 per person-in-poverty —

55 percent less than West LA

28 percent less than Central LA

22 percent less than the Valley

(Source: *LA Weekly,* 12/30/88)

neighborhood-based organizations led by local people. The Student Non-Violent Coordinating Committee of the early '60s and the Model Cities Project of the late '60s have both been spoken of disparagingly since their time. But in different ways, each managed to bring poor and working-class people of color to an appreciation of their power as citizens. This, in turn, stretched prevailing notions of democracy — that officeholders are supposed to speak as though they are college-educated and as though they share an identity of interests with the rich and middle class.

Organization from the bottom up will be crucial in reform, and it will deliver an important lesson we are perhaps ready to hear. South Central Los Angeles, like many inner cities in the U.S., is no longer a study of monoliths coded in black and white. For better or for worse, the '80s proved that black conservatives do indeed exist. Clarence Thomas, Anita Hill and their friends demolished completely easy equations of blackness with the liberal wing of the Democratic party — with any wing of the Democratic party. Working-class black people exhibit the same ideological heterogeneity.

The poor and working-class people who will need to organize toward the regeneration of their neighborhoods are also heterogeneous ethnically and racially. Effective organization, therefore, will need to reach out to people of many backgrounds. Allies from within and outside the inner-city neighborhoods who want to be of help can't afford to remain racially or ethnically parochial. We are accustomed to using the language of race to talk about class, but recent experience shows that poverty and joblessness have more than a black face.

Rebuilding South Central Los Angeles in these recession-ridden, post-industrial times will prove challenging in the extreme, but the path may already be discerned. It leads from one beaten black body to a rainbow coalition organized from the grassroots. ■

Nell Painter teaches history at Princeton. This column first appeared in In These Times.

Los Angeles: Larry Hirshowitz

Social Disease

by Richard Gaines

n retrospect, the greater horror and tragedy resided in the national somnolence.

If we knew — at some level — about the failure of our political system, which allowed determinant power and influence to be concentrated in the hands of an anonymous lobby, we stoically bore that knowledge as if it were an inevitable condition of life in American democracy.

If we knew of the moral failure of our economic system, which concentrated

unaccountable wealth in the hands of a few and doomed countless millions to unconscionable destitution, we stoically bore that knowledge as if it were an unavoidable inefficiency in a capitalistic system that had proved its mettle in the century's great ideological showdown.

If we knew that Martin Luther King, Jr.'s dream of racial harmony had proved to be a mirage, we came to accept the racial fissures as an unfortunate law of imperfect life.

A generation that had defined itself in

opposition to these social malignancies expended itself, its energy and the nation's billions fruitlessly seeking to build the New Deal into the Great Society. Exhausted and frustrated, in the '80s we dimmed the lights and retreated into a romanticized Hollywood fantasy, desiring to forget — or at least ignore. When the eight-year extravaganza ended, we asked for a rerun. And we puffed with self-satisfaction when external events in China and, later, in the Soviet Union and Eastern Europe gave us reason to feel superior. The battle cry of the '60s,

"Tune in, turn on, drop out," transformed in the mundanity of modern life to become "Turn it off, tune in, drop out."

This the American public did with increasing determination. We turned off to the festering social failures that seemed as irradicable as AIDS. We tuned in to *The Cosby Show*, a lying exemplar of black middle-class assimilation (which, ironically and appropriately, ended its own eight-year run on the worst night of the riots in South Central LA). And we dropped out of a democratic politics grown pathetically irrelevant. We had become a nation adrift, inured to mediocrity, understandably convinced that our fate was fixed and there was damn little we could do about it.

What we wanted and what we got was distraction. *Lifestyles of the Rich and Famous, E.T., Rescue 911, Unsolved Mysteries*: Individual, isolated sagas of triumph and tragedy served our need. The appetite for these distractions was all the greater because the realities from which we were seeking refuge were so troubling and seemingly immutable.

The educator John Silber, president of Boston University, diagnosed the national distemper in his prophetic 1989 book, *Straight Shooting*. "Our society is in trouble and we all know it," he wrote. "We know that something is terribly wrong — the way we might know in our own bodies that we are seriously ill. When we have an internal intimation of serious illness, it is hard even to talk about the way we feel. We sense that talking about it might make it worse."

Now, thanks to Rodney King, four cops, 12 jurors and countless anonymous thieves, arsonists and murderers, whose collective actions have produced a pyre that even Cecil B. DeMille could not have conjured, we have been given a wake-up call. Belated though it may be, it is one we can no longer ignore.

It matters little whether King (who should not ever be confused with the martyr of the same name) deserved the merciless beating he received. Or whether the cops technically violated a California criminal law by inflicting the blows on their hapless victim. Or whether the jury

was motivated by a determination to apply the evidence to the law without racist instincts. Or even whether the mobs that sacked and burned Los Angeles did so out of uncontrollable rage or greed.

All of them, in their actions in sequence and together, unleashed a manifestation of ills of biblical clarity. First the tape, then the verdict, then the fires. The death and destruction that turned Tinseltown into Locustland may finally have roused us from our grand delusion. The sinfully unjust distribution of wealth, power and opportunity, the inequities between white and non-white, the failures of the political system — not mere moles on the face of the nation, but cancerous, possibly fatal lesions — have finally penetrated the American consciousness.

Ills that previously have been treated in isolation and with precarious results, from Boston to Brooklyn to Miami, now, as a result of these events, will demand and possibly receive the nation's full attention. Talking about it now can't make it any worse, however fervently the entrenched powers might wish otherwise. As Los Angeles burned, White House Press Secretary Marlin Fitzwater, in a transparently pre-emptive move, accused likely Democratic presidential nominee Bill Clinton of politicizing the verdict and the riots. As if, thanks to Rodney King, et al., the fundamental failures of the nation — ignored, overlooked and rationalized since the other King ignited moral outrage a generation ago — had not become the only real political issues before the American people, now suddenly awakened from a restless sleep.

Now. There's plenty to talk about, argue about, debate and vote on. Plenty to do.

Now. The unseen hand of history has dragged Bush and Clinton and all of us toward a rendezvous we couldn't have imagined not long ago.

Now. We're all in Hollywood. With the cameras rolling. And, as they said in the '60s, the whole world is watching. ■

Richard Gaines is co-author of the unauthorized biography, Dukakis: The Man Who Would Be President. *This column first appeared in the* Miami New Times.

A Hundred Excuses

by Steve Erickson

I never smelled the smoke of Watts. Watts was just a little far away then. Only 27 years later do we understand just how far and, at the same time, just how close it was. I was 15 and living in the north end of the San Fernando Valley at the border of fear, where the new suburbia still felt afraid enough to arm itself when the Other Los Angeles came advancing across the Cahuenga Pass. But one didn't see the flames from the rooftops then, as I saw them this time, and one didn't smell the smoke then as I did when it finally wafted through my window last Thursday night, 24 hours after the verdict was delivered.

Now we're caught in a middle ground that goes beyond simply white or black or right or left or have or don't. America hurtles on to the ever-clearer division between those who feel the individual is never accountable for anything, especially his violence, and those who feel he's accountable for everything, including getting the fuck beat out of him by a dozen cops. Accountability has always been a clear-cut issue for Americans because Americans have no patience for anything that's

• • • • • • • • • • • • • • • •

Number of new jobs added in LA between 1980 and 1987:
420,000

Percentage of those jobs offering wages less than $15,000 annually:
40

(Source: Goetz Wolff, "Industry Trends in Los Angeles," LA Economic Roundtable, 1980)

making sense: commentary

Los Angeles: Ted Soqui

complicated; if there's one thing Americans hate, it's ambiguity. The left will make a hundred excuses for the carnival savagery with which a driver is hauled from his truck and cut to the very quick of his life; and, in the meantime, the jurors explain the verdict this way: "But it's hard to be a cop [an issue that was not on trial, since no trial would be needed to agree on it] and Rodney King was in control of the entire situation."

Hearing that, you have to feel as though you just fell down the rabbit's hole. Giving those 12 people the benefit of the doubt, assuming theirs was a good-faith effort to render a just verdict, you nonetheless have to wonder how many legal hairs got split to refute 81 seconds the entire world has seen; how deep into the trees they had to get to not see the forest — at which point it was inevitable that, in the light of examining a single leaf, the entire

forest would go up in fire. The jury's prototypical American disdain for ambiguity reduced a complicated truth to a simpler one, and the simplest truth of all — that a man on the ground was hit 56 times in 81 seconds — was twisted to an absurdity: Rodney King was in control of the entire situation.

In the spirit of moral ambiguity, let's not kid ourselves. What happened was not simply an assault on the mean cynicism of Reaganism by those at whose expense the rich have built their epoch; it was also an *expression* of Reaganism, or rather of the instinct Reaganism perversely raised to the stature of an ethic: You can have it if you can take it.

Americanism, once about justice and freedom, is, in the last smoking days of the 20th Century, about acquisition — and all that exists between what you want and what you have is whether the will to want it is powerful enough to overcome any inhibitions of civilized behavior. So from south to north and east to west, people took it. Oh, it appears they're giving away TVs today at the Circuit City up the street. Let's go get one. The point was less the object than the getting. The greatest lie of this political year is the one that says the people have been betrayed by the system and their politicians; we take righteous satisfaction in this lie, because the only alternative to believing it is admitting that we betrayed ourselves, allowing the system to justify what's most venal about us. We saw who we were, from Simi Valley to South Central LA, and though I don't sell short our ability to come up with a new lie to account for it, another generation from now we'll be smelling it not just through the apartment window but in our sleep: the smoke of a city that's never been an aberration of America, but rather the ultimate version of it. ∎

Steve Erickson is a contributing writer to the LA Weekly, *where this column first appeared.*

Los Angeles: John Goubeaux

The First Multicultural Riots

by Peter Kwong

I f you arrived in Los Angeles one week after the riots, the first thing you would have noticed wasn't the smoke from the fires, or even the tension between the many races that make up this most polyglot of American cities. It was the jacarandas, which blossomed just two or three days after the looting began. The brilliant, purplish-blue, waxy, artificial-looking flowers bloomed simultaneously all around LA, from the sunshine of upscale Westwood to the blackened walls of Crenshaw Boulevard.

By Mother's Day, the jacarandas had competition from dozens of sidewalk flower vendors in the Latino neighborhoods. On burnt-out intersections, surrounded by the debris of gutted stores, they pushed dyed carnations for $5 a bunch — just about the only economic activity in the area undisturbed by the riots.

If what happened here two weeks ago was a race riot of blacks against whites, it was an odd one that left many more blacks and Chicanos dead and injured than whites. "I wish this riot was only a black and white problem! It would be much easier to resolve," lamented Vibiana Andrade, regional counsel of the Mexican American Legal Defense and Educational Fund. At an angry neighborhood meeting called to discuss limiting the number of liquor stores that could be reopened in South Central, Alfred Livingston, a 34-year resident, said, "We just can't take it no more. Like wounded animals, we struck out...but we weren't aiming particularly at nobody. It just happened to be Koreans."

In fact, the rioters were aiming at business establishments. At the end of the fury, 1,867 Korean businesses were looted or burned. Korean businesses alone suffered an estimated $347 million in property damage — about one-half of the total loss from the riots. The worst damage to Korean property, however, did not occur in the African-American neighborhood of South Central LA — only 9 per cent of all Korean businesses in LA are located there. The heaviest loss occurred north of South Central, in Koreatown, which is inhabited mostly by poor Latino immigrants.

The Los Angeles riots were fueled by a reality much more complex than that presented by the national media — though you wouldn't know it from looking at *Newsweek*'s cover, "Beyond Black &

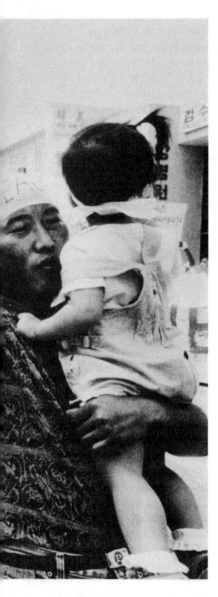

White," or *U.S. News and World Report*'s "Black vs. White." The fixation on black versus white is outdated and misleading. In fact, the Rodney King verdict was merely the match that lit the fuse of the first multiracial class riot in American history.

I Hate This Neighborhood

Jay Lee, who operated a home-appliance stall in a Los Angeles "swap meet" (a large, open floor space with individual counters used by various discount merchants), is quite clear about what happened to him during the riots. At 4:30

Thursday afternoon, April 30, a few hours after reports of the riots in South Central went on TV, his swap meet was surrounded by Latinos, mostly recent Central American immigrants who live in the rundown tenements nearby. Someone called the police for help. The LAPD came, but soon withdrew. The merchants blocked the entrance for a time, but when a burning bottle of gasoline was thrown through a window, the mob rushed past the shop owners and looted all the stalls.

As the fire spread, eventually engulfing the five-story building, Lee and the other merchants watched their livelihoods go up in smoke. Lee lost $70,000, of which he still owes $20,000 to his wholesale supplier. To make matters worse, in anticipation of increased sales over Mother's Day weekend, Lee had invested most of his liquid capital in new merchandise just before the riot. After paying the mortgage on his house, he has only $50 left.

Lee, who served in the U.S. Army for 10 years before starting his business, keeps asking, "Why me? They were my customers. I was nice to them. I know many are poor and they don't have legal status. When one of them had a death in the family, I donated $200 for the funeral. Now I really hate them," he adds bitterly. "I don't even want to go back to start the business at the same place again, but I'll have to. I'll get out of this [neighborhood] as soon as I've paid back my debts."

Lee's experience is not unique. Hundreds of Korean merchants, some with even more tragic stories, flooded into the three relief centers set up in Koreatown (one combined federal, state and city center, and two set up by Radio Korea and the Oriental Mission Church). They wanted to find out whether they were eligible for disaster-assistance grants from the government's Federal Emergency Management Administration, but they were particularly interested in the disaster loans from the Small Business Administration (SBA). To maintian an income, they had no option but to go back.

Most, like Lee, were not insured,

because their location was considered high risk even before the riot. Only 500 of the 1,867 Korean businesses destroyed by the riots had any coverage at all. The remaining uninsured owners of some 1,400 shops were left to contend with home-mortgage, credit-card, tax and car payments, not to mention things like school tuition and daily expenses. In two short days, these merchants were reduced to financial ruin — even though many of them drove back in German-built cars from the rubble of their shops in South LA to nice Glendale or San Gabriel homes.

But that tells only a part of the story. If half the businesses wiped out in the riots were owned by Koreans, between 30 and 40 percent were owned by Latinos, mostly Mexican-Americans and *Cubanos*. More than a third of those killed in the riots were Latino, and roughly a third of the 13,000 arrested during the week of violence were Hispanic (though most of those arrests were not for looting but for violating the curfew).

There is little hard evidence to support popular claims that undocumented Latinos are responsible for much of the looting, but at least 1,500 of those arrested were undocumented immigrants who were turned over to the Immigration and Naturalization Service for immediate deportation. The only obvious fact is that businesses in Koreatown located near poor immigrant Latino housing were devastated.

The Latino population in Southern California has swelled in recent years until it now constitutes about half of South LA — though there are no Hispanic elected officials from the riot-torn areas. And there are sharp class distinctions among Hispanics that create a cultural gulf nearly as wide as that between whites and Koreans. The Latinos who live around Koreatown are mostly poor, non-English-speaking new immigrants. Many who came from Mexico are undocumented, while those from the war-torn areas of El Salvador and Nicaragua live here legally but with only temporary status. Caught up in the melée two weeks ago, some war refugees were threatened by the INS with long jail terms if they refused to sign voluntary deportation orders.

When they can, the men get jobs by waiting on street corners each morning to be picked up as day laborers in construction or restaurant kitchens and for warehouses or for yard chores. If they do get picked up, which is not always the case, they make between $20 and $40 a day. Women work in child care or as maids. Some Latino men work as help in Korean businesses, and women also work as seamstresses in garment factories in downtown LA, where more than half of such factories are Korean-owned.

The role of the undocumented Latino community is the least understood of all the groups swept up in this riot. They are disenfranchised, at the bottom of the social order; their marginal status is in direct contrast to that of the upwardly mobile Korean immigrants (however relative that Korean position may be). Unlike black workers, they do not aggressively militate for higher wages, and they have no organizations to represent their interests — the established Latino groups in East LA do not work with undocumented immigrants. Until the riots, the tensions between the Latinos and the Korean-Americans went unarticulated, smothered at least in part by the struggle both immigrant groups were mounting to survive and prosper. Latinos were in no position to express racial animosity because of their legal and economic status, and the Koreans needed the Latinos, their most important clientele and a cheap source of labor to run their businesses. They would never have initiated the rioting, but, once it began, the Latinos did finally find a voice. However the major media try to define the violence as black on white or, to a lesser extent, as black on Korean, the real message for Asians in LA was sent by the undocumented immigrants living all around Koreatown.

A Divorce With No Alimony

Pundits are quite right to point to the abandonment of the inner cities by the American political elite as one of the chief causes of the riots. But what they don't say is that it's this very neglect that lured Korean immigrants to Los Angeles in the first place.

After the 1965 Watts riot, politicians made pious promises to improve conditions in the inner cities, yet few of the recommendations of the subsequent McCone Commission report were implemented. Instead, whites moved wholesale to the western part of city or plowed over desert land in all directions to build new, homogeneous (read: lily-white) suburban communities. The new suburbs are self-incorporated and have rules to keep "undesirables" from moving in. That left the city to the terribly poor and the terribly rich, the latter of whom built up walls, set up sophisticated electronic surveillance systems and hired private police to protect them. Los Angeles reemerged a scant 10 years later as an even more segregated city of isolated communities.

Then, in 1976, the white middle class launched a successful tax revolt — Proposition 13 — to lighten its burden for the support of the urban poor in the neighborhoods they had left behind. The result was not just a divorce between whites and the ghetto population, but a subsequent refusal to pay alimony. "We are all quite isolated in our own communities," a resident of Westwood, a mostly white middle-class neighborhood, explained. "We don't know and don't care about the problems in the inner-cities. Driving to work every day, most of us don't even know where South Central is — except many of us saw the fires from that direction when we were stuck in traffic on Thursday afternoon, after most offices let out their staffs early."

While Los Angeles as a whole has made dramatic economic progress, the inner-city has been left behind. In fact, the gap between whites and blacks has widened in the 27 years since the Watts riots. The poverty rate in the South Los Angeles area stands at 30.3 percent, three times the national average; dropouts from the labor force make up 41.8 percent of the adult population; some 24.9 percent are on welfare; and households headed by single women account for 15.8 percent. The statistics would be worse had this area not experienced a large influx of Latinos, who tend to be less dependent on welfare and have a higher rate of employment and family unity.

With no public investment in their education system thanks to Prop. 13, inner-city youth are no longer wanted by the economy. They are the "throwaway" generation, born into the underclass.

And the systematic oppression does not stop there. William Julius Wilson, the professor of sociology at the University of Chicago who popularized the term "underclass," gave a lecture to UCLA students the weekend after the riots. He told them Chicago employers would hire Mexicans, Hispanics or any Asian rather than African-Americans because of the latter's image as unreliable workers. The employers would say: "I can't afford to take a risk."

"Koreans were lured by developers to settle and do business in the inner-city" of Los Angeles, contends Royal Hong, executive director of Korean Immigrant Workers Advocates of Southern California. Anxious to escape from political instability and the high rate of unemployment at home, Korean professionals came in droves in the 1970s. They arrived with education, personal savings, military training (no one is allowed to emigrate from South Korea without first serving two years in the armed forces) and a willingness to work hard. These self-selected capitalists saw South LA as their stepping stone to the American Dream. They believed they would follow in the steps of those who started earlier, have already "made it" and now park their Mercedes beside homes built near affluent white neighborhoods. After a time, they would build up enough money to move their businesses out of the ghettos into more profitable white areas.

Korean businesses in South LA — mainly groceries, liquor stores and swap meet stands — were perfectly suited for the needs of the system. The ghetto may be poor, but that doesn't mean there isn't money to be made there: These new entrepreneurs provided valuable retail access to the ghetto for corporations like Brown Forman distilleries, R.J. Reynolds, General Foods and Coca-Cola. They also provided the major economic activity in impoverished neighborhoods and supplied essential merchandise to areas long abandoned by

earlier, often Jewish-owned, businesses. Best of all, they did this without putting whites at risk. During the long American recession, as the major corporations laid off employees, small businesses have become the chief source of new jobs, and many have been started by Asian immigrants. Some 38 percent of the retail outlets in LA County are Korean-owned, and Korean-American businesses in LA proper actually grew by 27 percent in the past two years. The cohesiveness of the community gives them a slight advantage in acquiring seed money — but not because, as some people in the neighborhood believe, they have been favored by white banks. Most Korean-Americans attain their capital in one of two ways: Either they labor at more than one job for up to 16 hours a day, as Jay Lee did for two years, or they participate in a community savings club known as a *kye*. In a kye, perhaps a few dozen families chip in between $500 and $1000 annually; each year, one family (decided by lot) gets that year's receipts to start a business.

By American rules, the Koreans have done nothing wrong. They are no different from the Jewish, Italian or any other kind of merchants who have made their living from the ghettos. That's why they were so shocked when they were attacked, and incensed when the police did nothing to

protect them. "Koreans escaped from political persecutions at home, and came here expecting to enjoy this country's respect for the rights of individuals," complains Edward Chang, professor of Ethnic and Women's Studies at California Polytechnic Pomona. "But our constitutional right of equal protection has been violated."

Korean Community Mobilizes

The uniquely homogenous nature of the Korean-American community is a direct consequence of the Korean War. When fighting disrupted the countryside in the early 1950s, millions of refugees flooded the cities of South Korea and quickly became urbanized. The children of these displaced peasants worked to obtain professional degrees but found their immature, export-oriented economy offered them few opportunities. So when U.S. immigration law was liberalized for professionals in 1965, they decamped in large numbers — and became one of the few immigrant groups in American history that was overwhelmingly urban, educated and unigenerational. They were also largely Christian. More than the language barrier, this unusual demographic similarity explains why the Koreans responded so quickly to their crisis. Overnight, AM

Radio Korea became a unifying force for the entire community, covering the riots and their aftermath in gory detail. Horrified, Korean-Americans quickly put away their differences and rallied to assist their countrymen. In less then a week, $2 million in emergency funds was raised and the Koreatown relief centers were set up to provide free groceries, rice, cooking oil, milk and fresh eggs to cash-short victims. Within 10 days after the riots, dozens of merchants gathered at the Oriental Mission Church relief center. They were absolutely panic-stricken as they tried to complete the complex government application forms for SBA disaster loans, but community translators and some 200 volunteer Korean CPAs pitched in immediately to speed the process.

On May 2, with less than 24-hours' notice, 30,000 Korean Americans and their supporters held a march at Ardmore Park in Koreatown to show their solidarity. There, the Korean leaders broke with their long-held — and conservative — attitudes toward the local black and Latino communities, attitudes that by and large have been shaped by Republican values about property. Notably, they blamed the police — and not the looters — for failing to protect Korean businesses in the crucial early hours of the riot. Even more significantly, they called for justice for Rodney King, thus relinquishing their confrontational stance against blacks. Most Koreans did not speak out about the case of Soon Ja Du, the grocer who was given a light probationary sentence for the videotaped killing of 15-year-old black teenager Latasha Harlins just two days after King's beating (Soon had suspected Harlins of stealing a bottle of orange juice).

As part of this sudden change, the Korean community placed the blame for urban violence on federal and state policies. In turn, they also came to see themselves — for the first time — as victims of white racism. "This is clearly racist," says Edna Bonacich, professor of sociology at UC-Riverside. "If the riots had spread into the northern white neighborhoods, the U.S. Army would have moved in."

The media's repeated juxtaposition of the Soon Ja Du shooting of Latasha

Harlins with the police beating of Rodney King made Korean-Americans feel intentionally marked for violence, and the frequently broadcast scenes of gun-wielding Korean vigilantes defending their businesses only reinforced their fears.

When Bush came to LA to inspect the riot damage, 24 Korean leaders met with him. Some were pleased when the president extended the meeting from the originally planned half-hour to 50 minutes. But Bush offered more sympathy than substance. He politely rejected the leaders' demand for reparations for all business losses suffered during the riots and offered no new ideas for the problems of South Central LA.

The argument for reparations came on the grounds that "this riot was not a natural disaster," as Edward Chang, one of the representatives who met with Bush, puts it. "It is a man-made one. It could have been avoided had law enforcement moved in earlier. The root cause, however, is the wrongheaded government social policy toward the urban poor in the first place."

These more realistic attitudes reflect the influence of the second and "1.5" (Korean-Americans not born in U.S., but who came here as children) generations. The crisis so overwhelmed the immigrant business people that they had to rely on their children — many of whom are not in the ethnic businesses — to help interpret reality and to speak out for them. Many of the younger

Koreans left their colleges or suburban jobs and came back home to protect their parents' shops, simultaneously experiencing overt racial threats for the first time in their lives. Many reacted with expressions of gratitude for all their parents had done for them. In that sense, the riots had an even more profound effect on Korean-Americans than on blacks — it bridged growing cultural gaps within families.

We Are All Trapped

Despite the devastation and racism, many of the merchants will return to South LA. "They don't have the capital to compete with larger stores in other areas," Professor Chang explains, "so they'll have to go back. They don't have any choice."

Going back, however, is not going to be easy. Chang Park, of Korean Immigrant Workers Advocates of Southern California, suspects that many of the merchants will not be able to get government loans. Swap-meet operators, who after the grocery markets suffered the second-largest loss (a total of $54,941,300), are particularly vulnerable because of their poor record-keeping and high turnover rates. Most of them will not have adequate documentation to qualify for assistance. In fact, Chang Park accuses the Korean leaders who are not ghetto businessmen for "instilling false hope in the victims."

But the scarcity of loans is not as problematic as lingering racial tensions. There is no getting around the class issues. Koreans don't live in the areas where they do business; Asians constitute only 1.9 percent of population in South LA. The African-American community can't help but see them as outsiders sucking profit out of the community.

There are other sticky issues on which the two sides may never reach compromise. The problem of Korean liquor stores in the ghetto is a key one. According to the Korean Grocers Association, there are 184 Korean liquor stores in South Central LA — practically two stores per block. During the riots, local residents reported that all of them were burned down.

In the days following the riots, community and church organizations lobbied the city's Planning Commission to pass legislation limiting the number of rebuilding permits for liquor stores. The Korean community cried foul. After all, liquor sales are by far the most lucrative legitimate ghetto business. On the day of the public hearing, hundreds of leaders from both sides addressed their concerns in front of the commissioners.

One Korean leader justified the high number of liquor stores as a service to older people who often do not have cars to travel to wealthier neighborhoods to shop. A female liquor store owner broke down and cried during her testimony, begging the commissioners not to repeal her liquor permit: "I have been here for 10 years working every day from seven in the morning to 10 at night. I do not ask for welfare, and I am providing services for the community. Why does anyone want to destroy my livelihood?"

But a black South Central resident, Arlene Palona, countered: "Alcohol is the blight of the community. You cry for your lost business, but I cry every time I see men laying wasted and dying slowly from the poison, and I cry every time I see our young men hooked on the bottle that saps all their youth. Moreover, you worked 10 years to build your business, but we waited 300 years to be free. We in the community do not believe that business interests should come first." Operating liquor stores in the black ghettos *is* a serious moral issue. But, as Chang Park asserts, the problem lies not so much with the urge to profit as it does with the structural poverty and racism hemming in the neighborhood. "It would be unfair to expect of Koreans to carry the burden of all that is wrong with this country."

They Still Don't Get It

The American establishment is still trying to find an easy villain to blame. Even before the fires had been put out, Police Chief Daryl Gates accused undocumented immigrants of being major participants in the rioting. The LAPD, in collaboration with the INS, has engaged in "sweep-up" operations to deport the "illegals," particularly those in Central American and Mexican neighborhoods — often without following proper legal procedures. These indiscriminate, racially tinted "arrests" seriously undermine the civil rights of all people living in the Latino communities, be they legal or undocumented.

Since the riots, "white flight" from the city has intensified. Real-estate agencies in Ventura County north of LA (a solidly white middle-class suburb where Simi Valley is located) have reported a 75 percent increase in inquiries for housing from people presently living in the city. Others are purchasing guns for protection. LA gun shops reported the highest-recorded eight-day sales period ever immediately after the uprising. Many purchasers are actually moving up to more powerful weaponry.

Middle-class flight and heightened fears of racial violence are certainly not prescriptions for future community accord. Professor William Julius Wilson predicts that Californians are not only waiting for the next big earthquake; they are also, he believes, waiting for another, possibly larger quake along the "social fault line." In Los Angeles, Chang Park of the Korean Immigrant Workers Advocates only hopes that, next time, the black community will be better organized and have a higher political consciousness — one that will finally target the right enemy. ∎

Peter Kwong contributes to the Village Voice, *where a version of this story first appeared.*

Looking for Hope

by Katharine Fong

Among the horrifying images caught on national television from South Central Los Angeles during the riots were the scenes of armed Korean-American merchants firing on predominantly African-American rioters and looters who threatened their shops. Indeed, scores of Korean businesses were vandalized or destroyed by the raging protesters — who in many cases left nearby black-owned businesses untouched — and Koreans and other Asians were reportedly harassed and shot at. Relations between the two groups have been tense for some time, and not only in LA; but the ugly footage played over and over on TV screens was a grim reminder that "the race problem" exists not only between whites and blacks.

Friction between Asian-Americans and African-Americans has been on the increase in recent years. Across the country, community leaders from both minority groups are painfully aware of the need to bridge divisive racial gaps, particularly in the wake of last week's violence. "It's difficult to talk about hope right now," says Bong Hwan Kim, executive director of the Korean Youth Center in LA. "It's amazingly tragic for the Korean community to be in South Central at this time in history. [Koreans and African-Americans] are two disenfranchised groups competing for the remaining crumbs after the status quo has finished and left the table."

But Kim has been trying to foster communication between Koreans and African-Americans. He is co-chair of the Black-Korean Alliance, a community-based organization that focuses on substantive solutions. "We're a *de facto* speakers bureau going into schools and the community," says Kim. "Kids especially have accepted the stereotypes of each other perpetuated through mainstream media and parental attitudes. We establish a dialogue where Koreans, who might think blacks are all gang members or substance abusers, can talk to black attorneys, ministers and vice versa. It turns the stereotypes on their heads." Kim hopes the Alliance will become a pilot program for other cities. He also sees joint economic development as another solution, where state and federal governments institute programs to match funds when partners from two or more minority groups go into business together. But it's of primary importance, according to Kim and other Korean-Americans throughout the country, that their communities be organized and vocal, and that other Asian-Americans not presume to speak for them.

In San Francisco, community leaders have been working to defuse racial tensions in such hot spots as Washington and Lincoln High Schools, where some students carry weapons; just days ago, a black student shot a Vietnamese student. Noting Rodney King's plea to work out our problems, since "we're stuck together for awhile," Rev. Amos Brown of the Third Baptist Church says, "We've got to talk to each other. What happened in Simi Valley is that those people never talked to black people. We've got to acknowledge that we each have mutual needs, that we've each got something to offer one another." Brown wants more racial interaction among parents and business and professional leaders in schools and churches, suggesting that churches and other organizations "adopt a school."

Such formal and informal programs may not be enough to counter virulent and pervasive racism in America, made so apparent by the Rodney King verdict and its aftermath. Ronald Takaki, professor of Asian-American Studies at UC-Berkeley, despairs over what he terms the "let-them-flip-hamburgers" attitude of whites toward African-Americans. But he maintains that animosity between minority racial groups is the result of ignorance of each other's history and culture. For instance, "most Asians don't realize that, were it not for the passage of the Civil Rights Act in 1964, they wouldn't be here. The civil-rights movement led to questioning discrimination in U.S. immigration practices, which led to the Immigration Act of 1965."

On the other hand, Takaki objects to the continued media portrayal of Asian-Americans as one-dimensional. "Even in films like *Do the Right Thing*," he says, "the black and white characters come off as complex. But there's no complexity to Mr. Lee, the Korean grocer. I wish the director had taken the camera into the store, inside to where we could have seen Mr. Lee's diploma on the wall from Seoul University."

Like Kim and Brown, Takaki suggests workshops and cultural events to promote racial understanding. All three express concern about the white backlash against minority communities. President Bush, argues Takaki, has already put a spin on events that emphasizes the looting and destruction instead of the issues of racial injustice, poverty and unemployment. "All the detailed statistics on troops were like Desert Storm all over again — as in 'Saddam Hussein will not stand,' " says Takaki. "Bush was the white knight against the dark forces, the barbarians. The nervousness across white America is such that whites everywhere identified with him. It may work toward his re-election."

Takaki points out, however, that the absence of strong moral leadership within minority communities contributed to the "deregulation" of the King verdict protests; while the fury of the mob was understandable, it was in stark contrast to the non-violent mass demonstrations and civil disobedience advocated by leaders such as Martin Luther King, Jr. What happened on the San Francisco Bay Bridge was an exception, "a small price for commuters to pay," says Takaki, "and better than burning down shops."

Rev. Amos Brown was on the bridge during the protest. "I saw people getting fidgety, angry, because they couldn't move," he says. "But I thought, well, this is how black people have felt for 300 years — they're stuck, they can't move. This has been our experience."

When protesters in San Francisco were reported to be heading from Nob Hill toward Chinatown on Thursday evening, the second night of the riots, Henry Der, executive director of Chinese for Affirmative Action (CAA), received phone calls from people asking if he felt Asians were being targeted. "There was a fear," Der says. "But looked at as a whole, what happened everywhere was that rioters were striking out at whatever was in front of them.

"It's a constant struggle to make institutions responsible and accountable in their actions to minorities," he continues. "But concurrently, there must be dialogue among minorities — in school, in the workplace, in social settings. I don't know if racism will ever be eradicated, but to maintain our sanity, we have to hope to overcome it. We've got to find common ground."

Certainly, victimization and stereotyping make for common ground. But some see the chasm between people of color growing wider. African-Americans, for instance, were incensed over the paucity of Asian-American reaction to the light sentence given the Korean storeowner convicted of shooting a black teenager in LA. "That incident eroded my compassion for Asians as minorities," says columnist Julianne Malveaux. "Asians needed to make a public statement then, and most didn't. They were angry about the injustice in the Vincent Chin [murder]. Why not this case? I consider it a breaking of the faith."

• • • • • • • • • • • • • • • •

Number of check-cashing facilities in South Central LA: 132

Percentage of LA banks that will not cash government benefit checks for non-depositors: 94

Percentage of banks that do not offer low-cost checking to the non-elderly poor: 50

(Source: "Economic State of the City"; Paul Ong, Legal Aid Survey; "Taking It To The Bank," Western Center on Law and Poverty)

Malveaux further assails some Asian-Americans for enjoying their status as "honorary whites" who think themselves better than blacks. "I understand that when people come to this racist society, where blacks are the lowest on the ladder, they emulate its values," she says. "I've seen people here who can barely speak English, yet they can say 'nigger.' "

"There is a pecking order in racism," acknowledges Henry Der. "Because of Asians' higher socioeconomic status, they tend to be regarded as higher." A "hierarchy" in racial minorities' status brings into question Asian-Americans' responsibilities to other communities of color. Whether Asians should act in solidarity with African-Americans, Latinos, Native Americans — and, for that matter, other Asians — is a volatile issue, made more complex by false outside assumptions that minority groups are somehow monolithic. The myth of the "model minority," after all, has blurred severe problems among Asian-Americans generated by differences in class, ethnicity and income, and has been used as a wedge between Asians and other minorities.

"We can't turn our backs; we can't bash affirmative action," urges Henry Der, "because we'll pay the price in a social context."

"Asian-Americans must speak out against being used this way," agrees Ronald Takaki. "We need to support affirmative action for others because we support justice, and because we know about discrimination."

As the U.S. Civil Rights Commission has found, Asians still face an uphill climb, many struggling with living, working and raising their families in an enormously complex, multi-layered society.

"My parents — and other immigrant parents are the same — told me that all I needed to do in this country was to study hard, attend class, and that would protect me from racism and the mentality that would hold me back," says Bong Hwan Kim. "But there is no social infrastructure to deal with racism and other problems in American society. I only hope it will improve with the generations." ∎

Katharine Fong is an associate editor of San Francisco Focus and a contributing editor to SF Weekly, where a version of this story first appeared.

Between Black Rage and White Power *by Nora Choi*

Michael Schumann/SABA

When Los Angeles, home to the country's largest Korean-American community, ignited early this month in an angry response to the Rodney King verdict, Koreans all over the world were rudely awakened to the harsh realities of race and class in the United States.

In the aftermath, Koreans on the streets are angry and distrustful of both blacks and whites. According to Dong Soo Lee, a Korean-American reporter for the *Los Angeles Times* who has interviewed dozens of Korean merchants since the uprising, "Koreans feels anger toward blacks because, although at times they have not helped to improve the situation of blacks in this country, they certainly didn't create the inequality either." Most Korean-Americans acknowledge that some in their community are prejudiced against African-Americans, but they point out that the prejudice often flows in both directions. Koreans also maintain that angry blacks missed the target when they participated in the destruction of Los Angeles's Koreatown.

Annie Cho, executive director of the Korean-American Grocers Association, a national group based in Los Angeles, says, "We understand that the underlying problem is economic and is a result of blacks being isolated from the rest of society....It was a class revolt over the lack of health care, job opportunities and affordable housing, and the increase in crime and drugs. But we cannot exist as a United States...as long as we allow the system to [divide] us in this way."

Koreans began to immigrate to this country in large numbers in the mid-1970s, when immigration laws loosened. Tens of thousands settled in cities like Los Angeles, New York and Chicago, pursuing their version of the American Dream. The immigrants, few of whom spoke English,

began businesses in the poorest, toughest neighborhoods, often predominantly black, where rents were low and there was little competition. Once merchants succeeded, they often moved on to "less dangerous" areas, continuing the cycle until they made it to the suburbs. Until then, as Cho puts it, "We live with the threat of being robbed and killed every day that we open up our stores. It's an occupational hazard."

While Korean-Americans have justifiable fears, African-American customers say they often feel shop owners judge them guilty of being criminals the minute they walk in the door. To blacks with sharply limited access to economic empowerment, it seems outrageous that a new immigrant group can move so easily up the economic ladder. Korean-Americans say the keys to their success are a no-interest lending system financed by monthly dues and run through family, church and social networks, and the unpaid labor of store owners' family members.

The targeting of Koreatown shocked Korean-Americans, forcing them to look beyond their storefronts and to society's injustices. Finding themselves scapegoated for what is essentially a black-and-white and class issue, Korean-Americans are even angrier at white institutions: the media, the police and politicians.

Yong Wha Kim, publisher of the Chicago edition of the national daily *Korea Times*, asks, "Why did the LA police not respond to the repeated request of Korean-Americans for assistance in protecting their businesses, when at the same time they were so quick to guard other sections of the city like Hollywood?" According to Judy Han, a staffer at the national Korean-American Grocers Association, the lack of police response prompted some store owners to organize their own security forces.

Korean-Americans are also angered by press coverage they say portrayed them as racists and vigilantes. According to the *Korea Times*'s Kim, "The mainstream media repeatedly showed pictures of gun-toting Korean-American merchants, without explaining that they were forced to respond in this desperate way because of the failure of local and state law-enforcement forces to respond to requests for help."

As Koreatown begins rebuilding, observers wonder if relations with African-Americans will improve. Some enlightened Asian leaders have been talking about making links with the black community, but the majority, according to Times reporter Dong Soo Lee, feel no sense of solidarity — yet. In fact, fearing future violence, many Koreans are buying guns because they realize that armed store owners survived the recent attacks. Lee fears that, unless Koreans are able to reach out, their community will become more insular and parochial.

Small signs of hope do seem to be appearing, however, as thousands of store owners, their families and volunteers sift through the ashes to start reconstruction. Koreatown has been flooded with volunteers and donations of food, supplies and money, raised by Koreans in other cities and countries. For a community normally plagued by factionalism and infighting (partially a reflection of the division of Korea itself), this new unity is a hopeful sign.

Jay Kim, vice president of Chicago Korean Broadcasting and Publishing, says, "It's tremendous how this has brought together first- and second-generation Koreans. Our children are bilingual, bicultural, and we are seeing them act as a crucial link for us. Seeing our children understand the situation so much better than we do is a sign of great hope out of all of this." Still, the hope is tempered with caution. "We need to wait and see whether leaders are going to make the changes needed to address the needs of the black community," says Cho.

Until then, Koreans are taking steps to guarantee long-term justice. Korean-Americans everywhere are talking about becoming more politically involved — not just registering to vote, but also holding elected officials accountable. For a relatively conservative community used to observing rather than participating in U.S. politics, that is a big change. "We learned several valuable lessons from LA," says Daniel Lee. "One of them is that Koreans don't have much political clout." As Jay Kim puts it, "Koreans need to look more closely at candidates like Jesse Jackson and become more active in their campaigns, as well as continually organize ourselves so that we can be more effective in having our voices heard."

Jai Lee Wong of the Los Angeles County Human Relations Commission says the challenge is for Korean and black leaders to find commonalities on an individual as well as community level. "People are saying the healing has already begun," she adds, "but I find that to be a dangerous approach because the anger is still there.

"On the street level," she adds, "this is just the beginning of things to come until the fundamental issues of racial and economic injustice in this country are addressed. On the streets, Koreans will continue to be afraid" — continuing to pay the price of being caught in the middle. ■

Nora Choi, a Korean-American activist, is a former co-news editor of the Guardian News Weekly, *where this story first appeared.*

The armored personnel carrier squats on the corner like *un gransapo feo* — "a big ugly toad" — according to nine-year-old Emerio. His parents talk anxiously, almost in a whisper, about the *desaparecidos*: Raul from Tepic, big Mario, the younger Flores girl and the cousin from Ahuachapan. Like all Salvadorans, they know about those who "disappear"; they remember the headless corpses and the man whose tongue had been pulled through the hole in his throat like a necktie. That is why they came here — to zip code 90057, Los Angeles, California.

Now they are counting their friends and neighbors, Salvadoran and Mexican, who are suddenly gone. Some are still in the County Jail on Bauchet Street, brown grains of sand lost among the 13,000 other alleged *saqueadores* (looters) and *incendarios* (arsonists) detained after the most violent American civil disturbance since the Irish poor burned Manhattan in 1863. Those without papers are probably already back in Tijuana, broke and disconsolate, cut off from their families and new lives. Violating city policy, the police and Sheriff's Department fed hundreds of hapless undocumented *saqueadores* to the INS for deportation before the ACLU or immigrant-rights groups even realized they had been arrested.

For many days, the television talked

making sense: who are the looters?

Michael Schumann/SABA

Burning All Illusions in LA

by Mike Davis

their tenements, talking about their new burden of trouble. In a neighborhood far more crowded than mid-Manhattan and more dangerous than downtown Detroit, with more crack addicts and gang-bangers than registered voters, *la gente* know how to laugh away every disaster except the final one. Yet there was a new melancholy in the air.

Too many people had been losing their jobs: their *pinche* $5.25-an-hour jobs as seamstresses, laborers, busboys and factory workers. In two years of recession, unemployment has tripled in LA's immigrant neighborhoods. At Christmas, more than 20,000 predominantly Latina women and children from throughout the central city waited all night in the cold to collect a free turkey and a blanket from charities. Other visible barometers of distress are the rapidly growing colonies of homeless *compañeros* on the desolate flanks of Crown Hill and in the concrete bed of the LA River, where people are forced to use sewage water for bathing and cooking.

The neighbors in MacArthur Park

only of the "South Central riot," "black rage" and the "Crips and Bloods." But Emerio's parents know that thousands of their neighbors from the MacArthur Park district — home to nearly one-tenth of all the Salvadorans in the world — also looted, burned, stayed out past curfew and went to jail. (An analysis of the first 5,000 arrests from all around the city revealed that 52 percent were poor Latinos, 10 percent whites and only 38 percent blacks.) They also know that the nation's first multiracial riot was as much about empty bellies and broken hearts as it was about police batons and Rodney King.

The week before the riot was unseasonably hot. At night the people lingered outside on the stoops and sidewalks of

whom I interviewed, such as Emerio's parents, all speak of this gathering sense of unease, a perception of a future already looted. For them, the riot arrived like a magic dispensation. People were initially shocked by the violence, then mesmerized by the televised images of biracial crowds in South Central LA helping themselves to mountains of desirable goods without interference from the police. The next day, Thursday, April 30, the authorities blundered twice: first by suspending school and releasing the kids into the streets, and second by announcing that the National Guard was on the way to help enforce a dusk-to-dawn curfew.

Thousands immediately interpreted this as a last call to participate in the general redistribution of wealth in progress. Looting spread with explosive force throughout Hollywood and MacArthur Park, as well as parts of Echo Park, Van Nuys and Huntington Park. Although arsonists spread terrifying destruction, the looting crowds were governed by a visible moral economy. As one middle-aged lady explained to me, "Stealing is a sin, but this is like a television game show where everyone in the audience gets to win." Unlike the looters in Hollywood (some on skateboards) who stole Madonna's bustier and all the crotchless panties from Frederick's, the masses of MacArthur Park concentrated on the prosaic necessities of life like cockroach spray and Pampers.

A week after the riots, MacArthur Park finds itself in a state of siege. A special "We Tip" hotline invites people to inform on neighbors or acquaintances suspected of looting. Elite LAPD Metro Squad units, supported by the National Guard, sweep through the tenements in search of stolen goods, while Border Patrolmen from as far away as Texas prowl the streets. Frantic parents search for missing kids, like mentally retarded 14-year-old Zuly Estrada, who is believed to have been deported to Mexico.

Meanwhile, thousands of *saqueadores*, many of them pathetic scavengers captured in the charred ruins the day after the looting, languish in County Jail, unable to meet absurdly high bails. One man, caught with a packet of sunflower seeds and two cartons of milk, is being held on $15,000; hundreds of others face felony indictments and possible two-year prison terms. Prosecutors demand 30-day jail sentences for curfew violators, despite the fact that many of those are either homeless street people or Spanish-speakers unaware of the curfew. These are the "weeds" that George Bush says we must pull from the soil of our cities before it can be sown with the regenerating "seeds" of enterprise zones and tax breaks for private capital.

There is rising apprehension that the entire community will become a scapegoat. An ugly, seal-the-border nativism has been growing like crabgrass in Southern California since the start of the recession. A lynch mob of Orange County Republicans, led by Representative Dana Rohrabacher of Huntington Beach, demands the immediate deportation of all the undocumented immigrants arrested in the disturbance, while liberal Democrat Anthony Beilenson, sounding like the San Fernando Valley's Son-of-Le Pen, proposes to strip citizenship from the U.S.-born children of illegals. According to Roberto Lovato of MacArthur Park's Central American Refugee Center, "We are

becoming the guinea pigs, the Jews, in the militarized laboratory where George Bush is inventing his new urban order."

Little Gangster Tak can't get over his amazement that he is actually standing in the same room of Brother Aziz's mosque as a bunch of Inglewood Crips. The handsome, 22-year-old Tak, a "straight up" Inglewood Blood who looks like a black angel by Michelangelo, still has two Crip bullets in his body, and "they still carry a few of mine." Some of the Crips and Bloods, whose blue or red gang colors have been virtual tribal flags, remember one another from school playground days, but mainly they have met over the barrels of automatics in a war that has divided Inglewood — the pleasant, black-majority city southwest of LA where the Lakers play — by a river of teenage blood.

Now, as Tak explains, "Everybody knows what time it is. If we don't end the killing now and unite as black men, we never will."

Although Imam Aziz and the Nation of Islam have provided the formal auspices for peacemaking, the real hands that have "tied the red and blue rags together into a 'black thang'" are in Simi Valley. Within a few hours of the first attack on white motorists, which started in Eight-Trey (83rd Street) Gangster Crip territory near Florence and Normandie, the insatiable war between the Crips and Bloods, fueled by a thousand neighborhood vendettas and dead homeboys, was "put on hold" throughout Los Angeles and the adjacent black suburbs of Compton and Inglewood.

Unlike the 1965 rebellion, which broke out south of Watts and remained primarily focused on the poorer east side of the ghetto, the 1992 riot reached its maximum temperature along Crenshaw Boulevard — the very heart of black Los Angeles's more affluent Westside. Despite the illusion of full-immersion "actuality" provided by the mini-cam and the helicopter, television's coverage of the riot's angry edge was even more twisted than the melted steel of Crenshaw's devastated shopping centers. Most reporters — "image looters," as they are now being

called in South Central — merely lip-synched suburban clichés as they tramped through the ruins of lives they had no desire to understand.

Local television unwittingly mimed the McCone Commission's summary judgment that the August 1965 Watts riot was primarily the act of a hoodlum fringe. In that case, a subsequent UCLA study revealed that the "riot of the riffraff" was in fact a popular uprising involving at least 50,000 working-class adults and their teenage children. When the arrest records of this latest uprising are finally analyzed, they will probably also vindicate the judgment of many residents that all segments of black youth, gang and non-gang, "buppie" as well as underclass, took part in the disorder.

Although in Los Angeles, as elsewhere, the new black middle class has socially and spatially pulled farther apart from the de-industrialized black working class, the LAPD's Operation Hammer and other anti-gang dragnets that arrested kids at random (entering their names and addresses into an electronic gang roster that is now proving useful in house-to-house searches for riot "ringleaders") have tended to criminalize black youth without class distinction. Between 1987 and 1990, the combined sweeps of the LAPD and the County Sheriff's Office ensnared 50,000 "suspects." Even the children of doctors and lawyers from View Park and Windsor Hills have had to "kiss the pavement" and occasionally endure some of the humiliations that the homeboys in the flats face every day — experiences that reinforce the reputation of the gangs (and their poets laureate, gangster rappers like Ice Cube and N.W.A.) as the heroes of an outlaw generation.

Yet if the riot had a broad social base, it was the participation of the gangs — or, rather, their cooperation — that gave it constant momentum and direction. If the 1965 rebellion was a hurricane, leveling 100 blocks of Central Avenue from Vernon to the Imperial Highway, the 1992 riot was a tornado, no less destructive but snaking a zigzag course through the commercial areas of the ghetto and beyond. Most of the media saw no pattern in its path, just blind, nihilistic destruction.

In fact, the arson was ruthlessly sys-

Los Angeles: John Goubeaux

tematic. By Friday morning, 90 percent of the myriad Korean-owned liquor stores, markets and swap meets in South Central LA had been wiped out. Deserted by the LAPD, which made no attempt to defend small businesses, the Koreans suffered damage or destruction to almost 2,000 stores from Compton to the heart of Koreatown itself. One of the first to be attacked (although, ironically, it survived) was the grocery store where 15-year-old Latasha Harlins was shot in the back of the head last year by Korean grocer Soon Ja Du in a dispute over a $1.79 bottle of orange juice. The girl died with the money for her purchase in her hand.

Latasha Harlins. A name that was scarcely mentioned on television was the key to the catastrophic collapse of relations between LA's black and Korean communities. Ever since white judge Joyce Karlin let Du off with a $500 fine and some community service — a sentence that declared that the taking of a black child's life was scarcely more serious than drunk driving — some inter-ethnic explosion has been virtually inevitable. The several near-

riots at the Compton courthouse this winter were early warning signals of the black community's unassuaged grief over Harlins's murder. On the streets of South Central Wednesday and Thursday, I was repeatedly told, "This is for our baby sister. This is for Latasha."

The balance of grievances in the community is complex. Rodney King is the symbol that links unleashed police racism in Los Angeles to the crisis of black life everywhere, from Las Vegas to Toronto. Indeed, it is becoming clear that the King case may be almost as much of a watershed in American history as Dred Scott, a test of the very meaning of the citizenship for which African-Americans have struggled for 400 years..

But on the grass-roots level, especially among gang youth, Rodney King may not have quite the same profound resonance. As one of the Inglewood Bloods told me, "Rodney King? Shit, my homies be beat like dogs by the police every day. This riot is about all the homeboys *murdered* by the police, about the little sister killed by the Koreans, about 27 years of oppression.

Rodney King is just the trigger."

At the same time, those who predicted that the next LA riot would be a literal Armageddon have been proved wrong. Despite a thousand Day Glo exhortations on the walls of South Central to "Kill the Police," the gangs have refrained from the deadly guerrilla warfare that they are so formidably equipped to conduct. As in 1965, there has not been a single LAPD fatality, and indeed few serious police injuries of any kind.

There may be other agendas as well. I saw graffiti in South Central that advocated "Day one: burn them out. Day two: we rebuild." The only national leader whom most Crips and Bloods seem to take seriously is Louis Farrakhan, and his goal of black economic self-determination is broadly embraced. (Farrakhan, it should be emphasized, has never advocated violence as a means to this end.) At the Inglewood gang summit, which took place May 5, there were repeated references to a renaissance of black capitalism out of the ashes of Korean businesses. "After all," an ex-Crip told me later, "we didn't burn our community, just their stores."

In the meantime, the police and military occupiers of Los Angeles give no credence to any peaceful, let alone entrepreneurial, transformation of LA's black gang cultures. The ecumenical movement of the Crips and Bloods is their worst imagining: gang violence no longer random, but politicized into a black *intifada*. The LAPD remembers only too well that a generation ago the Watts rebellion produced a gang peace, out of which grew the Los Angeles branch of the Black Panther

Party. As if to prove their suspicions, the police have circulated a copy of an anonymous and possibly spurious leaflet calling for gang unity and "an eye for an eye.... If LAPD hurt a black we'll kill two."

For its part, the Bush Administration has federalized the repression in LA with an eye to the spectacle of the president marching in triumph, like a Roman emperor, with captured Crips and Bloods in chains. Thus, the Justice Department has dispatched to LA the same elite task force of federal marshals who captured Manuel Noriega in Panama as reinforcements for LAPD and FBI efforts to track down the supposed gang instigators of the riot. But as a veteran of the 1965 riot said while watching SWAT teams arrest some of the hundreds of rival gang members trying to meet peacefully at Watts's Jordan Downs Housing Project, "That ole fool Bush think we as dumb as Saddam. Land Marines in Compton and get hisself re-elected. But this ain't Iraq. This is Vietnam, Jack."

A core grievance fueling the Watts rebellion and the subsequent urban insurrections of 1967-68 was rising black unemployment in the midst of a boom economy. What contemporary journalists fearfully described as the beginning of the "Second Civil War" was as much a protest against black America's exclusion from the military-Keynesian expansion of the 1960s as it was an uprising against police racism and de facto segregation in schools and housing. The 1992 riot and its possible progenies must likewise be understood as insurrections against an intolerable political-economic order. As even the *Los Angeles Times*, main cheerleader for "World City LA," now editorially acknowledges, the "globalization of Los Angeles" has produced "devastating poverty for those weak in skills and resources."

Although the $1 billion worth of liquor stores and mini-malls destroyed in LA may seem like chump change next to the $2.6 trillion recently annihilated on the Tokyo Stock Exchange, the burning of Oz probably fits into the same Hegelian niche with the bursting of the Bubble Economy: not the "end of history" at the seacoast of Malibu but the beginning of an ominous dialectic on the rim of the Pacific. It was a hallucination in the first place to imagine that the wheel of the world economy could be turned indefinitely by U.S. trade deficits and a fictitious yen.

This structural crisis of the Japan-California "co-prosperity sphere," however, threatens to translate class contradictions into inter-ethnic conflict on both the national and local level. In the case of Los Angeles, it was, tragically, the neighborhood Korean liquor store, not the skyscraper corporate fortress downtown, that became the symbol of a despised new world order. On their side, the half-million Korean-Americans in LA have been psychologically lacerated by the failure of the state to protect them against black rage. Indeed, several young Koreans told me that they were especially bitter that the South Central shopping malls controlled by Alexander Haagen, a wealthy contributor to local politics, were quickly defended by the police and National Guard, while their stores were leisurely ransacked and burned to the ground.

The prospects for a multicultural reconciliation in Los Angeles depend much less on white knight Peter Ueberroth's committee of corporate rebuilders than upon a general economic recovery in Southern California. As the *Los Angeles Business Journal* complained (after noting that LA had lost 100,000 manufacturing jobs during the past three years), "The riots are like poison administered to a sick patient."

• • • • • • • • • • • • • • • • • •

by an-y means nec-es-sary

[archaic, origins uncertain]

Printed on T-shirt of man filmed kicking fallen trucker at intersection of Normandie and Florence; believed to be slogan taken from LAPD training manual.

(Source: *LA Weekly*, May 8, 1992)

Forecasts still under wraps at the Southern California Association of Governments paint a dark future for the Land of Sunshine, as job growth, slowed by the decline of aerospace as well as manufacturing shifts to Mexico, lags far behind population increase. Unemployment rates — not counting the estimated 40,000 jobs lost as a result of the riots, and the uprising's impact on the business climate — are predicted to remain at 8 to 10 percent (and 40 to 50 percent for minority youth) for the next generation, while the housing crisis, already the most acute in the nation, will spill over into new waves of homelessness. Thus, the "widening divide" of income inequality in Los Angeles County, described in a landmark 1988 study by UCLA professor Paul Ong, will become an unbridgeable chasm. Southern California's endless summer is finally over.

Affluent Angelenos instinctively sensed this as they patrolled their Hancock Park estates with shotguns or bolted in their BMWs for white sanctuaries in Orange and Ventura counties. From Palm Springs poolsides, they anxiously awaited news of the burning of Beverly Hills by the Crips and Bloods and fretted over the extra set of house keys they had foolishly entrusted to the Latina maid. Was she now an incendiarist? Although their fears were hysterically magnified, tentacles of disorder did penetrate such sanctums of white life as the Beverly Center and Westwood Village, as well as the Melrose and Fairfax neighborhoods. Most alarmingly, the LAPD's "thin blue line," which had protected them in 1965, was now little more than a defunct metaphor — the last of Chief Daryl Gates's bad jokes. ■

Mike Davis is an LA-based writer and political activist and the author of City of Quartz: Excavating the Future in Los Angeles. *This story first appeared in* The Nation.

THE TRICKLE-DOWN THEORY OF LOOTING

Illustration by R.J. Matson/The New York Observer

Real-Life Looters *by Richard Rothstein*

The television reporter on the scene was incredulous. A looter, unconcerned about TV cameras, police or the stares of fellow neighborhood residents, walked by, arms laden with stolen property. The reporter raced, trying to shove her microphone in the looter's face: "Why are you doing this?" The looter shrugged. "Don't you feel guilty?" the reporter pleaded. "No," the looter said matter-of-factly, and walked off.

Another looter came by, also laden with someone else's property. "Why are you doing this?" This time, the looter turned to the reporter and gloated, "Because it's free!"

Back to the news anchors. "Of course it's not free," one of them pontificated. The cost of looting, he said, is enormous: businesses destroyed, jobs lost to the community, lives wasted, children destined to go hungry, a generation's opportunities devastated. No, it's not free.

The looters, those grinning, laden-down, amoral thieves, didn't stop to give their names to our on-the-scene television reporter. Who might they have been? We can only guess at their identities. But let's try. Perhaps we've run across them before.

One of the looters seemed to emerge from a store that sold electronic devices. Could he have been John Welch, Jr., chairman of General Electric, who oversaw the increasing growth of RCA production work at his plant in Kuala Lumpur, Malaysia, where unions are illegal; where teenage girls from rural villages can be had for factory assembly work at a wage of 45 cents an hour, so long as their fingers are nimble; and where the supply of other girls to replace them is seemingly limitless? Did Welch feel guilty about the devastation of communities like Bloomington, Indiana, where 500 RCA workers lost their jobs in the 1980s? Welch may have thought the profits were free. Perhaps the TV anchor wanted to remind him of the cost to Malaysian girls crowded with a dozen others into one-room dormitories so they can work round-the clock shifts. Or perhaps the anchor was thinking of a Bloomington woman, forced to sell her home after being laid off because the only job available now is table-waiting, at one-third her former wages.

Could one of the looters have been Raymond Hay, chairman and chief executive officer of the LTV Corporation, who put his firm into bankruptcy in 1986, claiming it couldn't afford to pay $2 billion in debt to its employee pension fund? Hay expected the government's pension-insurance plan to make up the difference, and it did. But within a year, when LTV returned to profitability, the company refused to resume responsibility for the pension payments. What the hey! said Hay. We thought pensions for our 100,000 steelworkers were free! We'll let sucker taxpayers underwrite them. And no, we don't feel guilty about taking our profits home.

Was one of the looters John Nevin, chief executive of Firestone Tire and Rubber Company, who collected a $5.6-million bonus payment in 1986, two years before Firestone was sold to a Japanese firm? Nevin had certainly earned his bonus

making sense: who are the looters?

Los Angeles: Cynthia Wiggins

— by shrinking the company payroll by almost 60,000 workers during the previous seven years alone. Perhaps the TV anchor was trying to remind this looter that $5.6 million can never really be free. Firestone once had a plant in Los Angeles, employing approximately 3,000 workers under a union contract that provided decent wages, health benefits and pension protection. Was our on-the-scene reporter trying to ascertain whether Nevin felt guilty about today's desperate residents of South Central Los Angeles, who no longer have the industrial jobs with which families can be supported in decency? Or was she asking about the fact that Firestone took Nevin's $5.6 million as a business expense tax deduction, helping to starve our public coffers of the funds needed for education, health care and public safety?

Perhaps the looter was Frank Shrontz, chairman and chief executive of Boeing in Seattle, or Shrontz's vice president, Forest Coffey. Boeing is Washington state's largest employer and, like other giant corporations, threatens to relocate unless it can avoid taxes that ordinary businesses must pay. During the last two years alone, Washington paid blackmail of $900 million to Boeing in sales-tax exemptions. If Coffey had been asked whether he felt any guilt about stealing $900 million from Washington's public schools, he might have responded, as he did

last year, "Why should I give [the schools] more money? What do I get?"

Was Don Dixon, owner of a savings and loan in Texas, one of the looters spotted by our shocked reporter? Dixon took depositors' money and "lent" it to friends who had no means of repayment — the loans were for as much as $90 million each. For this kind of hard work, Vernon Savings and Loan paid Dixon more than $2 million per year in salary and bonuses in the mid-1980s, not including outright gifts to Dixon of a $2-million beach house and a $5.5-million art collection. On second thought, though, the looter on TV probably wasn't Dixon. Dixon could never have claimed his loot was "free" — Vernon S&L paid out almost $50,000 to host fundraising parties on a yacht in the Potomac for congressmen who might influence S&L regulators.

Perhaps the interviewer had run across one of South Central Los Angeles's most notorious looters, Meshulam Riklis, husband of singer Pia Zadora. Eight years ago, Riklis, owner of the McCrory retail chain, took over Zody's discount stores, which provided merchandise as well as hundreds of jobs to South Central residents. Though profitable, Zody's cash flow was not as lucrative as the real estate on which the stores sat, so Riklis eliminated Zody's severance-pay policy for its 3,000 employees,

then closed the stores and sold the land. Meanwhile, Riklis rewarded himself with a gift from McCrory of stock in a McCrory subsidiary. Three years later, he sold the stock, clearing more than $1 billion. Riklis proved it: Loot really is for free.

Or perhaps the looter was F. Ross Johnson, once president of RJR Nabisco, who "put the company into play" by trying to buy his own firm from its stockholders for $17 billion. As president, Johnson presumably knew what his company was worth, and in the bidding war that followed raised his offer to $25 billion. Was our on-the-scene reporter trying to find out whether Johnson felt guilty about trying to trick his own stockholders into selling their shares for $8 billion less than he knew those shares were worth? Or was the reporter trying to find out how Johnson felt when he lost the bidding war to merger artists (who bought the company with borrowed money) pledged to sell off most of the company in pieces to pay off their debts? Johnson probably didn't feel too bad. He also got some loot for free — as president, he had committed the company to give him $4 million in severance pay if control of the company changed.

Newscasters last week were shocked at the "carnival atmosphere" in which looters smashed store windows and walked off with all the merchandise they could carry. Where have the newscasters been for the last 10 years? The Reagan and Bush administrations have encouraged a decade-long carnival of looters, and the cost was high, paid mostly by former industrial workers who saw their jobs turned into gambling chips in a deregulated financial casino.

Can we have a civilized society if looting is the norm and getting something for free the ideal? As events last week in Los Angeles showed, probably not. ■

Richard Rothstein is a research associate of the Economic Policy Institute and a columnist for the LA Weekly, *where this column first appeared.*

Nobody Listens

by David Weir

Editor's note: A few days after the rioting stopped in LA and San Francisco, a man called the office of Mother Jones *magazine in San Francisco to say that he wanted to return a computer he had looted from a local store, and that he had chosen the magazine for help because he liked its May/June cover story, "Race." He told managing editor David Weir his story.*

When I saw white people being beaten in the street on TV, I smiled ear to ear and jumped up and down with glee, because it told me that I'm not crazy. I hate to say I did that, because I have white friends, but I've been screaming for a long time and nobody has been listening.

I grew up in South Central LA, two miles from the epicenter. I moved to San Francisco because I didn't want to be in the gangs. I called my mother, and she asked if I got a TV. Everyone went for TVs down there. Up here, I went for a computer. I've been trying to get a computer for two years. Nowadays, if you don't have one, you can't compete. You can just end up in the streets, and I don't want that to happen to me.

I've been thinking for a long time that I'm crazy. There was one day, about a year ago, that I felt like going out and killing somebody. The denial in this country about what's really going on is so deep. For black men, we thought we were going crazy. But this event [the LA riot] convinced me I was not nuts.

I watch the news all the time, and they're going back to talking that same talk as before: "Law and order. Keep the peace." They're not putting the blame on the right people. The people rioting are not guilty. This country sacrificed these people.

I believe those jurors in the King case believed they were doing their job sincerely. They are not racists in that old way. Nowadays, everyone says this is all so senseless. But we're screaming at the top of our lungs.

It wasn't senseless. The cause and effect were perfect. We've all been reading in the paper that all of those store owners want more cops. They are scared of the black guys who are sleeping in the doorways of their stores. And they sic the cops on us, and the cops are vicious. Is anyone amazed that they grabbed this stuff?

Personally, I stopped because I was touched by Rodney King's plea. I didn't want to hurt him anymore. Look at Rodney King. Look at the black-and-white photo a year ago and the man we have now. I'm trying to make that transition. It took him a year to make it. The beating he got was a good thing for him, because it got him to a place where people care about him and are helping him. I'm trying to get to that place. But even Rodney King, in his plea, he started to say "I love everybody," but he stopped himself. He couldn't say it yet. He said he loved "people of color." I'm trying to get to that place where I can love everybody.

What I want to say is that reparations is the only way. It's guilt with honor. It's the only answer for this particular problem. Blacks would have money and we could empower ourselves. Rebuild our own businesses.

It's all there in hip-hop. Ice Cube warned you. Ice-T warned you. To the

● ● ● ● ● ● ● ● ● ● ● ● ● ● ● ● ● ● ●

In the mid-'60s, LA's auto-manufacturing industry, then the second-largest in the country, employed approximately 15,000 workers. The Van Nuys GM plant's upcoming shutdown will bring that number to zero.

(Source: *LA Weekly,* 5/8/92)

Koreans, "Give respect to the black fist or we'll burn your store to a crisp." It's not really their fault, the Koreans, we know that; but they don't have to be so rude.

The envelope was turned inside out for us, and we could see the seams. The riots straightened everything out. If the powers-that-be don't do something, if they don't pick up the ball and run in the right direction, there's no reason for us not to do it again. If you're not going to let us live, then nobody is going to live. Listen to me! That scared me! But I'll be there. I don't have any options.

One day my brother, when he was 27, came home wearing only boxer shorts and one sock, and he had tire tracks, car-tire tracks, across his chest. When I asked him what happened, he said he didn't know. He didn't know what happened to him. Later on, he was shot in the arm, and he lost the use of his arm. That's what it's like to live in South Central. My sister was raped by nine guys. It's that desperate a situation. That's what happens there every day. I'm gone from there, but I carry it with me. I see white people, and they're living in a different world, man, a dreamworld.

I think I've lost the ability to cry. My lip will tremble and my eyes get hot, but no tears will fall anymore. Now they say, "We gotta have peace." That makes me mad. If they [the feds] acquit those four cops, it will take the lid off like you've never seen. They just got a warning. That's all. Rodney King is not going to stop it next time.

They look at us like we're a bunch of killers — that we're waiting for the chance to kill people. We're a bunch of people waiting for a chance to live. I stole the computer that I've been wanting. It was my chance to get it. But then I decided I don't want to get it this way.

We talk this way about whites: "You know the way they are. Why are they that way?" That's what we say to each other. My question for you is: What is wrong with white people? Why don't they see us?" ■

David Weir is the managing editor of Mother Jones, *where this interview first appeared.*

Peace Pact

by April Lynch

Los Angeles: Ted Soqui

Bandit, his red shirttail hanging out beneath the hem of his black jacket, grabbed a younger member of his gang by the shoulder and gave the "baby g" a hard shove.

"Why do we have to go with some truce thing right now?" the younger boy, 15, was asking angrily, trying to shake Bandit's grasp. "Why now? The Crabs [Crips] have been smoking us for years. *Years*, man! Why should we respect them now?"

Bandit, a 21-year-old member of the Inglewood Queen Street Bloods, gave the boy another push, staring him straight in the eyes.

"Why? Why the hell not? Do you know how many homies I've seen go down? We've all grown up spending our time hanging at the f——— funeral home!

"We've got to stop now if we have a chance," Bandit continued, shoving the younger Blood a third time. "Otherwise, people are going to start getting rolled [killed] again. And if the rolling starts, you, my man, will be one of them that goes down."

Throughout the streets of Los Angeles County, such arguments resound as all eyes follow the truce between Bloods and Crips in South Central Los Angeles that began on the heels of last month's riots.

More than 900 street gangs claim turf in the county, according to estimates by the Los Angeles District Attorney. More than 770 people died in gang-related violence last year. In a sprawling, extremely diverse region like Los Angeles, the term "gang" can mean many things, and from gang to gang the idea of a truce can mean something very different.

Members of the mostly black sets, or gang factions, involved in the truce are working to give the peace effort direction and momentum. Other black gangs in areas like Compton and Inglewood are not officially part of the cease-fire but are following and respecting the truce.

Police from Los Angeles to Lynwood said there have been no deaths related to Blood-Crip rivalries in the month since the truce was declared. Law-enforcement officers, who doubt the truce will last or spread, at least say they are relieved that the deadly gang violence they usually see every day has stopped in one part of the city.

"A lot of these guys are hard-core, and I don't believe everything that has gone on here can turn around just like that," said one police officer as he sat in his patrol car on a corner of Western Avenue in South Central. "But I haven't had to call an ambulance for a drive-by shooting in a couple of weeks, and that's good."

Still, among Latinos, Asians and whites in gangs removed from the truce, fights and shootings continue. Young men in Latino and Asian gangs are watching the fragile peace between black gangs with curiosity and skepticism.

At the heart of the truce are two sets of Bloods and five sets of Crips from South Central. Altogether, the seven sets represent thousands of gang members, "baby g-sters" and "wannabes" (younger kids who spend time with gang members but have not officially joined a set).

Thousands of Bloods and Crips, who have been battling and killing each other on Los Angeles streets for more than 20 years, have gotten together for highly publicized parties and picnics in recent weeks. Leaders of the truce campaign know, however, that it will take more than partying to keep the peace going.

"It's been beautiful," said Q. Bone, a 27-year-old Crip from the 5-Deuce Broadway set. "People I used to fight — well, I'm hugging them now. Out of the rioting, something good came into the world. But we need to work to make this last. Only we can do that. We came from the street. We've got the foundations to work with the street."

Q. Bone, whose given name is Charles Rachal, has seen more pain and death on those streets than he cares to remember. He has seen deadly gunfire between Crips and Bloods and among rival Crip sets. He has served time in state prison. Until a few weeks ago, even visiting his six-year-old daughter, Quanish, was a cause for battle, since she and her mother live in a Blood neighborhood. Before the truce, Q. Bone had to sneak into their area; now he takes Quanish to a park near her house without fear.

He and other older gang members are trying to put job programs together for

making sense:who are the looters?

their neighborhoods, where the unemployment rate among young people is more than 45 percent. "We've got to show people that this eye-for-an-eye stuff is out the door," Q. Bone said. "But we have to do it ourselves. All that hand-out stuff from the '60s was messed up. We're the generation of the '90s, and we've got to show action."

The people who need to see the action most, according to older gang members, are the younger members. Younger "g's" in their early and mid-teens are still proving themselves, and they are usually among the first to seek angry revenge when a member of their set has been shot or killed.

Lemonhead, a 17-year-old member of a Blood set called the Pueblo Bishops, checked with his "bigger homeboys" when a group of outside gang members showed up at his housing project to talk about the truce a few weeks ago. Now, he said, he and his gang are "part of the peace."

"The gangs will still be here," he said. "It's part of where you live and where you're from. But now people are more at ease."

"I figure this is the time to come together," he said. "If the guys have been willing to die for red and blue before, they should be willing to die for black now. Some g's may not agree, but it's something everyone will have to realize for themselves."

Besides the Bloods and Crips, however, many gang members doubt such a truce will ever spread to their groups. For some Latino gangs in South Central, who share the streets with Crips and Bloods, the current peace among black gang members has opened up room for Latino gangs to settle scores with other Latino rivals.

"The Rodney King thing put the blacks together, but it wasn't necessarily our issue, said Hecter, 19, who uses the name "Savior" when he cruises with a Latino gang in the South Park area of South Central. "We all know about the police and brutality and we also all know how many of the homeboys have been killed by guys from outside. That is something no one can forget or forgive. No one."

In the Mexican and Mexican-American barrios of East Los Angeles, where the city's first street gangs were formed more than 20 years ago to protect local youngsters from groups of hostile whites, talk of the South Central truce can be heard in parks, in living rooms and on street corners.

But much of the talk is laced with skepticism: "I don't think the truce is going to last," said Johnny, a gang member who just got out of "the joint" a few weeks ago. It will be like what happens here — some people stay cool, but then some crazy loser will go and start something up."

Johnny and his homeboys live and hang out at the Varrio Nueva Estrada Courts housing project, one of the largest in the East Los Angeles area. The walls of the project's two-story wood buildings are decorated with vivid murals reflecting the area's strong pride in its Mexican and Chicano heritage. One wall is painted with scenes from Aztec mythology. Another proclaims in large letters: "We Are Not A Minority!" Others are covered with highly stylized letters reading "VNE" — the mark of the neighborhood gang.

On a clear day, westward from Varrio Nueva Estrada, the glass office towers of downtown Los Angeles can be seen glistening in the sun only a few miles away. But many of the young men who live in the project have never even been there.

"We don't go looking for trouble," said Johnny. He is taller, stronger and older than the other young men, and they quickly fall silent when he speaks. "But if someone comes down from another neighborhood, we'll protect ourselves."

More than 30 miles away in Long Beach, the faces of the gangs are different, but feelings about the truce are much the same. Unemployment has skyrocketed in

• • • • • • • • • • • • • • • • • • • •

AFDC receipents, 1990

South Central LA: 96,238, or 18 percent of residents
LA County: 592,403, or 7 percent of residents

(Source: United Way)

the struggling industrial and shipping center as factories have shut down or moved out of state.

Families of Cambodian immigrants began moving to the city's black and Latino "Anaheim Corridor" neighborhood about 10 years ago. The new arrivals were looking for affordable housing. They also found street gangs. Cambodian-American youths, after being beaten up in school, quickly formed gangs of their own. Now shoot-outs between Cambodian and Latino gangs have become a regular part of life in the neighborhood, and the gang members don't expect the violence to end anytime soon.

"We've all heard about the Bloods-Crips truce, but I don't think it will come here," said one 17-year-old Cambodian-American, as he watched his little brother play in a sandbox in a local park. The young man's street name is Solo. Members of the Asian Boyz gang call him that, he said, because he only hangs out with them "part-time, for protection, and the rest of the time I'm by myself or at home. I have to help my family out."

"It would be nice to see no more killing," he said. "But who would stop it? There is too much distrust."

Crips and Bloods in South Central said they understand such feelings. Until recently, they lived with them every day. Some young men struggle with distrust and bitter memories as they reach out to shake hands with former enemies. But now, they say, they at least have to try to promote the peace.

"Check out this guy," said Lemonhead, pointing to a young man wearing sunglasses and tapping a thin white cane on the ground before him as he walked into a meeting of Bloods and Crips. "He's blind. He got shot in the face, right in the eyes with 29 buckshots from a 12-gauge shotgun. If he can accept the truce idea, then other people can, too. They just have to open their minds and see what's going on for themselves." ■

April Lynch is a staff writer for the San Francisco Chronicle, *where a version of this story first appeared.*

105

Among the most glaring deficiencies unearthed in the tumult surrounding the Rodney King verdict was the absence of credible African-American leadership. And although black mayors now reign in several of the cities where violence erupted, their pleas for peace were just as ineffective as were the entreaties of their white predecessors during the fire of the '60s.

The angry and alienated African-American youth who made up the core — though surely not the entirety — of those wreaking destruction in their own South Central Los Angeles neighborhoods paid little heed to Mayor Tom Bradley's appeals for calm. "Black youth hate the ghetto," noted Los Angeles rap artist Ice-T. "It's as simple as that; they're only living here, for the most part, because their parents are too poor to live somewhere else." For many of these young people, Ice-T said, the destruction of their neighborhoods is no great loss. That black youth could reach such a conclusion is testament to the level of their social isolation. That such isolation is common even in a city run by a black mayor is an increasingly frustrating reality.

Photo of Malcolm X: UPI/Bettmann

Leaders Lacking in a Black and White World

by Salim Muwakkil

Despite the clear evidence that black electoral successes have done little to ease the deepening crisis in black America, most black leaders continue to focus their mobilization efforts on the political arena. Even a putatively independent leader like Rev. Jesse Jackson, shadow Senator for Washington, D.C., and president of the National Rainbow Coalition (NRC), drops his anchor in political waters. While African-Americans are being buried beneath an avalanche of negative statistics, the most visible black leaders seemingly are pushing strategies that mean little to

making sense: where's the leadership?

their beleaguered constituents.

"Those young black brothers out there in the street don't listen to the so-called black leaders because they know they aren't leading anyone but themselves," notes Maulana Karenga, professor of Black Studies at California State University-Long Beach and leader of a black nationalist group that for many years has worked with the youth in South Central LA. "They're simply fed up with preachers and politicians who seem to have no understanding of their situation and of the reasons for their rebellion."

And it's not just the ideologically committed who have duly noted black youth's contempt for more recognized African-American leaders. "There is a major communication gap betweeen our so-called leaders and these people who have taken to the streets," Johnnie Cochran, a black Los Angeles attorney, told *Time* magazine. "Nobody can talk to these people in the streets. Even their parents can't talk to them," he said.

This lack of leadership stood in bold relief after the King verdict when officials in cities across the country began pondering the possibility of trouble erupting in their own backyards. In Chicago, for example, city officials hastily devised plans to help keep their city cool. They knew that, in disputes aggravated by racial grievances, one of the most effective calming measures is an appeal for peace from a leader whom black youth respect. But in Chicago, and probably in other cities as well, there are few leaders who qualified. One name surfaced consistently, however: Louis Farrakhan. Needless to say, city officials were reluctant to request his assistance.

"I can't think of any black leader other than Minister Farrakhan who could command the attention of our angry and frustrated black youth," said black Chicago Alderwoman Dorothy Tillman. Tillman had provoked local controversy for refusing to urge her constituents to remain calm in the wake of the King verdict. "Not only could Minister Farrakhan get young people's attention, but he also can transform them from a criminal preying on their own neighborhood to a hard-working asset to the neighborhood."

But many black analysts insist the focus on leadership is misguided. "Who are the Chinese or Japanese leaders?" asks Walter Williams, a conservative economics professor at George Mason University in Virginia. "Who are the Irish leaders? Can you name them? The assumption that black people need leaders to show them where to go is demeaning and wrong."

Karenga's characterization of the LA insurrection as a "rebellion," while the mainstream media and most comentators have settled on "riot," recalls similar divisions from the '60s. For those involved in the black movement of that period, the word "riot" was politically incorrect; the words "rebellion," "insurrection" or even "revolution" were *de rigueur*. This time around, except for ideologues like Karenga, not much fuss is made over such semantic distinctions.

But according to many observers, the word rebellion may be even more appropriate now than in the '60s. "I can tell you for sure that a lot of gang-bangers had detailed plans for what to do if those cops were found innocent," said Lawrence Fortenberry, a Los Angeles writer. "These brothers hate the police with all their hearts, and in many cases they're better armed." He said the war between the police gang and the street gang is the underlying reality of the unrest in Los Angeles.

When Ted Koppel interviewed reputed gang members on the *Nightline* program of May 4, two of them expressed their determination to fight in what they conceived to be their war against the police, comparing themselves to the rock-throwing Palestinian youth of the *intifada*. In fact, many observers familiar with LA's gang culture discern an increase in political sophistication.

According to Fortenberry, some gang leaders have even noted that the U.S. Marines sent to staging areas in the city were Gulf war veterans, and that the Army troops were members of a unit that invaded Panama. "They are making connections between military and police and concluding that both of these representatives of U.S. power spend most of their time subduing non-white people," he said. Interestingly, Israel joined much of the world in criticizing the U.S. for its treatment of African-Americans. But then, without a hint of irony, it compared South Central LA to its own Occupied Territories.

Tensions between the city's police and African-American and Latino youth have always been high, but the economic and social distress of recent years have exacerbated those divisions. Add to that the paramilitary proclivities of disgraced Police Chief Daryl Gates, and the line between the police and minority hoodlums thickens.

The image of the police as a thin blue line of protection against the criminal anarchy seething in America's black ghettos resonates in middle-class neighborhoods. It was also an image cleverly evoked by the defense attorneys for the four officers charged in the King beating. Fear of black crime is at epidemic levels throughout the land, and the Bush Administration's highly vaunted war on drugs has magnified the menace and exaggerated the fear.

Rodney King's neighborhood, mostly black and with an unemployment rate approaching 50 percent, is virtually bereft of economic opportunities. For young black men there, vocational choices often break down to a choice between McJobs or crack jobs. And King's neighborhood is not unique. All across the country, America's inner-cities are beleaguered by a dizzying array of economic and social afflictions. With the U.S. government drastically reducing resource allocations to financially strapped cities during the last 12 years, it is truly remarkable that urban America has not exploded already.

But none of this is new. Rap artists, of course, have been chronicling the deterioration of life in the inner-city for many years. Yet their dispatches from the war zone were often dismissed as raucous exaggerations or as mindless celebrations of ghetto pathology. In addition to rappers' grass roots testimony, scholars have weighed in with research data demonstrating the declining fortunes of the black working and lower classes, even as highly educated African-Americans gain more access to the mainstream.

Faced with the naked fact that 12 years of Reagan-Bush have viciously disinvested resources from those areas of the inner-cities most in need, the president's men have already seized the opportunity to criticize social-welfare programs from Lyndon Johnson's era and push their own approach. Loosely labeled the New Paradigm, these Republican strategies that stress ownership and "empowerment" are promoted most effectively by Secretary of Housing and Urban Development Jack Kemp, who, after being literally ignored during Bush's early years, will now likely serve as the administration's point man on urban issues. Undoubtedly, the voices of black conservatives such as Robert Woodson of the National Center for Neighborhood Enterprise (NCNE), who urges entrepreneurial solutions to the problems of African-Americans, and George Mason University's Williams, who blames most of blacks' ills on a coercive government, will be amplified.

Yet without massive amounts of resources rerouted in their direction, the problems in America's inner-cities will only multiply. Next time, however, the fire may be too hot to handle. ∎

Salim Muwakkil is a senior editor for In These Times, *where this story first appeared.*

Photo of Martin Luther King, Jr.: UPI/Bettmann

LA Leaderless *by Harold Meyerson*

At 8:30 p.m., Wednesday, April 29 — the first night of the Los Angeles riots — Deputy Mayor Mark Fabiani and veteran Tom Bradley aide Phil Depoian huddled in an anteroom of the First A.M.E. Church, deliberating how the hell to get their boss safely out of the building.

In the parking lot outside the church, a crowd of perhaps 1,000 had gathered, which on any other night would have viewed Bradley with anything from affection to indifference. Professionals in suits, matrons holding their grandchildren, young men (none in gang regalia) from across the city, mainstream and fringe

activists, nearly all of them black, they had come to A.M.E. for what had been billed as a meeting to formulate a response to the acquittals that had come down earlier that day in Simi Valley. With the church full before their arrival, those outside listened to their own ad hoc collection of speakers and debated strategies. Just a few blocks away, looting had already begun.

"Don't do it in our community!" one speaker implored. Across the parking lot, people took up chants proposing alternative targets. "Beverly Hills!" shouted one cluster. "Parker Center!" yelled another. A disproportionate number of the suits in the parking lot crowd tried again to enter the church. Inside, Tom Bradley's staffers searched

for a way to get him out.

From the reports Fabiani was receiving, much of the city was going up in flames. Bradley had already cancelled his appearance on *Nightline*; he had to return to City Hall. After about 10 minutes in the anteroom, Fabiani, Depoian and Co. concluded that there wasn't going to be a lull in the parking lot action. With that, Bradley bent down and quick-stepped in an almost Groucho-like crouch toward his limo. He made it, and the car lurched out of the lot as demonstrators banged on the roof and the hood.

In the aftermath of the largest civic disorder in American history, Los Angeles is leaderless. The 1965 Watts riots may have signalled the eclipse of the conservative WASP order personified by then-Mayor Sam Yorty and Police Chief William Parker. But by the mid-'60s, a new governing coalition was already emerging, linking the black and Jewish communities, liberal on social issues, friendly to corporate priorities and soon to be presided over by Tom Bradley.

By contrast, the '92 riot has left only casualties. It's ended Daryl Gates's tenure as leader of California's law-and-order right, recasting him in the mold of the *Pirates of Penzance* police sergeant whose men — taran-ta *ra*! — never advanced. It has dramatized the self-subverting essence of Gatesism: the creation of a police force so committed to the military repression of the inner-city that merely to deploy it is to risk inciting total conflagration. It has revealed the limits of Bradley's regime, forever expanding to include the elites of one new group after another, but powerless to arrest the growth of poverty and of a savagely alienated underclass.

Even worse, unlike 1965, there's no new order on deck. Tom Bradley's

appointment of Peter Ueberroth to head up the rebuilding of South Central is less strategic than nostalgic: a hope that the magic man of the '84 Olympics can convince the very corporations that have abandoned LA over the past two decades to re-industrialize it. And minority Los Angeles emerges from the riots terribly balkanized: blacks and Koreans seething at one another, Chicanos disdaining the Salvadorans who took part in the looting.

In 1966, Ronald Reagan made it to the statehouse in large part due to the reaction to Watts — a harbinger of the national conservative ascendancy that began two years later and persists to this day. The Bush administration is already trying to lay blame for the riots of '92 at the doorstep of '60s liberalism. It may not be as easy a sell this time around. Discussions around town in the riot's aftermath have uncovered a predictable backlash — but also a surprisingly widespread acknowledgement that the downward spiral of the inner-city is linked to the same Reagan-Bush policies of national neglect that in less drastic ways have also injured the white middle class.

Deputy Mayor Mark Fabiani says that the Ueberroth Commission will produce nothing less than "a Marshall Plan for LA." But a Marshall Plan in one city, in an age when corporations routinely flee across state and national borders in search of cheaper labor, is no more credible than "socialism in one country." Banks and corporations will doubtless make a few investments in Los Angeles that they might otherwise have shunned. But absent a federal industrial policy, education policy, and adequate incomes, the notion that businesses will create the kind of high-skill, high-wage jobs required to rebuild the inner-city is sheerest fantasy. The fires of '92 can only be quenched by the elections of '92, and by an electorate determined to create a more cohesive nation. ■

Harold Meyerson is executive editor of the LA Weekly, *where a version of this story first appeared.*

Rodney King and MLK

by Harvey Wasserman

Nearly a quarter-century — within a year and a few days — passed between the murder of Martin Luther King and the acquittal of the cops who beat Rodney King.

What progress has been made in the interim?

The inner-cities ravaged in the uprisings following the King murder were never rebuilt by the time of the King verdict.

We have traded Thurgood Marshall for Clarence Thomas.

Lyndon Johnson for George Bush.

The Vietnam War is over, but its residual cancer has spread to every corner of American life.

We wait for our current rulers to pick another lethal skirmish like Panama or Iraq to boost ratings just in time for the election.

A random, seething ghetto discontent that occasionally exploded into violence has been transformed by a new generation of totally alienated, heavily armed ghetto youth into ceaseless, gut-wrenching, senseless slaughter.

Thanks to the National Rifle Association and the gutless politicians who bend to its every whim, the nation has become a collage of armed camps. The city gangs now operate with arsenals available only to actual armies 25 years ago. They come around in drive-by shootings, the quintessential expression of a nation that in an average eight-hour stretch can witness several dozen equally senseless TV killings with no blood, no pain, no human connection whatsoever. This, since the death of Dr. King, has become the core of our culture.

The Uzis on the street corners. The 15-year-old boy in Cincinnati who walked up to a car and ended 24-year-old pro footballer Shane Curry's life with a bullet to the head. When, in Dr. King's time, did 15-year-olds of any race or creed walk American streets shooting people they never met for no reason at all?

A quarter-century of cynical pillage and uncaring rape at the top has trickled thoroughly, pervasively down.

It has yielded the sickening knowledge that nowhere in America is really safe. Not the downtown streets. Not the white suburbs. Not even the national parks, where a crime wave is now polluting remote wilderness campsites.

Above all, it is defined by the inescapable knowledge that those on top not only don't care about the poor and the non-white, they are more than happy to use them, openly and cynically, at every opportunity.

Willie Horton.

The Thomas nomination.

The "quota" issue.

The nauseating alacrity with which that intellectual giant, White House Press Secretary Marlin Fitzwater, blamed the Los Angeles uprising on "too much welfare." Next week he will blame the famine in Ethiopia on "too much food."

"F—k the Jews," Jim Baker said recently of the supporters of Israel. "They don't vote for us anyway."

"F—k the blacks and poor," Fitzwater was adding. "Most likely they won't vote at all."

Predictably, the saturation media coverage focused on the "looters" walking out of the trashed stores with the TV sets, VCRs and other currency of the electronic age. Perhaps the most material culture on the face of the earth, whose most basic unit of self-worth is access to television, clucked about how an "unruly mob" could be so "lawless."

Sadly, predictably, on the streets it became once again minority against minority. Blacks against Koreans against Hispanics. The usual divide and conquer.

But remember *Dallas? Dynasty?* The sincere honesty of Richard Nixon? The open-hearted warmth and generosity of Nancy Reagan?

Who have been our role models for the past quarter-century?

How about Congress, which just failed to cut a paltry $4 billion from history's most bloated military pork barrel? Bush whined that in a post-Cold War era, with not a credible enemy in sight, a cut of less than 2 percent would tear too much "muscle" out of the armed forces. A supine, corrupt legislature bent over and let it happen.

Together they slashed housing, education, inoculation programs, AIDS prevention, nutrition for small children, sex education for teenagers. Meanwhile, their rich friends and relatives looted the public treasury with worthless weapons programs and at the limitless trough of the S&L catastrophe.

Like Neil Bush. For his pivotal role in the theft of at least $100 million from a Colorado S&L, the president's son was — horror of horrors — barred from investment banking.

How many VCR-equivalents did he carry unseen out of that bank? How many TV sets? How many Pampers, for which desperate mothers risked their lives on the mean streets?

Anyone convicted of looting during the chaos should be administered the "Neil Bush sentence" — they should barred from investment banking for life. That would teach them! But who will teach Bush?

The best coverage of all in the wake of the uprising belonged to Ted Koppel. Like a gritty old-time honest journalist — a thoroughly endangered species — Koppel actually took his mikes to South Central. He actually spoke to a group of the "homeboys," those terrifying black men who have so petrified mainstream Americans for four centuries.

What he heard was articulate, informed critiques, one after the other, about what is wrong with America, where the uprising originated, how they love their

• • • • • • • • • • • • • • • • • • •

Average home price, Los Angeles, 1990: $224,000

Average home price, South Central LA, 1990: $127,000

Maximum home price eligible for federal housing loans: $124,000

(Source: *LA Weekly*, May 8, 1992)

children, how the Rodney King verdict was anticipated by everyone in the city except the Chief of Police, and how the gangs that used to decimate each other are now working together.

A more upscale group at a nearby church was slightly less articulate, except for a rap poet who promised "No Justice/No Peace."

And for Maxine Waters, former City Councilwoman, now the area's Congresswoman. She chided a local man who asked Koppel to "send a message to George Bush."

"The president is a right-wing Republican," she fairly screamed. "He doesn't care! You don't send a message to George Bush. You get rid of him!"

In a quarter-century, what lessons have been learned from the death of Martin Luther King? His leadership has never been replaced. The lethal uprisings that followed his murder helped no one, translated into no positive action, raised no conscience or lasting consciousness among the nation's decision-makers. What came instead was a deep-seated neighborhood hopelessness, fought off with great difficulty by community organizers, but exploited ever since by the likes of Nixon, Reagan and Bush.

Those pundits who smugly argue that non-violence would have accomplished more than rioting ignore what happened to the last great African-American apostle of such methods, and what would almost certainly happen to another who might attain his level of power. It's not easy to preach non-violence with a bullet in the throat.

And it *is* easy to forget that, for non-violence to ultimately work, it requires a civilized response from those in power.

Twenty-four years after the loss of our greatest preacher of non-violent direct action, do we see any evidence of that moral or mental capacity in our government?

And, if not, what right do we have to be surprised when the torches and bullets once again fly, deadlier than ever? ∎

Harvey Wasserman is senior advisor to the Greenpeace Atmosphere and Energy Campaign and the author of Harvey Wasserman's History of the U.S. *This column first appeared in* Columbus Alive!

Los Angeles: Ted Soqui

Surrendering to Poverty

by John Judis

Before holding a cabinet meeting May 4 to discuss his administration's response to the Los Angeles riots, Bush was asked by reporters whether he really had a program to address the festering poverty and unemployment in cities like Los Angeles. The administration had, Bush said, "some very good proposals out on the table right now, proposals who [sic] clearly have come of age." Pressed to be more specific, he mentioned exactly one — home ownership for tenants of public housing.

Later, Press Secretary Marlin Fitzwater mentioned one other initiative — enterprise zones. This program would create Hong Kong-like tax-free zones within depressed towns and cities.

But here are two sad truths about the administration's urban policy. First, until that cabinet meeting, Bush and his chief economic advisors had never offered anything but the most token support either to tenant home ownership or enterprise zones — proposals dear to those conservatives like Secretary of Housing and Urban Development Jack Kemp, who favor a new "war on poverty." Indeed, once the smoke clears from Los Angeles, Bush will probably once again ignore these initiatives.

Secondly, even if Bush does back the programs enthusiastically, they do not add up to an urban strategy. Tenant ownership no more addresses the plight of the millions of Americans who lack adequate housing than enterprise zones come to terms with joblessness in areas like Los Angeles's Watts or Crenshaw districts.

Prior to the riots, several administration officials, including Kemp and White House policy aide James Pinkerton, pressed for anti-poverty measures, but they met continued resistance from Bush's chief domestic policy-makers and indifference from Bush himself. In January 1989, after Kemp took office at HUD, he urged Bush and Chief of Staff John Sununu to adopt the concept of a "conservative war on poverty." But Bush and Sununu believed that making an issue of poverty would benefit the Democrats.

Bush did agree to continue the Low Income Opportunity Board, but the chief administration domestic policy-makers, led by Sununu, Richard Darman, director of the Office of Management and Budget, and Nicholas Brady, the Secretary of the Treasury, ignored its recommendations. In July 1990, the *New York Times* reported that the White House had decided against any new poverty initiatives. "Keep playing with the same toys. But let's paint them a little shinier," was how one White House official summed up the administration's position.

When Kemp loudly protested this statement, Bush agreed to create a new Economic Empowerment Task Force with Kemp as its chairman. But instead of announcing the task force at a press conference with Kemp present, Bush merely initialed an executive order. And during the next two years, the administration ignored the raft of anti-poverty proposals that the task force produced. By the beginning of this year, the task force was defunct.

Ignoring Programs

Bush now claims that the administration championed enterprise zones, but the fact is that, besides Kemp, the measure's most enthusiastic supporters were black Democrats like New York Representative Charles Rangel. In 1990, Rangel, at Kemp's behest, introduced legislation that set up 10-pilot project enterprise zones, where new employers would be exempted from capital-gains taxes and granted tax credits for wages they paid employees.

Treasury officials immediately put out a report warning that the program — even though it planned to encourage businesses where few or none existed — would cost more than a billion dollars. Then, in that October's budget talks, the White House eliminated the proposal for enterprise zones from the final budget agreement.

In this year's State of the Union address, Bush mentioned enterprise zones as one of his domestic initiatives, but in the instruc-

making sense: where's the leadership?

tions that the White House sent the House and Senate budget committees, it put creating enterprise zones well below cutting capital-gains tax rates on its list of priorities.

Kemp's proposal for tenant management and ownership — dubbed HOPE, or Home Ownership and Opportunity for People Everywhere — has suffered a similar fate at Bush's hands. In 1990, Kemp got provisions for HOPE included in the National Affordable Housing Act of 1990, but Congress did not allocate any funds for it. Without money, the program could not go forward, since before buying their own apartments, tenants had to have the funds to rehabilitate and restore them.

The Bush Administration asked supplemental appropriations for HOPE the next January, but in the course of trying to win extra funds for the Gulf War, failed to lobby for HOPE, and it once again received no money. The next fall, Kemp asked for $861 million, but got $361 million. And he got that much only because of the last-minute intercession of another black Democrat, Mississippi Representative Michael Espy. The White House, which is now taking credit for the program, did not lobby for the funds.

Less Hope Today

But what if both programs were fully funded? What difference would they make? Both enterprise zones and HOPE are worthwhile proposals, but by themselves they would do little to alleviate poverty.

During the 1980s, 37 states initiated enterprise-zone programs, and Los Angeles itself set up five enterprise zones inside city limits. But these zones have tended to succeed only in areas that do not already suffer from crime, divided families, low high-school graduation rates and crumbling streets and sanitation.

In California, as a December 1990 *Los Angeles Times* survey discovered, enterprise zones were working in smaller central California towns like Porterville and Madera. But they failed abysmally in Watts. "Watts is a tough sell. Outsiders

know there are better places to set up shop," Paul Hiller, head of the state zone program for the California Department of Commerce, told the *Los Angeles Times*.

During the last decade, while it has had an enterprise zone, unemployment in Watts has grown. Jasper Williams, who was in charge of the Watts zone, told the *Los Angeles Times* in 1990, "The disenchantment is more obvious and people have less hope today."

To have a chance of succeeding in central cities, enterprise zones need to be combined with strong local leadership and major investment in education and infrastructure. "You really have to target the people rather than the geography," says David Osborne, co-author of *Reinventing Government*. But the Bush administration refuses to contemplate spending large amounts of money on inner-city education, transportation, streets and sewers.

Tenant ownership suffers from exactly the same problem. Where it is feasible, it can clearly be beneficial. The new owners of Washington's Kenilworth-Parkside housing project have largely driven drugs and crime out of their neighborhood.

But too few tenants are ready or able to buy their own homes. Public housing tenants average about $600 a month income — often insufficient to pay the utilities, let alone the upkeep of an apartment. And about a third of tenants are senior citizens living on fixed incomes.

Tenant ownership could be an important part of a larger program that included significant funds for new housing and for rent vouchers for the estimated 5 million families that need but are not getting housing assistance. Yet here, too, the Bush administration and conservatives are simply unwilling to spend money.

As the Bush Administration promotes them, both enterprise zones and tenant ownership are palliatives, not solutions. They are political gestures, rather than real policy commitments. But the real irony is that, if the riots had not occurred, Bush would not even have been interested in making gestures. ■

John Judis is a senior editor for In These Times, *where this story first appeared.*

Leaving the Mess to the Cops

by James Ridgeway

I figure Dr. King died for nothing.
— Tee Barnett, a South Los Angeles data control clerk

The Los Angeles riots were bound to happen. The country is always at war over race and class.

The Republicans have played with race since Richard Nixon's Southern Strategy broke the Democrats' 40-year hold on the presidency in 1968. During the Reagan Revolution, they laid siege to the very idea of modern government with an ideological attack on its underlying concept. Their intent was to wreck the last vestiges of the New Deal's social contract; since they couldn't do that frontally, they sabotaged it from within, gutting programs like Legal Services, treating public housing (in the Housing and Urban Development scandal) as little more than a mammoth excuse for looting by yuppie debutantes, setting up a multi-billion-dollar rip-off of the S&L industry and, in the Iran-Contra scandal, creating an unconstitutional, officially underground foreign policy. The looting in the streets of Los Angeles was nothing compared to the massive theft openly conducted during the past 12 years by political officials of the Reagan and Bush administrations — a theft that will hinder the future of the nation for decades, forcing ordinary citizens to pay for the lifestyles of the new renter class.

They have taunted the population with images of black convicted rapist Willie Horton and sought to pit the races against one another with attacks on affirmative action. The Republicans have engaged in every conceivable form of dissembling civil-rights legislation, decrying each proposal as a "quota bill." David Duke didn't decide to join the Republican Party for nothing — his emergence on the national scene opened the way for Pat Buchanan, whose campaign, as everyone knew from the very beginning, had little or nothing to do with becoming president but was aimed at dragging George Bush to the right.

The Republicans' greatest successes have come right where the LA riots began — in the judicial system. Frustrated by the slow pace of dismantling government, conservative Republicans — first through the nomination of Robert Bork, and later through those of Scalia, Souter and Thomas — sought to institutionalize the goals of the New Right through the courts. In the Rodney King case, as in countless civil-rights cases during the 1960s, people all across the country, from every walk of life, every race and every class, have looked to the federal courts as the source of ultimate justice in the United States. With all its faults, the federal judiciary has been a true foundation post of American democracy. Most of us believed, even when the Supreme Court came to reflect ideologically conservative views, that surely the federal system as a whole would remain a fire-wall against the Robespierres of the Reagan Revolution.

Most people believe that now, even after Chief Justice Rehnquist has taken it upon himself unilaterally to rewrite the concept of habeas corpus. And they continue to believe it even as the high court is about to undo the emancipation of women.

Yet the sad truth is that President Bush has been conducting guerrilla attacks on the district and appeals court levels with such success that the federal system has already begun to resemble a cornball caricature of patronage. Since the federal courts will be the next course of redress in the Rodney King case, consider for a moment how far down the road of Reaganaut reaction the court system has already traveled: Reagan/Bush judges are overwhelmingly white, male and wealthy, without a commitment to serving the underclass, according to the Alliance for Justice, a group of non-profits based in Washington. More than three out of every four nominees has a net worth of more than $500,000, and most have little pro bono

experience. Some nominees go so far as to list their work for the Republican Party as evidence of their commitment to the poor.

Reagan/Bush judges already hold nearly two-thirds of the appellate bench, with majorities on 11 of 13 circuit courts and pluralities on the remaining two. Of President Bush's 39 circuit-court nominees, 21 were first appointed by his predecessor to lower courts, and an additional five served in the Reagan administration. More than half of the 837 federal judgeships are now held by Reagan/Bush appointees — a figure that could rise to 62 per cent before the year is out.

The Democrats dealt with race in 1988 by beating Jesse Jackson's campaign for the presidency to the ground, arguing that the Rainbow Coalition he sought to mobilize was just a catchall of quarreling and insignificant minorities. The conservative mainliners in the Democratic Party insisted that concerns for the underclass must come second to the interests of the real constituency — the white suburbanites who had become the core of Republican electoral victories. Although Jackson's constituency accounted for millions of Democratic votes in 1988, he and his demands for a rational approach toward care for America's underclass were dismissed by the party. Governor Bill Clinton's nomination is the obvious beneficiary of that dismissal.

Increasingly, all the politicians — liberal, conservative, moderate — whose role it is to hammer out the compromises that make life possible in American society won't do their jobs. In Congress, representatives of both parties just gave up. They won't deal with education. They won't deal with the declining economic position of minorities. They don't care about women with small children. They abandoned the cities. They turned their backs on health care. And as members of both parties longed to win with the Republican constituency, they followed the lead of the Reagan and Bush administrations, always ducking the hard questions of how to make democracy work, avoiding the job they had been elected to do.

They have virtually declared a strike against the American people. They have left the mess to the cops. And as one

Rodney King case after another attests, the cops routinely go outside the law, intimidate, beat up, shoot and kill the innocent to maintain the semblance of peace.

And the politicians? They revived an old game. They went motor-mouth on race, rediscovering how they could use racial innuendo to advance their own narrow, unprincipled interests.

Given this context, it's perfectly understandable why former Los Angeles Police Chief Daryl Gates looked the other way when the riot started. Why should he shoulder the entire responsibility for the irresponsible behavior of the Los Angeles political establishment? In the middle of the violence, according to the *Los Angeles Times*, Gates "congratulated rioters for smashing windows at the *Times* building — then said hastily, "Joke, joke, joke."

When Arthur Fletcher, the chairman of the Civil Rights Commission, suggested on TV last Sunday that the problem lay in the failure of government officials promptly and expeditiously to enforce the laws enacted by Congress, he was shushed into the background. But Fletcher was right. The American economy is a huge mixed machine that is directed from Washington by government. When it comes to building an army, organizing the banking industry, bailing out the savings-and-loan industry, or saving the auto and electronics industries, few politicians talk about bootstrap capitalism.

The government has to take a firm lead position in creating jobs and providing the social and physical infrastructures of city life. Neither George Bush nor the small group of people who now make up the Democratic Party show any signs of doing this. Last weekend, both the Bush and Clinton camps argued over "how to respond" to the Los Angeles riots. How to respond? That's code talk for figuring out how the television footage of the truck driver who was beaten up will play in 30-second ads come the fall. Just how many white votes in the suburbs is the beating worth? Will it do for 1992 what Willie Horton did for 1988? That's what the riot is all about, and that's politics in America. ∎

James Ridgeway is the Washington, D.C., correspondent for the Village Voice, *where a version of this story first appeared.*

Do You Fear the Coming Darkness?

by Tom Carson

Los Angeles: Debra DiPoalo

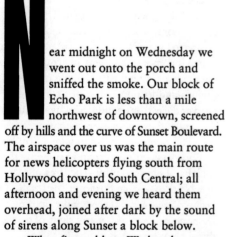

Near midnight on Wednesday we went out onto the porch and sniffed the smoke. Our block of Echo Park is less than a mile northwest of downtown, screened off by hills and the curve of Sunset Boulevard. The airspace over us was the main route for news helicopters flying south from Hollywood toward South Central; all afternoon and evening we heard them overhead, joined after dark by the sound of sirens along Sunset a block below.

What first told me Wednesday was a red-letter day for my adopted hometown? Mayor Tom Bradley's press conference in the late afternoon, a couple of hours after the Rodney King trial ended. The mayor's attack on the verdict, and his call for the officers just acquitted to be fired from the LAPD, was above all a well-crafted (though, as events proved, inadequate) tactical move: a bid to stifle street anger by wrapping it in officialdom's cloak. But even so, for Bradley to sound stalwart on any topic was a novel experience. When asked how the verdict made him feel "as a

black man," there was even an expression closely akin to feeling on his flesh-armored Madame Tussaud face. By the next day Bradley had reverted to form, unarousable by any issue other than threats to his own perks and good name.

Still, within minutes of Bradley's comments, local news helicopters had begun hovering above the intersection of Florence and Normandie — where *it* was starting. Spidery figures, in foreshortened zoom-lens perspective from on high, were darting in and out of Tom's Liquor. Soon the choppers had to expand their sweeps to take in the action at the gas station across the street. On each pass, you could glimpse two cars slewed into a V at the crosswalk. Abruptly the skycams flitted east, where something else was up.

The spectacle provided by modern-day instant news coverage may well have been a first: a God's-eye view of how riots grow. From moment to moment, we could track the deteriorating situation around Florence and Normandie — the assault on the dazed driver of the gravel

truck stopped at the intersection; the near-by beating of another motorist, instantly and forever known to us all as "the guy in the Bronco" (with "Asian" inserted in carets later on), by a bigger mob; the first fire (a mattress on the street). Cut to Parker Center: a growing crowd faced a line of cops — the first sight of riot gear — outside police headquarters. With each cutaway, the crowd's mood visibly changed from peaceful to taunting. As night fell our screens split: On the left-hand side, the speakers at the A.M.E. Church were struggling with increasing futility to contain their own fury as they called for restraint, and the choir sang and stomped. On the right, the earliest blazes turned the tube bright orange.

Among other things, the omnipresent cameras enabled even the most incurious viewer to gauge, from moment to moment, the police response — or non-response. Even the local anchors wondered about it: "We're not trying to judge the LAPD," Channel 7's Paul Moyer hedged, although he, his colleagues and everyone watching could hardly avoid doing just that.

In sober — that is, depoliticized — fact, the LAPD's decision to hold off on committing its resources until the size of the problem was clear probably made oodles of sense. But life is never depoliticized. The cynicism of the plan was that it turned the residents of South Central into pawns. Everyone knew that if the corner of Florence and Normandie were a white neighborhood, the cops would have been on it like lightning bugs as soon as the trouble started, and worries about premature allocations of force could go hang. (Politically, it would also have been typical of Daryl Gates's cunning to realize that, once things had been allowed to escalate into a full-blown riot, nobody would be in much of a mood to criticize whatever tactics his men used.) Nevertheless, by the time Hollywood got hit on Thursday, there weren't enough cops to go around.

As a rule, on Wednesday, the people who should have been the focus of attention — the rioters themselves — stayed weirdly dim figures on TV, with not only their motives but their specific actions all but impossible to get a handle on. This was mainly because, much like the LAPD, most local news operations delayed sending their crews out onto the street; early on they preferred to stay aloft.

Instead, the local anchors moved into the vacuum left by the city's (other) institutions, categorizing the nature of the event before anyone could have independently understood it, and in the process making it clear that they serve "the public" less than the social order. KABC's Moyer was the worst offender, flatly declaring as early as Wednesday evening that "This has nothing to do with the Rodney King verdict" (how in hell would *he* know?), and branding the rioters with abusive terms that were either purely rhetorical ("thugs," "hooligans") or as yet unsupported by any evidence ("gang-bangers").

Throughout the riot, the most comprehensive coverage was probably on Channel 2 — despite the presence of the execrable Bree Walker, whose solemn "Oh, the humanity" expression was to keep slipping all through the next 48 hours into a peeved sorority treasurer's "I may *barf*" look. The CBS affiliate was the station that found Greg Williams, the black man who'd rescued the Bronco's driver. (Walker and Michael Tuck were also almost pathetically eager to pump up the admirable Williams into the riot's official hero — only to drop him as soon as it became evident that moments of civic heroism, from the scruffy crowds helping with fire hoses to Edward James Olmos to Rodney King himself, were hardly going to be in short supply.) And so far as I noticed, KCBS was the only local newscast to carry a late-Wednesday interview with the city's self-appointed Roman proconsul, the vain, cruel man singly most responsible for LA's disaster, who, on being asked if he'd yet spoken with his successor-designate Willie Williams, audibly chortled before saying no. (According to the *LA Times*, at one point during the holocaust Gates also mockingly congratulated rioters for trashing the *Times* building.)

The steadiest coverage, however, came from the independent stations, my own favorite being KTLA Channel 5, with anchor Hal Fishman and, among others on the street, the superbly unflappable Warren Wilson. Unexpectedly, the indies' much-derided staffs of middle-aged, paunchy vets, the broadcast equivalent of beat-up old cars, came to look like a source of doughty stability. For one thing, unlike their more youthfully glamorous counterparts at the affiliates — not to mention a good many of their viewers, and most certainly an East Coast parvenu like me — a lot of them had actually been living and working in LA in 1965. That meant they'd seen riots before.

Thursday was a long day. That was the day people as yet unaffected awoke feeling a half-edgy, half-wishful calm, only to spend the afternoon plunged into endless, channel-clicking footage of one fire after another hiding the sky, to a Pet Shop Boys rhythm of rotor blades, all of it unexpectedly feeling somehow more natural, or at any rate familiar, than the calm had. It was the day so many of us spent fielding worried calls from other cities, some of which weren't to end the day in such great shape themselves.

It was a day of ingenuously stumbling across the reality behind clichés we'd never supposed could actually describe something. My own discovery, made on a quick jaunt to the Pioneer supermarket at the corner of Sunset and Echo Park to beat the curfew, could not have been more banal: a Mood of Ominous Expectation. The Bank of America there was locked, with a handwritten sign beginning, "Due to this state of emergency...." At least a dozen people were queueing for the ATM. Inside Pioneer: long lines. I tried not to dramatize the gassy sullenness in the air. Tried not to read foreboding into the faces around me, yet they wouldn't stop looking expectant, worried, grim. And back in my living room, a woman reporter — Jodie Baskerville? Do I remember a bow? — shoved a microphone in the face of a begrimed fireman and asked, "Do you fear the coming darkness?"

In early afternoon, a few black, windborne flecks of soot began to swirl down out of the sky. The newscasters, bizarrely oblivious to the fact that they were marking off a box around *us*, kept reporting fires and rioting ever nearer: Third and Vermont, Santa Monica and Western.

As soon as the rioting spread beyond the inner-city Thursday afternoon, the troubles in Hollywood and other predominantly white areas got the lion's share of the live TV coverage. Even at the riot's geographic high tide, it was apparent that the quantity of buildings being torched south of Interstate 10 still dwarfed the relatively small number of fires to its north. Yet once the Anglo neighborhoods were threatened, South Central and Crenshaw could have burned to a crisp without anyone watching television being any the wiser — and Hollywood Boulevard, with its two burning buildings, got more footage on TV than the dozens of other fires then raging in the city put together. When the KNBC helicopter pilot, trying to pinpoint the location of the big fire at Wilcox and Hollywood, mentioned Musso & Frank's, anchor Kelly Lange, thinking the restaurant itself was ablaze, gasped audibly, "*Oh, no!*"

Until Friday morning, when things slowed down and the community in question asserted itself, almost no one on TV caught on that if there was such a thing as a uniquely painful local tragedy in the middle of the city's larger tragedy, it certainly hadn't happened in Hollywood. It was the devastation of Koreatown and of the complicated relationships in the inner-city, already made livid in recent months by the Soon Ja Du case, between Asian- and African-Americans. The rioters' frequent targeting of Asian-owned businesses was heart- breaking not least because it was such a classic case of scapegoating — that is, of being so blinded by despair as to mistake the thorn in one's side for the barbed wire at one's throat. Surely it's plain as day that Asian merchants are now prevalent in poor urban neighborhoods only because white businesses won't go in there anymore. Like the inner-city Jewish landlords and shopkeepers cast in the same role of WASP proxies in the East Coast ghettos in the '60s, Koreatown's merchants were stand-ins for an authority too remote to see or touch.

Movie-conditioned as I am, I couldn't avoid responding to the sight, increasingly common in Thursday's TV coverage, of armed Asian-Americans banding together to protect their stores. They just seemed cool in a quietly badass, *High Noon* sort of way; or at least like the only people that week who knew for sure what they were doing. This particular bit of audience appreciation got nixed fast by the hypnotic footage of one merchant up on his rooftop with a rifle, (crazily? furiously?) loading and firing, reloading and firing again, at — what? Nothing? Everything? (We never saw his target.) Ultimately, the shopkeeper I liked best was the one who got asked, during Friday morning's aftermath, if he now felt hostile toward African-Americans. He said no; his store had been

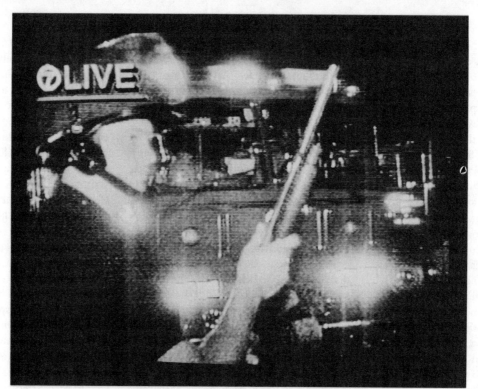
Los Angeles: Debra DiPoalo

looted, he assured his interviewer, by people of all races.

That line is a key to one story of the riot that we were all able to see on TV, despite the anchors' persistent attempts to convince us we ought to be seeing something else. The crowd at Parker Center looked to be equal parts Anglo, black and Latino; in none of the neighborhoods lit by firelight were the faces exclusively black, and in some, non-blacks predominated. One of Thursday night's surreal and oddly cheering TV moments was the sight of a plump white guy in a ball cap being interviewed along with his black neighbors near the burnt-out Thrifty at La Brea and Rodeo in Crenshaw, talking firmly about "our community."

One conclusion could be drawn from this: In our society's current polarization, class may ultimately count for more than even race. At its lower economic levels, damned if Los Angeles isn't more integrated than many of us ever suspected. The Watts riots' confined physical area and the almost exclusively black skin color of those involved made it easy for the rest of LA to pigeonhole the 1965 upheaval as

a straight case of us against them. Watching the mix-up of races and ethnicities in the riot of '92 — blacks facing off against Asians, black cops arresting Latino looters, Hollywood white trash junking Hollywood white bread — the Valley may well have decided that this time it was them against them and a plague on both. But for many inside the city proper, it became movingly unmistakable that this time it was us against us.

But while the images told their own story, nothing to that effect was being said on TV. By Thursday, all the stations were bearing down hard on the thugs-and-hooligans line. (Lest anyone think I'd have preferred the anchors to have talked about "heroic revolutionaries" or some such, let me make it clear that, for news purposes, "looters," "arsonists" and even "snipers" would have done the journalistic job quite nicely.)

On the other hand, there *was* something that poor Bree Walker, especially, just couldn't stop wondering about. How on earth, she kept fretting, could anyone do this *to their own community*? Well, look, Brie — excuse me, Bree — it's like this: if people live in a place that makes it absolutely clear their society finds them worthless, and from which they have virtually no prospect of escaping, a fair percentage of those people, particularly if their education and family life have been a farce, are unlikely to feel that there's a whole lot that makes said place worth living in. Much less *for*. And as a purely practical matter, even the hardiest or craziest Crenshaw youths tempted to firebomb or for that matter sightsee in Beverly Hills, where you're no doubt worried about the new Armani store going up, are going to think twice about having to get home through 10 or 15 miles of alien if not hostile white neighborhoods.

Like the other anchors, Walker was appalled that the looters were acting so happy. God knows, the images of mindless exultation were disturbing — one eerie bit of KNBC film of a young black girl grinning as she flitted through a trashed supermarket will probably stay with me for decades. But even so, has anyone ever seen *depressed*-looking looters? I bet that even the most virtuous middle-class types aren't immune to how tantalizing it would be to just up and kick out a plate-glass window for the hell of it. Combine everybody's inner looter with more alienation and material and moral barrenness than any middle-class person will ever have to endure, and you will quickly find that you've all but run out of arguments for keeping the window intact. Isn't pity the right response to people so fucked over that an act as stupid and wanton — as *puny* — as showing off a 99-cent roll of stolen toilet paper for the cameras is the closest they may ever come to feeling in charge of their lives?

In my perfect world, where Michael Bolton shovels French fries at MacDonald's until he's fired for sloppy hygiene and a putzy attitude, those are the questions I would have liked to see TV raise last week. Fat chance. What happened instead was a classic example of the confusion of roles — dispenser of information versus guardian of order — that compromises television news in a crisis. Repeatedly, when those interviewed on the street brought up militant black grievances, and especially if they suggested that there was a lot more fueling this riot than the King verdict, reporters would shush them or the cameras would quickly cut back to the studio, on the grounds that such talk risked "inflaming" the situation. One exception came late Thursday afternoon, when KNBC's Linda Douglass, with admirable determination, started to talk on the air about the exclusion from society that can make young African-American males feel they've got nothing to lose. But she got put down fast by anchor Jess

Marlow, who contemptuously asked if they felt better now. (This was, by the way, a lovely demonstration of the patriarchal structure of the anchor-field reporter relationship: Daddy Jess was bringing a rude child to heel for company's benefit.)

Marlow was pretty visibly fraying by that point. But to be fair, he may have been disgruntled because he already knew about the week's most scandalously irresponsible journalistic decision — KNBC's ratings-goaded insistence on cutting away from the riots to air the finale of *The Cosby Show*. When the anchorman came back on the air afterward, he looked as if he'd kept himself occupied during the hour-long break by developing an ulcer. Any self-respecting journalist would have.

As always, TV remained obliging whenever an opportunity came up to cede its regency over public morals to official authority. But during most of the riot, with the exception of the firemen — whose egoless common sense and staunchness were so awesome that I wondered what kind of pay raise would persuade them to switch gigs with the LAPD — authority wasn't any too forthcoming. After his one flicker of gumption on Wednesday, Bradley wound up seeming like some huge, hollow kettledrum being rolled here and there for the cameras. Filling the gap, California Governor Pete Wilson cemented his rep as a man who would have failed to convince passengers on the *Titanic* that there were compelling reasons to board a lifeboat.

Until Bush spoke on Friday, that left Police Chief Daryl Gates. True to form, he managed one astonishingly provocative gesture. Although he normally wears civvies in public, he appeared Thursday clad in full dress uniform — black shirt, four stars on each lapel, huge badge. He looked as happy as Mussolini invading Ethiopia. Luckily the riot had all but burned itself out by the time Gates uncorked

• • • • • • • • • • • • • • • • • • • •

Percentage of the poor, by race,
who live in low-income census tracts
in the 100 largest American cities:
African-American: 83
Latinos: 73
Anglos: 33

(Source: Paul Ong, "Justice for Janitors," *Los Angeles Should Work for Everyone*, 1989)

his most reckless zinger, declaring out of the blue that illegal aliens were among the main agents of the riot, including, naturally, many criminals. Did any TV reporter query the chief about what data, if any, supported his contention? Did some bright Jimmy Olsen question that QED link in Gates' mental circuitry between aliens and criminals? Huh! What city do *you* live in?

Well, not Algiers, however many Anglo Angelenos must have suddenly and disturbingly seen themselves as French colonial *pied-noirs*. And not Beirut, no matter how often TV invoked the name. It doesn't minimize the horrors we lived or watched last week to point out that it's ignorant hyperbole to compare Los Angeles to a war zone, considering that basic services (water, telephones, the like) kept functioning throughout the crisis, food was never scarce even at its height and easily three-quarters of the citizens would have been as much in harm's way had they been vacationing in Iowa.

And then? Yeahcumon, tell us, Pops. There's an hour till the bus comes. Then?

Oh — then it ended. By early Friday afternoon some stations were returning to regular programming; there were Gomez and Morticia cavorting on Channel 11 in the same moldy black-and-white as the old clips of the Watts riot that TV had been showing during lulls.

The media age may have come to exert a decisive effect on not only the tempo but the duration of events — the Gulf War, this. They end once we've grown saturated with their imagery. Or perhaps TV's influence was more prosaic: So many ordinary citizens of LA were immediately able to see the dimensions of the disaster that their reaction time was sped up. Maybe the reason that the leadership's response seemed as slow as elephants underwater was that they were out of sync, operating in old-fashioned real time and not, like the rest of us, in TV time.

The failure of leadership at the city level on Wednesday was matched by an equally visible failure at the state level on Thursday, which may account for why Wilson's Friday press conference was unexpectedly conciliatory, his tough crack-down talk of the night before replaced by chastened rhetoric about neighborhood investment and economic dignity. My hunch is that the main outside factor pressuring Wilson to back off from his earlier hard line was Jesse Jackson, a major presence in the city and on the airwaves, and at his vigorous, lucid, adamant best.

But the catharsis the city desperately needed came from another source — when the dazed, fragile, sorrowing man whose victimization 14 months ago had sent Los Angeles up in smoke became for the first time not only a face but a voice on our sets. Rodney King's family had apparently worried up to the last minute about whether he'd be able to face the cameras at all; by all reports, in the last year this traumatized man's sanity has been hanging by a paper clip. Yet in the bravest act I've ever witnessed on television, American history's second black man named King held his courage and his mind together long enough to stammer out the plea that had lost none of its power to move and haunt the 10th time I saw it that night. In the 60-some hours since the riot had begun, Rodney King was the first person to express grief for the dead.

Grief — but what about hope? It quickly became the riot's final cliché, as Korean-Americans gathered near the Wiltern to call for peace, and volunteer clean-up crews spontaneously banded together up and down the wrecked streets, brooms in hand. Amid the fine words and deeds, no one knew if the reconciliation had a chance of outliving the looming white backlash against the riots, a backlash which may well guarantee George Bush's re-election.

Judging from the crafty grin that kept twitching at one corner of Bush's mouth during his harsh speech Friday night, he knows as much. Hope? I listened to Bush denounce the people rioting in my adopted hometown and offer scarcely a word about reconstruction or understanding or economic justice, and I thought: Fuck you, you dingbat. You outsider. Don't you dare talk that way about our city. ■

Tom Carson is a staff writer for the LA Weekly, *where a version of this story first appeared.*

Simi Valley: Cynthia Wiggins

The Verdict *by Doug Ireland*

The LA riots began less than 24 hours after the Republicans staged their $9-million rent-a-Cabinet-member Washington dinner, a self-congratulatory orgy of privileged white economic power whose organizers and contributors were shown to have, at a minimum, skirted the law to help fill the party's coffers. As Woody Guthrie used to sing, some will rob you with a six-gun, some with a fountain pen. Between the presidential PAC-rats assembled in that Washington banquet hall and the clients of the soup kitchens in South Central Los Angeles yawns a chasm of difference in perception about what defines this nation.

When the putative leader of the free world finally deigned to address the agony in LA on the little screen Friday night, he once again institutionalized that difference as a matter of national policy: "What we saw last night and the night before in Los Angeles is not about civil rights....It's not a message of protest. It's been the brutality

of the mob, pure and simple....We must understand that no one in Los Angeles or any other city has rendered a verdict on America." Not about civil rights? Then why the need for a federal investigation of the four thugs-in-uniform who beat a black man senseless? Not a protest? Why did a member of the president's own Cabinet, Jack Kemp, admit (on CNN's *Newsmaker Sunday*) that the events in LA were, as he put it, "a cry for help"? Not a verdict on America? That's *exactly* what they were.

One expects this sort of abhorrent nonsense and denial of reality from a man who began his political career running for the Senate in 1964 by campaigning against the Civil Rights Act. But one hoped for better from the editorialists at our national dailies; Sunday's *New York Times* complacently argued that "President Bush skillfully gave equal weight to order and justice," while the same day's *Washington Post* found that "the federal response to the stunning verdict and the outbreak of indiscriminate violence and wholesale law-lessness in Los Angeles" was "reassuring."

In Meg Greenfield's well-tailored world, it was perhaps "reassuring" that the president began his address not with a word of understanding or compassion, but in full blame-the-victims George Bush mode. Maxine Waters, the admirable congresswoman from South Central LA who was justly propelled into media stardom by the riots, nailed it on Friday's *Nightline*: To loud applause from an audience of well-dressed blacks gathered at the First A.M.E. Church, she put her finger on the speech's offensive tonalities. "The president," she said, "had the audacity to try and use what has happened here as a chance to prove again how tough he is....Instead of his get-tough, second-Persian Gulf message, what he should have been doing is talking about the peace dividend for reinvestment in America....He has dropped off America's agenda the inner-cities, where there are no jobs, there's little or no job training. Industries have gotten tax credits from him and his kind [but] they've taken the profit, put it in their pockets, didn't reinvest it in the state-of-the-art equipment so that they could have more jobs, exported the jobs to Third-World countries for cheap labor markets, and he's got the *audacity* to tell us...how *tough* he's going to be? He's inflaming the situation."

Slick Willie had a chance to revivify his sagging campaign and redefine himself in contrast to Bush, but he blew it, big: Clinton's moral bankruptcy was confirmed for all to see in his ad-libbed ABC appearance after the president's talk, for which he had nothing but praise. What would *he* do? asked Peter Jennings. "First, I would sign the crime bill," Clinton answered in what Roger Wilkins — in a Sunday *Washington Post* "Outlook" piece — correctly labeled "a naked bid to rip the law-and-order mantle from the Republicans." Wilkins called for "leaders who have the moral clarity and the courage to lead us out of our racist slumber." That ain't Slick Willie, who — even though he's proclaimed himself the candidate of "healing" and the "change agent" — showed himself to be nearly as empty of

imagination as H. Ross Perot (who found little more to say than, "I would go to LA").

New Yorkers on the dawn patrol before their TV sets vicariously shared the experience of Angeleno riot potatoes thanks to WNBC, which provided continuous live and unedited coverage picked up from its sister station in Los Angeles all through the first three nights. The seven LA TV stations had a dozen "telecopters" in the air, and KNBC's provided endless aerial views of the disorders. On Wednesday, the night of the worst violence, there was a near-total absence of voices from the affected communities during what, in LA, was the prime viewing time. Worse, the overly-coiffed co-anchor, Kelly Lange, kept breathlessly editorializing — or, more accurately, emoting — against the rioters and the arsonists, but never whispered a word that I heard about the jury's decision or the social conditions that caused it all. If *I* found Lange's intrusive commentaries offensive, what must the people of color who lived there have thought?

Time's Richard Schickel said it best in a cracking-good commentary: "Los Angeles television just kept pouring raw footage from the remote units onto the screen. It was roughly the equivalent of dumping raw sewage into Santa Monica Bay. In effect, intelligent life-forms — those organisms struggling to make sense of tragic chaos — found the oxygen supply to their brains cut off....TV needed to offer perspective. Anchors everywhere plied field reporters with Big Picture questions. But that wasn't their job. Their job was to create a mythical city, a sort of Beirut West, views of which would keep many viewers frozen in fear to their Barcaloungers. And, incidentally, send a few of them out to join in the vicious fun....TV itself needed... interruptions of its uninterruptedness, so it could sort out its information, make sense of it in sensibly edited and narrated reports. The basic function of journalism is selection. It is through that skill that a medium earns civic responsibility and achieves public trust."

On the national grids, the same lack of systemic analysis and insight prevailed. Not until Friday night, an hour before

Bush's speech, did any of the Big Three offer prime-time programming on the events. And though the title of CBS's Rather-hosted special was *Beyond the Rage*, the show provided little that moved beyond the spot-news and human-interest stories to the root causes of it all until a truncated exchange of soundbites in the last 10 minutes featuring Shelby Steele (the black neo-con), John Kerry and Eleanor Holmes Norton, who made a point I heard nowhere else. "Now the president," she pointed out, "who is against affirmative action, is being helped this very evening [in preventing the spread of rioting to other cities] because affirmative action has begun to integrate the people who patrol the very streets that he has done so little for."

What will be the political fall-out from all this? History gives little cause for optimism. The 1965 Watts riots led directly to the election of California Governor Ronald Reagan and launched his national political career. The 1968 riots in the wake of Martin Luther King, Jr.'s death led directly to the election of President Richard Nixon. And the national opinion polls taken since the underclass's latest inchoate rebellion show there is still a white majority that refuses to recognize racism as endemic to our institutions and that at the same time is susceptible to the blandishments of skin-privileged forms of repression.

If the verdict in the trial of the men who assaulted Rodney King was obscene, so too has been the response of those who wield political power. As *The Progressive*'s Erwin Knoll put it on *MacNeil/Lehrer*, "The leadership of this country is content to condemn and consign the poor [and] the minorities to the hell which is their daily existence and doesn't want to do anything about the problems that are reflected in these terrible outbursts."

Oh well, *I* can always renew my passport. The folks in the South Centrals of this land aren't so lucky. ■

Doug Ireland is a columnist for the Village Voice, *where a version of this column first appeared.*

The Inner-City Non-Issue

by Jeff Cohen and Norman Solomon

Los Angeles: Debra DiPoalo

It was an amazing discovery for network TV and other national news media. Within hours of the Rodney King verdict, they unearthed millions of people living in America's desperate inner-cities. What followed were rare TV specials and magazine cover stories about urban poverty and neglect. Ted Koppel even hosted a *Nightline in South Central*. If many Americans had been stunned by the Los Angeles riots, no one was caught more off-guard than national news outlets. That America's poor urban areas are powder kegs ready to explode has been highlighted in other mediums. You could hear it in rap music, or see it in such movies as *Do The Right Thing* and *Boyz N The Hood*. But in most national news media, this reality was invisible — despite the fact that we're in the middle of an election campaign, when our most pressing problems are supposed to receive a full hearing.

Until LA erupted, the inner-city was a non-issue in campaign '92. Political journalists regularly dismissed black people as just another selfish "special-interest" group — sort of like the natural gas lobby. Media pundits openly instructed candidates to ignore the concerns of blacks, Latinos and the poor and appeal instead to "the middle class" — a code-phrase that began to sound like "just us white folks."

Cutting against the orthodoxy of the pundits, Jesse Jackson has tried for months — with little success — to get presidential candidates like Bill Clinton forthrightly to discuss "the urban agenda." Jackson's efforts have earned him the scorn of national media. Days before the Rodney King riots, a supposedly objective *New York Times* news article began, "Jesse Jackson, who has twice run for President and knows a thing or two about creating mischief within the Democratic party, avoided endorsing Gov. Bill Clinton today...." When calling upon the Democrats to stand for racial justice is portrayed as "creating mischief" — and constituencies such as blacks and Latinos (20 percent of the country) are dismissed as "special interests" — media bias is clearly evident.

In fact, since 1990, many news outlets have seemed less concerned about racism than about the allegedly overzealous activists who challenge inequality — denounced as "politically correct" in countless stories. A computer search of the term "politically correct" found that the *Los Angeles Times* published 252 articles containing this put-down in the last six months alone.

The media obsession with disparaging activists helped obscure the fact that racial bigotry and hate crimes have been on the rise. A National Opinion Research Center

• • • • • • • • • • • • • • • • • • • •

Earnings gap between comparable Chicano and Anglo males in LA, 1986-87:
20 percent

Earnings gap between comparable African-American and Anglo males in LA, 1988:
30 percent

(Source: Paul Ong, based on 1980 Census Data)

poll in 1990 showed widespread prejudice against every racial minority group, especially blacks: 53 percent of non-black respondents thought African-Americans were less intelligent than whites; 56 percent believed them to be more violence-prone; and 78 percent said they were more likely to "prefer to live off welfare" than to be self-supporting. The poll offers clues to the racial attitudes the 12 jurors took with them into the Simi Valley jury room.

Far from raising consciousness about racism, news media have often reinforced stereotypes. Little has changed since a 1987 *Columbia Journalism Review* study conducted by researcher Kirk Johnson found that mainstream media coverage of two black neighborhoods in Boston focused overwhelmingly on stories involving crime, violence and drugs: "85 percent reinforced negative stereotypes of blacks." By contrast, Boston's African-American media during the same period provided a more multifaceted story, which — while not ignoring crime — revealed "a black community thirsty for educational advancement and entrepreneurial achievement, and eager to remedy poor living conditions made worse by bureaucratic neglect." ∎

Jeff Cohen is the executive director of FAIR, the New York-based media-watch group. Norman Solomon is the author of The Power of Babble: The Politician's Dictionary of Buzzwords and Doubletalk for Every Occasion.

Helicopter Journalism

by Carol Tice

The television coverage of Los Angeles in the aftermath of the acquittal of the four officers who beat Rodney King was dizzying.

Not dizzying in its analysis or complexity, but in its use of endless helicopter shots circling over fires and looting. The meaning of what was happening, the root causes for such a staggering explosion, remained as remote as the endless live, on-location broadcasts.

In their hunger for images, television news values called for incessant shots of fires. Even when press conferences were held by officials, Governor Pete Wilson, Police Chief Daryl Gates, Mayor Tom Bradley and even President George Bush became tiny talking heads against a background of flame — or, on some networks, disappeared altogether.

The men became unwitting narrators of a live tapestry of destruction, their words often taking on ironic meaning against the backdrop of chaos. As Wilson quoted Dr. Martin Luther King, Jr., on KCBS Channel 2, he was a disembodied voice narrating a horror show of looting, violence and fires. His words served only to highlight the futility of all good intentions in the face of such an enraged and disenfranchised populace.

The presence of TV crews seemed to exacerbate the eerie carnival atmosphere at looting sites. At a scene where a man had been shot with his own gun and was lying dead in his car, KCAL Channel 9's reporter tried in vain to describe the gruesome situation while a crowd of black teenagers laughed, frolicked and mugged for the camera behind him. Mortified, the reporter gave up, saying grimly, "There's a dead person here and it's a big joke. Back to you."

Unlike the Watts riot, during which many stations had to draft their first black reporter on the spot, everyone seemed to have capable women and minorities in the field. Back in the studio, though, the anchors were almost universally white — and utterly mystified by the events they saw on their monitors.

No one commented on the macabre vision of our consumer culture being turned on its head. When the poor get angry in Los Angeles, the poor go shopping. These were the riots that weren't riots; no angry mobs marching down the street, shaking their fists and smashing windows. This was simply people shopping and people setting fires. What turned ordinary people into thieves? Statistics about the economic plight of the neighborhoods that exploded were nowhere to be found, despite hours of round-the-clock coverage. Along with the lack of hard data on the economic state of South Central LA was an astounding lack of persistent questioning of officials. How, after weeks of planning, could the National Guard be caught short on ammunition, delaying their deployment by many hours? Gov. Wilson lamely replied, "This ammunition problem has not happened before and will not happen again." (Imagine a fire chief saying, "Oops, sorry. Next time the fire hydrants will have water.")

When police were mysteriously unavailable during the first few hours of the crisis — not even a few units could be found to escort emergency medical vehicles to get beaten motorists off the streets — Chief Gates was allowed to get away with "I only work here" mumbles. "I asked the same question — where were the police?" he told the press corps.

One black woman interviewed on Hancock Park Street seemed to grasp the incident better than any of the mostly white anchors back in the studios, and made a wry comment on the level of TV coverage as well. "This isn't expressing anything," she said. "This is just stupid." ∎

Carol Tice is a Los Angeles-based writer whose commentaries are heard regularly on KPPK Radio. A version of this story first appeared in the Los Angeles Reader.

What You Didn't Hear on Television

by Gary Davis

Pictures of violence sell TV news, and LA viewers have had no shortage of those in the last week. But the full sound of the violence rarely accompanied the images, and that helped us stay comfortably detached as we stared through our living room peepholes.

As any moviegoer knows, THX or Dolby stereo add enormous impact to a film. Watch a scene from *Lethal Weapon* or *Star Wars* with the sound turned down, and you may wonder what all the excitement is about. But that's excactly what TV news does: puts its all-important reporter's chatter in the center of the action, with the real sound turned off or just low enough that the pictures don't seem unnatural. Hailing back to the days of radio news, the TV norm assumes we won't maintain interest if they don't continually describe what we're seeing. The "live" label and continuous coverage is supposed to guarantee the broadcast's impartiality, but in fact this is a deceptive comfort. By turning the real sound down or off, TV news provides a strange emotional detachment from the events it shows. The riots many be happening to "them" but not "us."

Using a home satellite dish to intercept network broadcasts, I was able to witness many of the same "live" events, but with their original sound intact. Wednesday night's coverage of the attack in Parker Center, for example, showed rioters hurling trash cans into the large glass doors. But the sounds of metal striking metal, glass shattering, boots kicking reinforced

Los Angeles: Debra DiPoalo

panes, fires crackling and the crowd's angry yells were all but deleted in the TV control rooms. Believe me, the impact of watching the same scene with Hollywood-quality sound was gut-wrenching.

The other reason natural sound disappears is language. There are a few words which, though frequently used in every-day speech, have been ruled unacceptable by the mainstream media and will never be seen in print or heard on broadcast television. (In fact, it was rather surprising to see those words in a photo on the front page of last Friday's *Los Angeles Times*. Where are the photo retouchers when you really need them?) Here, without apologies, are some uncensored transcriptions of citizens' angry reactions:

During the attack on Parker Center: "Chaos, motherfuckers, chaos!" "Yes! Get those pig motherfuckers." "Damn, somebody did it to them." "Check the fucking bus!" "Motherfuckers!" "This is for Rodney!" (Also deleted was the sound of people cheering: We were not supposed to know that some people *approved* of the violence.)

At a Seattle riot: "See what's goin' on here in motherfucking Seattle. We mad at all you motherfuckers, all you guys, all you government, Mr. Daryl Gates, you messed up, so you better do something, 'cause Seattle's pissed off!" Reporter: "So what you're saying is that justice doesn't work, so you have to take it into your own hands?" Protester: "Yeah, what the fuck else? What's left? We keep twisting the motherfucker, we keep twisting your peckerwood and you fucked up!"

I don't know exactly what he meant, but I do know that on TV news you'll never get a clue. ■

Gary Davis contributes to the Los Angeles Reader, *where a version of this story first appeared.*

Truth, Justice and Videotape

by Andrew Goodwin

Two months ago, while I was teaching at the University of California at San Diego, a colleague stormed into my office to complain about my supervision of a graduate student. The student was working on the aesthetics of Madonna's video clip "Cherish," and had written about the use of editing, lighting and visual framing to create meaning and, yes, beauty in the clip. My colleague's complaint was that I had taken this aesthetic level too seriously, when what I should have done was steer the student towards what really mattered — the clip's sexism.

Analyzing the aesthetics of a Madonna clip and ignoring the "content," I was informed, was like taking the videotape of Rodney King's beating and using it to talk about camera angles. My reply (which, typically, I came up with so late that it was only delivered in my imagination) was that of course the camera angles in the Rodney King clip do matter. That was when I started thinking about the dangers of believing in that piece of "evidence." When a colleague who should have known better assumed that a piece of videotape involves no mediation, no point of view, then you know that something strange is happening. The tape's meaning was, apparently, transparent. Until last Wednesday.

The relationship between truth, justice and videotape is a tricky one, but in the case of the beating of Rodney King by four LAPD officers, it did seem at first glance to be deceptively simple. For once, the media evidence seemed to be on "our" side. After years and years of complaining that the cam-

era does indeed lie, here were some images the left could believe in: irrefutable evidence, it seemed, of police brutality and racism.

Even before the verdict came in, this attitude made me nervous. As a white person, I plead guilty to stupidity for being at all taken aback by the decision. But as a media critic, I'm innocent of all charges: I never brought the argument that the camcorder clip of Rodney King's beating was sufficient proof of the police officers' guilt.

The King video clip put left and radical critics of the media in a strange dilemma; having argued for more than a decade that media analysis shows the partial and manipulated nature of media representations, some now took the contrary position — that the clip was essentially "true." Think about this for a moment. It is a preposterous and impossible position. The unaestheticized images of smart bombing during the Gulf war were in some literal sense "true"; yet we know they also lied by omission. The wallpapering of images of commuter strife in Germany during the recent transportation strikes captured something that actually happened; yet, in focusing exclusively on the consequences of a strike, without showing us anything of its causes, television once again performed its time-honored role of delegitimizing industrial action.

Now think about the video of Rodney King's beating. Imagine how that sequence might be started or stopped in different places to create quite different impressions. Imagine how changes in the angle and positioning of the camera could tell us more or less about what occurred. Imagine how watching the clip in different circumstances, with different people, might change the way you view it. Yes, something did really, actually happen out there that night. And I do not doubt that it involved brutality and racism. But the camera didn't teach me that.

Many people were shocked by the jury's verdict because it seemed to be clearly at odds with "reality" — or rather with a videotaped version of that reality. Savvy media critics should not have been surprised at all. The juror who explained her own reasoning by suggesting that King "asked for it," that he was "in control" at every stage, and that the LAPD officers merely responded to King's actions, just proves what sophisticated media research has been saying for the last two decades. Images are never innocent — not at the point of production (they always embody a point of view) and not at the point of consumption (they can be "read" in different ways). All Orwellian theses about the overreaching power of TV (Neil Postman, etc.) collapse on this point. They assume that TV has terrible powers to frame our views. Instead we discover that a juror looking at a brief segment of apparently self-evident evidence sees something entirely different than what we see.

What does she see? Of course she doesn't see what I see at all. She's a different reader, and what the juror sees on the tape is something that dovetails with her experience, with her attitudes, with her own already available frameworks of interpretation.

What did we see in the media coverage of the rioting that followed the verdict? Individuals looting stores. A group of black people beating a white truck driver almost to death. Buildings on fire. What does Pat Buchanan see? Out-of-control rioting that needs a firm hand. What does Daryl Gates see? "Illegal aliens" taking advantage, according to the *Los Angeles Times*. What does Jesse Jackson see? Years of humiliation and alienation expressed in self-destruction. What does a gang member from Compton see? I have no idea. Some people, driven insane by too much left-think, even saw "the revolution," and thought that it was going to be televised after all.

The most revealing post-verdict comment came from a juror who told a radio reporter that the jury was amazed by the response of the protesters and the looters, and might have reconsidered its verdict had they any clue that such an outcome would occur. Now, that the jury could be at all surprised by the response is a clue to the whole bizarre reading of the videotape. If you were already so out of touch with urban reality that cathartic anger and violence strikes you as an unusual way to react to the injustice of the verdict, then clearly your frameworks of interpretation are quite well attuned to what we might call the LAPD P.O.V. As the defending counsel pointed out, the trick was to get the jury to

covering the riots: media

view the events from the point of view of the police officers, and not Rodney King.

Common sense seems to say that this is all just words. That when you look at the tape there is a point beyond which the LAPD officers cross the line, and they are delivering a beating, not apprehending a suspect. And yet the jury did not see that. It contextualized the images differently. The juror's response to their critics was to suggest (as media critics generally do) that the images were being viewed out of context. You had to experience the whole trial, they said, in order to understand what the images really meant. It is no argument at all to respond to this by saying that we don't need any context because we know what the images mean just by looking at them. That, after all, is precisely the logic of the mass media's apologists.

A more credible critique of the juror's reading of the Rodney King video is that they used the wrong framework (the LAPD's, instead of the victim's) and provided the wrong context. They were, after all, chosen precisely for their competence in that area, and this was the basis for moving the trial out of LA and into Ventura County. Those two regions offered very different potential readers of the videotape. The jurors in Simi Valley were "wrong" not because they failed to see the self-evident truth of a piece of videotape, but because they were chosen for their propensity to read it a certain way.

Liberals, leftists and anti-racists want to pretend now, because it suits us, that our critique of the jury's decision derives from a superior "reality" that the camera innocently revealed. But it did no such thing. Arguing the whole case on the basis of the video clip proved to be a fatal strategy in the courtroom. In the wider arena of politics, radicals are onto a no-winner if they choose this moment suddenly to start believing in the simple veracity of mediated images. ■

Andrew Goodwin contributes to the East Bay Express, *where a version of this story first appeared.*

What's in a Word

by Bill Gaskins

One of the most frustrating aspects of what the media have done in the aftermath of the Rodney King verdict is that they have replaced the images of the police beating and the issues surrounding it with images of blacks as "looters" in the streets of LA. Emphasis has shifted from the violence of the King beating to the shock, astonishment and judgement by white America of blacks *reacting* to the blatant racism.

No white man, woman or child has to experience the collective insecurity that African-Americans feel in the face of a system of law enforcement and jurisprudence that applies different standards based on skin color. The Simi Valley jury indelibly confirmed and justified that insecurity for blacks, yet insensitive whites in and out of the media insist on telling black America how to react to this chronic injustice.

The widespread acts of vandalism and robbery were committed by whites, Latinos and blacks of all ages for a complex set of reasons, of which the King verdict is only one symptom. In spite of the complexity of the situation and the integrated composition of the participants in the violence, media images of the "looters" are dominated by black youths and adults. This kind of editing creates an insidious and unconscious word-image relationship that unfairly merges blacks with the nation's criminal image, becomes a dehumanizing tool and redefines the words we use to talk about race.

American news media use one standard of description, interpretation and evaluation when crimes are committed by blacks. When crimes are committed by

covering the riots: media

whites, a different language is used.

Let's examine the word "loot." *Webster's Third New International Dictionary* defines the word as follows: 1a) to plunder or sack (as in a conquered city) in war; b) to rob, especially on a large scale and usually by violence or corruption.

In the aftermath of the King verdict, a clear word-image relationship has been formed between blacks and the word *loot*. An example of how word-image relationships are formed when whites commit the same crime in a different manner was illustrated by a group of students in a photography course I teach at Ohio State University. While giving a lecture on how words form and support images in the minds of viewers, I used the media coverage of the LA riots as an example. I wrote three names on the board — Ivan Boesky, Michael Milken and Charles Keating — and asked the class whether they could tell me who these people are. After a pregnant pause, one student asked "Charles Keating is a writer, isn't he?" In reference to Boesky, another student said, "He's that Wall Street guy." I asked if anyone could tell me what "the Wall Street guy" did. No one answered. The students could not tell me who these men are; nor were they able to associate them with their criminal acts. Even though these three people have robbed on a larger scale than all of the black people on the streets of LA, the "looters" remain African-American in the words and images of the media. What's more, all three of the white looters will serve relatively light sentences. Already, Milken has written a cover story, "My Story," for *Business Week* magazine. Can movie rights be far away? White looters write the book, while black looters get booked.

The term "race problem" is another myopic interpretation of race in American culture, and implies that the mere presence of blacks is the problem. When blacks are not presented in acceptable, easily digested roles as entertainers, athletes or servants, the mass media frequently present African-Americans as a social problem in the form of questions such as, "What do we do about America's black underclass?" Such questions spring from a paternalistic and condescending attitude. One *does something* about a problem, not a group of people. America does not have a "race problem." America has a history of white males (often with white women at their side) seeking power and supremacy, and *they* have a problem with race.

A serious social analysis of our country that scrutinizes white males as the central problem of American culture rarely gets front-page status. A recent example of this truth was buried deep on page 25 of the Business Section of the Sunday *New York Times* (May 3, 1992). Dr. Jacqueline Jones, Harry S. Truman Professor of American Civilization at Brandeis University — who has completed a historical study of poverty from the Civil War to the present called *The Dispossessed* — makes clear, incisive remarks about the role of race in poverty, work and unemployment in America. Her study alludes to structural components in our society that explain poverty in America and that limit blacks, regardless of education or social strata. In the opening line of her study, Dr. Jones debunks the myth that blacks are a willful "underclass," as well as the notion that poverty is limited to urban blacks: "Poverty abides no line drawn by color or culture."

The article "When a White Collar Unravels," written by *New York Times* reporter Barbara Presley Noble, provides a summary of Dr. Jones's main points, citing the central role of race in the history of poverty in America: "...Since the Civil War, whites, especially white men, have been successful at constricting black opportunity. Early in this century, inexperienced whites applying for factory work were given preference over blacks, creating an economic foothold denied to blacks. Discrimination continued to preserve opportunities for white men by protecting them from competition."

In what appeared to be a forced press conference toward the end of the riots, Rodney King asked the question, "Can't we all get along?" The role of mainstream and alternative news media in how blacks and whites "get along" is crucial. The truth is a dangerous business, but lies are fatal. Mainstream news media has the combined agenda of reporting the news and making money. News editors are faced with making decisions between telling a story with in-depth coverage or appeasing viewers' limited attention span and endless appetite for the sensational image. Alternative journalism has the challenge of surviving and maintaining a product that attracts not only readers but advertisers. It is time for all who are in the business of news to realize their social responsibility at this fragile hour. And maybe it's time for business owners to devote their advertising dollars to publications that fulfill that social reponsibility, rather than supporting mainstream media that merely maintain the status quo.

Rodney King and all of black America were victimized by an all-white jury practicing a dual system of justice, one that comedian Richard Pryor has called "just-us justice." American media is simply another all-white jury that maintains a dual system of journalism.

A predominantly white and male industry presents visible white males committing invisible crimes, while relatively faceless blacks are presented committing crimes that are all too visible. Blacks are not the only ones affected by the media's portrayal of them as *the* public enemy. The entire nation suffers when the media support the notion that the only people who can invent, create, manage, govern and lead effectively are white. America's decline as a world power could be attributed to the wasted minds and potential of African-Americans and others who experience discrimination and discouragement from cradle to grave, regardless of their social standing or how hard they work.

No amount of singing, candlelight vigils or prayer meetings will have more of an effect on this episode of American history than ending the cycle of word-image relationships that villify blacks as the core of a so-called "race problem" in America. Recent events mandate both mainstream and alternative news media finally to seize the moment and lead the American people into social maturity. ∎

Bill Gaskins contributes to Columbus Alive!, *where a version of this story first appeared.*

Los Angeles: Debra DiPoalo

Through The Smoke Screen

by David M. Roth

Last Thursday night — the evening after all hell broke loose — I found myself morbidly transfixed by an ABC network show called *Top Cops*. This program's simplistic, venal outlook squares perfectly with that of the defendants in the Rodney King case, who believe that because it's a rotten, nasty world out there, we (white cops) had better do it to them before they (criminals, mostly of color) do it to us. The consequences of not following that credo were driven home chillingly in an episode where one member of a two-brother police team is shot in the face from the window of a car commandeered by four black men, who, like Rodney King, had been stopped for a traffic offense. The message: Black

males are a deadly force and should be dealt with accordingly.

Racist, rottenly timed programming? You bet. But there's more. Interspersed between episodes of *Top Cops* were promos for other programs filled with all manner of brutal, nightmarish violence. In other words, your basic TV fare. Problem was, when positioned against helicopter shots of LA burning, against plumes of black and gray smoke churning into the sky, against the gutted remains of family-owned businesses and against crowds of people gleefully looting, these crass juxtapositions led to two conclusions: one, that if this station were in LA, it, too, would probably be burning, and, two, that television is as much to blame for our depraved

state of affairs as our neglectful government.

One thing about TV, though: Like government, it's got a ready supply of chutzpah. It can mix good and evil without missing a beat. Directly on the heels of *Top Cops*, we had *Street Scenes*, a national newsmagazine hosted by Ed Bradley, the distinguished black journalist of *60 Minutes* fame, whose cool demeanor had been visibly eroded by the day's events. To a string of legal pundits, he posed one question repeatedly and with unmistakable rancor: "Did the jurors in the Rodney King case see something in that tape that the rest of America *didn't*?" None of the so-called legal experts offered anything that even approached a comprehensible answer, and Bradley's constant repetition of the question — as well as his rerunning of the damning footage — told viewers that something terribly wrong had happened in Simi Valley. And that something, whatever it was, was emblematic of the two-tiered system of social, economic and criminal justice that was literally tearing American cities apart. ■

David M. Roth is associate editor of the Sacramento News & Review, *where a version of this story first appeared.*

covering the riots: culture

Photo of Ice-T by Harrsion Funk

Interview with Ice-T

by Terry Gross

erry Gross: Ice T is from South Central LA, where the rioting first broke out. His lyrics are about gangs and street violence. He co-starred in the movie *New Jack City* as a renegade undercover cop trying to bust a crack house. But on his new record, *Body Count,* he has a track called "Cop Killer" about someone who has a gun and is ready to use it on a cop. The lyrics include words that aren't usually used on the radio. The chorus is, "Fuck the police for Daryl Gates, fuck the police for Rodney King."

We called Ice-T to talk about his inflammatory lyrics and his reaction to the rioting in LA. I asked him what he's thinking about now as watches his neighborhood go up in flames.

Ice-T: Well, it's a sad sight, you know, I saw a lot of places that I grew up around burned down, but at the same time it's something that I predicted. I knew it was going to happen sooner or later and I'm not surprised at all.

TG: Have you been out on the streets in the past couple of days?

IT: Yea, I've been out there and I have nothing but love out there. I go out there, I walk right amongst the people. They like, "What's up Ice," you know. I cannot stop them, the only person that could've stopped them was the person that would've got in there and got that guilty verdict.

TG: So what have you been doing on the streets?

IT: Just hanging out, talking, asking them to be careful, telling them to watch out for these National Guards. You know, it's my neigborbood. I'm not afraid because it's my people. And when I was up here in Hollywood cooling out, the gay people were rolling through Hollywood, Queer Nation, about 3,000 of them and they were like "get with us," and they're up here mad.

See the problem with this is, America was not prepared for so many people to be so angry. They were used to just being able to do something to somebody black and everybody else said, "It's OK." But the campuses, the schools and people are afraid. My attitude is, if you weren't prepared for this, if you didn't think it was going to happen, or if you are at all surprised, then it's your fault.

TG: Were you in a gang before you rapped?

IT: Yea.

TG: What was the worst that you did in a gang in terms of violence against a person?

IT: Whatever, you know, everything happens in a gang. And the day before this riot jumped off, the gangs in LA had called a truce.

And you got no national publicity for that. The Crips and the Bloods were hugging each other on TV. There were people that...you know, were like "OK, well the gangs stopped." I mean that was the biggest thing that happened in my life, was to see that happen, and then the next day... you know the problem is if these National Guards go into that neighborhood and they start shooting, it's not going to be like they're rounding up people from Omaha, Nebraska. They've got hardened people down there. These kids have been at war for the last 15 years and now they're together, they're going to run into some serious bloodshed down there.

TG: Let me ask you about your rap, "Cop Killer," which is about a character whose got his gun and is going to kill a cop and the chorus is "die, die, die, pig die. Fuck the police." Is that a rap that is supposed to be advocating people going out into the streets and doing that?

IT: No, it's a rap that lets you know that under certain situations you will push people to that attitude.

TG: I don't understand what you mean.

IT: OK, before this record came out, before this riot happened, you might have thought that there was one person who thought like that. Now, you're seeing the people out there who have that attitude.

It's a rap that says "Listen to me." The record goes, "I got my ski mask on, I got my black shirt on, I got my black gloves on, this shit has been too long. I got my twelve-gauge sawed off, my headlights turned off." And then the chorus is "cop killers, better you than me; cop killers, fuck police brutality." It's a record about rebellion against police brutality. It's a guy who said, "I am not going to allow you to whup on me." And if that's what it takes, then that's what it takes, because they are killing us out there and when they kill us they do not go to jail. A cop gets laid off for murdering somebody, they don't go to jail. Why?

TG: So do you feel that your record is encouraging people to take to the streets and do you want it to have that effect?

IT: No, nobody is listening to my record at this point. This is beyond my record. That record was just somebody... I'm letting you...I gave you warning, that record was warning. I can almost answer every question like "refer to album three, track one." Buy the *Iceberg* album and listen to album three, track one and I told you there was going to be marshal law. If you listen to the song "Body Count," I say what is a brother gotta do to get a message through? You know, you try to ban the AK, I got ten of them stashed with a case of hand grenades. The tension mounts. But up to now, "it was just a record," and it was "Oh, Ice-T running his mouth," but now you've seen it's real, it's like I don't even have to do nothing, now I can just sit back and you know, I'm some old Nostradamus and just watching it all unveil, I predicted it all. I predict this riot will continue all over the United States for at least another week.

TG: OK, so you feel like your records are predicting it, but on the other hand you can say that your records are helping to incite it.

IT: I could care less, because I want to see the people rise up. I am tired of Americans being cowards. I mean I am not just a rapper, rapping is something that I do, but I'm more of a person who really is sincerely mad at this system and how it has been treating people. I've got brothers in jail for four years for an ounce of weed. You

● ● ● ● ● ● ● ● ● ● ● ● ● ● ● ● ● ●

team coverage *n. Used by KFWB anchors to describe the station's riot reportage. The "team" simultaneously suggests sports and a sense of belonging to something. This last part is important in drawing the audiences because, unlike an earthquake, a field reporter can't rely on more than a few listeners to know — or care about — what they were doing when, say, Pep Boys burned down. "Team coverage" implies the listener is more than a spectator to history — he or she is a fan, rooting for widely scattered acts of heroism or booing similar moments of vandalism.*

(Source: *LA Weekly*, May 8, 1992)

know, people that I haven't seen.

TG: What have the cops done to you that you see them as the enemy?

IT: Put me in jail, kill a couple of my friends, beat me, harass me, look me in my eyes because I'm in my car and told me to get over, put me on the side of the road, laid me down in the street like a punk. All that has to do is happen to you once and you'll hate them.

You know, I live it. If you're not from LA you don't understand the Gestapo force of police that they have in LA. They're not humans. I just think white America, or the upper class, don't even have any way of understanding the injustices that go on in the ghetto, and until you do it's just a waste of my time explaining it to you. Do you have anybody in prison, any friends?

TG: Actually, I don't.

IT: See, I got buddies on death row. I get phone calls everyday from them, on death row, and they ain't killed nobody.

TG: Do you think that taking to the streets and burning down stores and carrying guns is a really a good solution to the problem?

IT: Is that how we had the first American revolution, where we broke away from the British, ain't that how we did it? Ain't that how they do it in the Persian Gulf, ain't that how they did it in Panama, isn't that how a revolution takes place?

TG: By destroying your own neighborhood? Not exactly.

IT: Well, they're moving to Beverly Hills right now. They just hit the Beverly Center last night. It ain't their own neighborhood, you know, it'll be your neighborhood next. It's going down, it's going down. ■

Terry Gross is host and executive producer of Fresh Air, *which is produced at WHYY-FM in Philadelphia and distributed via National Public Radio. This interview was taped on May 1, 1992.*

I Told You So

by Heather Mackey

When Chuck D says that rap music is like CNN for black people, it makes complete sense to me, because I use rap as a news source. My sources of information are different from the evening news — they have to be, because I don't watch a lot of TV.

Last week, something I heard over and over again from friends was how uncannily the violence in Los Angeles seemed to mirror songs in their record collections. Whether people thought they had heard it before in Ice Cube's lyrics or Public Enemy's, there was an uncomfortable feeling of *déjà vu*. I guess someone at National Public Radio had the same sensation. The day after the rioting in Los Angeles had reached its peak, I listened to *Fresh Air* correspondent Terry Gross interview Ice-T, who's from South Central. With my PCP-enhanced superhuman strength, I turned the radio volume on high and sat down to listen to white liberal America try to figure out whom to blame for the post-acquittal violence.

Later, after listening to the tape of it a couple of times, we all agreed that Gross made a noble sacrifice of herself. If she knew anything about rap, she gave no indication of it. If she knew anything about Ice-T, she pushed it aside. What she did was ask the kinds of questions that would get Ice-T exasperated enough to give a great interview.

In the time-honored tradition of trying to show that rap is a dangerous art form, Gross asked Ice-T if his music was inciting people to violence. First, she played the song "Cop Killer" to make her point. Isn't that a song that advocates violence, she asked? Well, listen to the lyrics, Ice-T replied: "Cop killer, better you than me/ Cop killer, fuck police brutality."

"Cop Killer," Ice-T explained, is a warning. It's a song about rebellion against police brutality: "They're killing us out there," he said, "and when they kill us, they don't go to jail. A cop gets laid off for murdering somebody. Why?"

"I predicted the whole thing," he says. "I can almost answer every question like, "Refer to album three, track one."

This little encounter between Gross and Ice-T is, in microcosm, the clash between two different information systems. Rap music tries to get a message out about the frustrating realities facing blacks today; mainstream media interprets that message as a threat. Ice-T is right when he says that "the violence in LA goes beyond my record," even though songs like "Body Count" seem to describe it. When Gross tries to tell him it's not going to make matters better if black people destroy their own neighborhoods, she's right, too. Gross asked Ice-T why he hates cops. He responded with a list of things that happened to him. He talked about his friends in jail. "I just think white America or the upper classes don't even have any way of understanding the injustices that go on in the ghetto," he said, "and until you do it's just wasting my time trying to explain it to you. Do you have anybody in prison?" he asked. "Actually, I don't," Gross answered, suddenly sounding a little embarassed.

Ice-T has a lot of bluster, but despite his tough-guy image, I don't think he's scary. Maybe I haven't been watching the same programs that other segments of white America have. "I'm not just a rapper," Ice-T said at the end of the interview. "Rapping is something that I do — but I'm more of a person who really is sincerely mad at this system." ■

Heather Mackey is a staff writer for the San Francisco Bay Guardian, *where a version of this column first appeared.*

Buy-It Riot

by Leslie Savan

Crisis calls for commercials. During the next few months, you may or may not see new economic programs sprouting up in the inner-cities of Los Angeles and other towns, but you will see the ads. "We can all work together" ads, "Intolerance is terrible" ads, even "Are you racist?" ads. Such public service announcements have run before, but only occasionally — advertising almost genetically avoids any message more hard-hitting than Hands Across the Ghetto. Even with cities ablaze, they still may not go much farther, but in the ad flurry everyone and his local anchorperson will at least know you shouldn't call other people names.

Of course, the first few days of the LA riots were a commercial emergency, and ads were on the scene quicker than the police. Los Angeles TV and radio stations ran spots asking people to stay cool, including clips of Martin Luther King, Jr.'s exhorting, "Build, baby, build." Tone-Loc and N.W.A.'s Ren refused to mouth "Stop the violence" in PSAs, but other rappers obliged.

Then *Ad Age* expanded the mission nationwide, running a front-page editorial — "A call to admen: Help stop riots." It implored companies (like sneaker firms) to make anti-violence ads, along the lines of the anti-drug spots by the Media-Advertising Partnership for a Drug-Free America. That dubious anti-drug ad blitz may serve as a role model for a campaign shaping up in Los Angeles. Last week, 15 top ad and media execs gathered to brainstorm ads that'll probably appear under the umbrella of Peter Ueberroth's Rebuild LA program. Meanwhile, Mingo, a black agency, and the Ad Council will soon air the first of a series of PSAs on racism. They'll be along the lines of "we have to ace what we've been denying — that discrimination exists — and we have to begin a dialogue," says a spokeswoman. Race suddenly has the media cachet drugs once did. "There is a window of opportunity right now insofar as media acceptance is concerned," says Ad Council president Ruth Wooden.

And though they've been in the works since Crown Heights, 250 brotherly love posters were installed in New York City phone booths the week after the riots. The following words run down black-and-white backgrounds: "You have a tumor. In your brain. A specialist is ready to operate. He's black. Is that a problem?" "Your son needs a new kidney. In 48 hours. They found a donor. He's white. Is that a problem?" A mite too drop-dead staccato (i.e. ad-like) for me, but as a declarative sentence, "You have a tumor" does rather grab your attention. And then forces you to wonder if you're racist. But only under extreme conditions. Is that a problem?

"There's so many stereotypical ideas of what a black person is or what a white person is," says Doug Raboy, who wrote the ads and who, along with his agency, Smith/Greenland, makes up "Citizens for Racial Harmony," which signed and paid for the posters. "So when you can twist it and give it a surprise, that's good. It's also supposed to show how silly racism is."

NYNEX's TV ad tries to show how childish it is. A bunch of green and blue marbles confront a bunch of orange and yellow marbles; they argue in cute, baby-like grunts. One blue and one orange marble finally break ranks and shake hands, so to speak. The marbles cheer, mingle in joy, and, as the camera pulls back, they have so mingled that they form — what else? — a globe. The whole ethnic peacefest gets a big fat NYNEX logo at the end. (This from the company that ran pro-Gulf war ads last year.) The spot was launched on Peter Jennings's (pre-verdict) children's special about prejudice, but the company bought extra time during riot week, because, says a spokeswoman, "NYNEX's mission is to help people communicate."

Unlike the marbles, Spike Lee's anti-racism spot for Nike uses the name-calling words, though they're the joke ones. "I

Los Angeles: Larry Hirshowitz

ain't playing ball with no ball-hoggin', gunnin', show-boatin', Nike-wearin', high-flyin', donut-dunkin', hip-hopping homeboy from Harlem," a white basketball player says to a black one, and so on. Spike ends on a note of peace and promo. "The mo' colors, the mo' better." The ad was filmed before the riots, but will be rushed onto the air sooner because of them. Ad people know they have the access to sell the right thing, but their industry has some major structural obstructions that militate against effective racism bashing. Advertising and TV are too complicit in the larger process that leads to Simi Valley denial and South Central looting.

Most obviously, ads help perpetuate a system that doesn't allow many people to live the good life the commercials tell them to. (Though guilt over this is almost palpable in the rush of post-riot advertising, that hardly means agencies will stop hyping the goods.) Advertising has also committed thousands of sins of image — to name just one example, luxury car-makers who resist putting blacks in their commercials because it would communicate "low status." A system that justifies itself as a democracy of money, that runs on the concept that the market is fair — an idea for which advertising is the frontline and that the LA riots defy — cannot spend too much energy proving otherwise. And

because it's in the interests of commercial culture to get us to think more or less alike — in order to sell millions of people the same product — advertising has a tough time promoting real differences between people. That puts it rather at odds with real racial harmony, which has to acknowledge *pluribus* before it can get to *unum*. Consider a current Ex-Lax commercial: A pretty woman with straight blond hair, the perfect median point between girl-next-door and model, further documents how normal she is by saying she jogs and swims but loves junk food. But even *she* sometimes gets constipated, she admits. "For regular people — who sometimes aren't," goes the tag line. If, as the very definition of "normal," she sometimes diverges, then it's OK for the rest of you to down Ex-Lax, too.

Shit happens, and television is always there to push it aside. The happy ending, the cute meet, the never-ending glamour glow of the big people in the big world we watch on our TVs send poverty and injustice far, far away.

If ads are going to attack racism at all, they've got to go for the structural jugular. Increase the pitch. ■

Leslie Savan writes the "Op Ad" column for the Village Voice, *where this article first appeared.*

129

in the aftermath: what's to be done

Los Angeles: Ted Soqui

Daughters of the Dust: Rebuilding Lives in LA *by Peter Noel*

Susan Cooper places her hungry, bawling four-month-old baby boy in a rickety crib parked in the middle of her water-soaked living room. Cooper's building in LA's Mid-Wilshire section blazed on April 30 after arsonists torched an adjacent apartment complex under construction. Now she maneuvers around a table cluttered with chairs, rumpled clothes, Pampers and rotting food in her one-bedroom, ground-floor apartment. With the names of her husband and two of her five small children tattooed on her left arm, Cooper, 28, sits down on a maroon suede couch and begins to chart the future of her family.

Meanwhile, Yvonne Davis, 30, who lived on the third floor in Cooper's building, is in an even worse predicament: Her one-bedroom apartment, which she shared with her three children, was gutted and looted "by strays" the day after the fire. One week later, she and her daughter Porsja, 10, have returned to the apartment on a salvage mission. Except for a few sentimental mementos, including a Bible and Nintendo cartridges, all was lost.

Rebuilding the lives of the two women and their families won't be easy in the wake of the revolt of LA's permanent underclass. Both Cooper and Davis are "welfare moms" who jack reluctantly to the humiliating dictates of LA's public-assistance programs. They are two out of 735,000 Los Angeles County residents who receive Aid for Families with Dependent Children. But if California Governor Pete Wilson has his way, benefits to some families would ultimately be reduced by 25 percent per household per month. A referendum proposing the cuts will be on the November ballot in California. The cuts would devastate the Cooper and Davis families — cutting roughly $200 a month from each of their incomes. Davis balances her "welfare budget," a $788 monthly check, "on my own back."

Cooper, a certified registered nurse, could not find work after her first child was born. Her husband, Michael, 30, is an unemployed maintenance man. They take turns watching the children and looking for work. "I get $928 every month," says Cooper, who picks up her 15-month-old boy and guides him around shards of glass "My rent is $535. Last year they cut $50 out of my money, and now they want to cut another 25 per cent. They are cutting aid to poor black people to try to compensate for the mess that they've made. And if you think people are angry now, imagine it that happens. Imagine them trying to 'Rebuild LA' without us. It's unrealistic."

Cooper is a self-described "amateur politician," but "a practical one." She blasted "the contrary direction" of official white outcry to black outrage over the Rodney King verdict, arguing that responsibility for the nation's worst civil unrest in this century begins and ends with President George Bush, whose spokesperson in turn blamed the Great Society welfare programs

130

designed by the Democrats in the '60s and '70s to rescue inner-city blacks from poverty.

And while conditions degenerated long before Bush became president in 1988, for Cooper, the whole Reagan-Bush era has been sort of a blur: "What about the years of urban neglect by Mr. Bush?" she asks. "In my opinion, the riots were a direct result of a plan by Mr. Bush to give some states the go-ahead to cut back on aid to mothers who get pregnant while they are on public assistance. The Rodney King verdict was the final kick in the butt." Cooper says she would return to the job market only if the government provides day care for her children — a proposal the shell-shocked Bush administration has squelched. "The government does not want to pay for day care, and that is why a lot of mothers I know prefer to stay on welfare."

Davis, who lost her job as a receptionist and check-cashing processor three years ago, says, "I want to get off public assistance but the government keeps jerking us around in this cycle of poverty, saying we're enjoying the ride and don't wanna get off. It's hard to keep up with the system or to get out when they keep changing the rules. And before you know it, people are gonna rise from the ashes like embers and spark more fury."

Twenty-four years ago, the Kerner Commission, which investigated the cause of the riots that inflamed black ghettos in 1965, concluded that "Our present system of public assistance contributes materially to the tensions and social disorganization that have led to civil disorders. The failures of the system alienate the taxpayers who support it. As one critic told the Commission, 'The welfare system is designed to save money instead of people and tragically ends up doing neither.'...It provides assistance well below the minimum necessary for a humane level of existence, and imposes restrictions that encourage continued dependency on welfare and undermine self-respect."

Yvonne Brathwaite Burke, a candidate for supervisor of Central LA's Second District, repeated a campaign promise to "do everything to urge the defeat of Governor Pete Wilson's plan to cut welfare" if she is elected in California's June 2 primary elections. "His plan is yet another massive shift of responsibility for the care of the indigent to California's county taxpayers whose taxes are already too high," says Burke, California's first African-American assemblywoman and the state's first African-American congresswoman. "This kind of action must be opposed, strongly and promptly, by everyone."

As Bush announced plans to tour riot-torn LA, Susan Cooper was busy tracking several food distribution sites and awaiting the arrival of workers hired by the building's management to come in with their giant fans to suck water out of the walls and replace her soggy carpet. "I wish the president would put the emphasis on rebuilding lives and not corporate LA; our babies gotta eat, too," she says.

Upstairs, Yvonne Davis talked about rising from the ruins of LA. "I am determined not to get lost in the awful depression that has intensified among black people since the rebellion," says Davis, who stuffed a supermarket cart full of items retrieved from her apartment.

"There is no hostility in my heart," says the woman, who is staying with friends until her apartment is repaired. "This is just the end of another struggle for me. I know what I have gone through these past few days."

Annie Henderson, 69, a neighbor for 15 years who lives on the second floor, drops by the burned-out apartment to see how Davis is holding up. "Now, you're lucky," the retired social worker tells Davis. "They [looters] didn't leave my couch. They took all of my clothes and didn't drop a hanger. It's like somebody dropped a bomb in there."

But Davis is more concerned about Henderson's psychological condition — not everyone in the building has reacted positively to the fire that destroyed 20 apartments. "I don't know how I feel," she says hesitantly. "It might hit me later." Davis urges Henderson to dump any pent-up bad feelings about the fire. "Well," says Henderson, "let me put it this way. I was raised up with my three brothers and they always told me not to worry about anything, just say, 'I don't care.' So that's the way I feel. I don't care."

Henderson says she isn't particularly concerned about rebuilding LA; she's hopeful, but skeptical that African-Americans will be awarded a fair share of the contracts to "build and rebuild" their communities. "I'm just glad I had fire insurance," she says. Three white insurance adjusters, who are surveying structural damage to the building during this conversation, ignore Henderson and hurriedly leave the floor. Shortly after, a white man who identifies himself as John approaches Davis and tries to get her to end her interview with a reporter and a photographer.

"The owner doesn't want any press in the building," John says. "Channel 5 was here on Saturday and started a riot; they just excited all these people who started yelling and screaming, and I had to be taken out of the building by four LAPD officers."

John refuses to say why the tenants, the majority of whom are black and Chicano single mothers, had reacted angrily toward him. "This appears to be the only apartment building that was burned down in the whole city," he snaps. Davis later tells the reporter that tenants had long complained about poor living conditions prior to the fire.

After John leaves, one of two "representatives of the lender" who helped finance the construction of the building asks Davis if, while fleeing the burning building, she remembered to set off the fire alarm as she raced down the stairs to safety. "I told everybody to get outta here. Wasn't that enough?"

Davis takes the investigators' question as a suggestion that she — and African-American Angelenos in general — would let her building burn as revenge against the white owners, even though tenants themselves would suffer the consequences. "They say it's not a racial thing," Davis tells a reporter, "but it is."

Porsja cuts in, with a barb that's a clear rebuke to the investigator's insinuation: "I want to be a lawyer, then president of the United States, because I want to help people instead of businesses." ■

Peter Noel is a staff investigative reporter for the Village Voice, *where a version of this story first appeared.*

Editor's note: Along with property destruction and loss of life, another casualty of the LA riots was individual constitutional rights. In many areas, LA's criminal-justice system proved woefully incapable of dealing fairly with chaos on such a grand scale: Undocumented aliens were summarily deported, homeless people were jailed, and many of those arrested remained imprisoned for days before hearing the charges against them. In response to widespread concern about such abuses, in late June the Southern California affiliate of the ACLU issued Civil Liberties in Crisis, *a report that offers a reform plan for dealing with future emergencies. The report's executive summary is excerpted below.*

Los Angeles: Larry Hirshowitz

Civil Liberties in Crisis

by the ACLU Foundation of Southern California

Although newspapers and television have been flooded with stories of the riots that swept Los Angeles, not enough attention has been paid to the quality of justice that was meted out during that time.

Practically every politician running for office this election year is promoting his or her "tough on crime" image by calling for maximum punishment for those swept up in the law-enforcement response to the civil unrest. But who were the people caught up in this widely cast net? What were they arrested for? Were they dealt with fairly? And, if this type of emergency should again arise, how should the city respond differently?

Civil Liberties in Crisis: Los Angeles During the Emergency, prepared by the staff of the ACLU Foundation of Southern California, attempts to answer these questions by providing, for the first time since the unrest, a comprehensive analysis of all available data and anecdotal information pertaining to the law-enforcement and judicial response to the emergency. In compiling this complex report, several things became clear.

First, neither complete blame nor congratulations are in order when it comes to the city's response to the disorder. Some areas worked well, and others completely fell apart under the burden of mass arrests, mass detentions and fear surrounding the unrest. In addition, because information, statistical and otherwise, pertaining to the disorder is difficult to come by and sometimes was never kept at all, a complete picture of the situation will probably never be available.

In many instances, people were treated unfairly by the overburdened system. Often serious civil-liberties violations, including a loss of individual rights, were tolerated and practiced in the name of mass efficiency and political vindictiveness.

Many areas need to be examined and changed so that if and when such an outbreak of unrest should occur again, the city will be prepared to respond in a more just and effective manner.

A growing body of evidence shows that police and federal agencies used the time of civil unrest to round up and deport people who they believed to be illegal immigrants. Reports by immigrants-rights community groups reveal that, during and after the unrest, the Los Angeles Police Department stopped and interrogated many Latinos regarding their immigration status, then turned many of them over to the Immigration and Naturalization Service (INS). These turnovers often occurred without the lodging of criminal charges.

Not only did LAPD officers spend valuable time during the unrest rounding up undocumented immigrants who were not involved in violence or looting, but they continued to do so after the conclusion of the unrest. The LA Sheriff's Department was also involved in this activity, far exceeding the number of immigration-related turnovers in which they are normally involved. Between April 29 and May 20, the LASD turned over 1,090 people to the INS, and the LAPD turned over another 452 people. Once given to the INS, many immigrants signed voluntary deportation orders when faced with the threat of long prison terms and $20,000 bail.

On April 30, Mayor Tom Bradley signed an ordinance putting into effect a dusk-to-dawn curfew which — broadly interpreted — allowed police officers to arrest virtually anyone out after dark for any reason.

Unfortunately, the terms of the curfew were not published in Spanish-language newspapers, nor accurately conveyed to the public in speeches or electronic broadcasts; hence, many people who believed they were not in violation of the curfew, because they had a valid reason for being outside, were arrested and jailed for up to a week.

Many people were arrested for curfew violations while coming from and going to work. There are also an estimated 70,000 homeless people in Los Angeles, and only 6,634 shelter beds. When the mayor instituted the curfew, hundreds of Angelenos with no place to go were arrested for simply being on the streets.

The ACLU believes that the application of the emergency curfew to homeless citizens violates the Eighth Amendment by enforcing criminal penalties against the homeless for their very status as people without homes. If there were sufficient shelter space available to house the homeless, many never would have faced jail sentences.

Many individuals who committed minor offenses — most arrested for simply being in the wrong place at the wrong time — found their lives turned upside down by the broad discretion practiced by police officers making arrests during the state of emergency. The combination of excessive levels of bail and the threat of harsh sentences, delays in arraignments and overcrowded jail facilities created conditions that caused hundreds of people to plead guilty to misdemeanor offenses — virtually all curfew violations — with which they should never have been charged in the first place.

In the period immediately following the emergency, civil-liberties violations combined to virtually ensure that hundreds of people — many of whom had no prior contact with law enforcement or the criminal-justice system — would be forced to plead guilty to avoid the damage of continuing pre-trial detentions. People who were arrested often spent several days in jail before even hearing the charges that were filed against them, and then were dealt with *en masse* in the courtroom. These people were then told they could plead guilty for their crime — whatever it was — and get out of jail in the next few days, or ask to see a lawyer and spend perhaps the next month in jail waiting for a trial. Thus,

thousands of people were virtually forced into pleading guilty and developing a criminal record — regardless of the crime or their guilt. In Inglewood, one person was charged with a felony and got $50,000 bail for stealing sunflower seeds from a convenience store.

For several weeks after Mayor Bradley's declaration of a state of emergency, the constitutional rights of peaceful demonstrators in public places were also severely restricted. Permits for protests, demonstrations, rallies or marches on public sidewalks and streets and in designated public forums were refused or ignored by police, and numerous peaceful and orderly demonstrators were jailed. Most disturbing is the fact that the police's treatment of such demonstrators seemed to depend upon the content of their message.

Some demonstrations, like the one held by the Korean community on Saturday, May 2, in the midst of the emergency, were permitted and protected while other marches or demonstrations with messages more critical of the LAPD or other government officials were suppressed.

Of the 45 people whose deaths were related to the Los Angeles violence, 10 were killed by law-enforcement officers or National Guard troops. Two of the decedents were shot in the back.

Although media reports speculated about more than 18,000 arrests, when arrest numbers were finally tabulated, only 12,545 individuals had been arrested during the emergency. Statistics also demonstrate a disparity between arrest rates for Latinos and for African-Americans — with Latinos suffering statistically higher arrests. Of the 5,633 arrests during the emergency included in this review, 51 percent are Latino and 36 percent are African-American.

Given the fear and uncertainty of the initial days of the emergency, it isn't surprising that some of the violations described in this report occurred. Law enforcement and the criminal-justice system were confronted with a situation that stretched the capacity of existing systems. The criminal-justice system did not have adequate plans to cope

with an emergency of this dimension. Clearly, one of the issues the system must address is the need for better planning in future emergencies to avoid such violations and problems. In this report, the ACLU makes more than 30 recommendations, a few of which are as follows:

•Assemble an independent task force or commission, with adequate staff and operating support, to examine the criminal-justice system's response to the unrest. This inquiry should focus on specific components of the criminal-justice system, including the courts, detention/custody and prosecuting agencies, bearing in mind the larger social context of the unrest.

•Terminate immediately the de facto practice of improperly turning people over to the U.S. Immigration and Naturalization Service.

•Develop realistic contingency plans for housing homeless people during emergencies. At a minimum, specific public facilities should be identified as places of refuge for homeless people who cannot be accommodated in existing shelters.

•Allow individuals sentenced for curfew violation during the first days of the recent disorder to withdraw their guilty pleas. These individuals should be allowed to contest the charges without the pressure of continued incarceration and have the benefit of counsel. If their cases are dismissed, their records should be expunged and destroyed. Prosecuting agencies must make every effort to locate homeless people convicted of curfew violation and readjudicate their cases.

•Consider legislation to reduce curfew violations from a misdemeanor to an infraction. Sentencing policies for simple curfew violation should be revised, favoring community service or fines instead of incarceration. These changes should apply retroactively to people already convicted in the recent unrest.

•Enact legislation to require local governments to maintain detailed emergency contingency plans as a precondition to qualifying for temporary legislative relief from court timetable rules. ∎

For further information, contact the ACLU Foundation of Southern California at (213) 977-9500.

Stop the Stereotyping

by Walter Stafford

For virtually all groups of color, the multicultural riots that shook Los Angeles were clear evidence of our country's growing inability to establish and maintain racial equality and justice. For blacks, who had already been migrating out of the inner-city and returning to the South for more than a decade, it confirmed longstanding expectations of urban racism. For Latinos, who along with blacks have been a particular focus of police brutality, the riots confirmed their invisibility: Despite the fact that more Latinos than blacks were among the initial arrests, the national press focused almost exclusively on blacks.

If groups of color saw the riots as confirmation of their usual fears, for whites the explosion was a warning about the future. Surveys in Los Angeles following the riots indicated that slightly more than two-thirds of LA residents expected further outbursts in the years to come. Already a city with one of the highest proportions of gun dealers in the country, Los Angeles also saw a mass rush to stock up on arms. With angry and defensive minorities arrayed on one side and aggressive and armed whites on the other, LA is turning from an already segregated and violent city into an armed camp.

Meanwhile, for the nation's policy-making elite — its politicians, think-tanks, academicians, policy analysts and journalists — the Rodney King verdict was just another instance of suburban whites voting to protect their distance from the ever-dangerous black male. Instead of seizing the opportunity to deal with the domestic policy issues underscored by the riots, many politicians pointed to the uprising as evidence not of institutionalized racism but of the absence of values among lower-income groups and the criminal propensities of the welfare-dependent underclass. Policymakers ignored surveys that made it clear racism was a major concern of both blacks and whites, and that the public felt increasingly strongly about helping inner-city communities. With the notable exceptions of Congresswoman Maxine Waters (D-CA) and Senator Bill Bradley (D-NJ), leaders of both parties took refuge in platitudes about law and order and moral values. Most seemed to believe that by painting a picture of America as a nation with fluid upward mobility and shared, successful values, they could undermine threats to their leadership that might coalesce around the issue of bigotry. Ultimately, what politicians in this country fear most is blacks and Latinos uniting to fight racism.

One of the many ironies of the events in Los Angeles is that they shattered the preception of national unity engendered by the Persian Gulf war. In fact, in United States history, it is not unusual for urban race riots to erupt in the wake of wars. Race riots flared in 1863, during the second half of the Civil War, in New York City; they also erupted around World Wars I and II, as well as during Vietnam. As during Vietnam, during the Gulf war politicians and policymakers used the nation's media to focus attention on smart bombs and other attention-grabbing military success stories, steering it away from such troubling issues as the racism involved in attacking Iraq or the disproportionate number of black and Latino troops. It was only coincidence that such issues were so perfectly crystallized by the video of the Rodney King beating, which flashed around the world only a few days after U.S.-led planes bombed retreating Iraqi soldiers in stalled vehicles.

Are any new lessons to be learned from the Los Angeles experience? Yes and no. Los Angeles residents showed great resilience and resourcefulness in developing options for their city after the riot. Yet none of the East Coast papers covered these options. Los Angeles newspapers published articles with ideas from urban planners, citizens, agency directors and gang members about how to redevelop South Central LA. The plans emphasized the need for contracts from city, state and federal governments to support redevelopment; year-round schools and new training centers; and funds for black credit unions, school improvement measures and constructive ways to fight crime.

Bending to pressure from polls suggesting the government needed to do something, the Bush administration offered enterprise zones — a concept the General Accounting Office has largely discredited — as the answer to the beleaguered inner-cities. It also came up with the scheme of selling the Los Angeles airport to pay for damage caused by the riots. Not surprisingly, Los Angeles officials scoffed at such suggestions.

If the rebellion in Los Angeles is going to have any long-term impact, the strategies being discussed in the city need to be linked to a broader federal framework. Cities where riots have occurred thus far, and cities where they are likely to occur in the future, should be designated as "filtering" cities. As such, they should be targeted for special grants, including funds to increase black and Hispanic economic development, establish bilingual training programs for all youth and encourage contracts for business development from international firms and incubators for new businesses.

But even if government were to endorse these plans, a fundamentally important issue remains to be addressed: the stereotype of black men as inherently violent. For it is this stereotype that allows police and the criminal-justice system the freedom to abuse. As a result of the stereotype, a disproportionate number of blacks as well as Hispanics are in prison, in jail or under supervision of the criminal-justice system. Amnesty International and Human Rights Watch have rightly identified this problem as an international issue, arguing that the disturbing social conditions of our cities require new, objective monitors. ∎

Walter Stafford is an associate professor at the Wagner School of Public Services at New York University.

what's to be done: reforming the cops

Prop. F Wins Big

by Laureen Lazarovici

On May 2, 1992, an impromptu, multiracial coalition of Angelenos took to the streets with brooms and shovels to clean up the mess left by the riots. On June 2, they took to the ballot boxes to clean up the mess left by decades of an aloof and often brutal police department by passing Charter Amendment F, the landmark police-reform measure. Proposition F was approved by an overwhelming 67 percent of the voters, a signal that LA's citizens are ready to begin what will be a long and painful healing process.

Prop. F was a compilation of the most far-reaching reforms to emerge from the Christopher Commission report, written by a blue-ribbon panel headed by former diplomat Warren Christopher, with members appointed by both Mayor Tom Bradley and Police Chief Daryl Gates. The charter amendment limits the police chief to two five-year terms, gives the mayor and City Council a greater role in choosing the chief, adds a civilian to the police conduct review board and provides more options for disciplining officers.

The measure's victory did not come as a surprise to either its supporters or detractors. A poll in the *Los Angeles Times* days before the election showed Prop. F leading with 61 percent in favor,

Illustration of Daryl Gates by Roman Genn

17 percent against and 22 percent undecided. In addition, the poll showed Gates's disapproval rating at a whopping 81 percent. Although Prop. F did not directly affect Gates's tenure at the LAPD (he had announced his June retirement date many months earlier), it was seen as a repudiation of the arrogant, imperious, controversial chief's performance both after the Rodney King beating (which he termed "an aberration") and the bungled police response to the riots.

The two sides spent roughly the same amount of money (about $500,000 each) on the campaign but pursued opposite strategies. The No on F forces relied mostly on TV, while the Yes on F side adopted an old-fashioned field operation. One of the ironies of the campaign is that the chief strategists on the No side were East Coast-based consultants Gerald Austin and

Henry Sheinkopf; Austin handled Jesse Jackson's 1988 presidential bid. They produced a controversial TV ad that featured footage of the infamous Reginald Denny beating. The commercial blames the riots on three political leaders, two of them black and one Jewish: Mayor Tom Bradley, Councilman Mark Ridley-Thomas and Police Commission President Stanley Sheinbaum. "The police wanted to do their job" on the night of the riots, the commercial says, as images of looters flash on the screen. "They weren't allowed." Within a week, all the local TV stations were refusing to run the ad.

While the LAPD officers' union, the Police Protective League, provided the overwhelming bulk of the money for the No on F campaign, the Yes on F forces, Citizens for Law Enforcement and Reform (CLEAR), raised money from the city's development, business, legal and entertainment industry elites. The amount raised, however, disappointed many activists. Insiders blame a host of factors for sapping funds: the recession, a large number of contested congressional races, complacency about F's seemingly inevitable passage and disaffection with elections in general.

The Yes campaign would have needed $2 million to run the kind of street campaign it wanted to and be on TV. "In a choice between the airwaves and the streets, we're taking it to the streets," said

Yes on F spokesman Fred MacFarlane. The campaign bypassed television in favor of phone banks, precinct walking and regional offices in strategic parts of the city, including the mostly white and middle-class San Fernando Valley.

There was a broad base of support for Prop. F, including established conservative leaders and organizations who believed F would make our city safer. The Yes on F campaign targeted Valley homeowner groups for support, viewing them as the crucial neighborhood organizations — like block clubs in South Central and churches in East LA — that provide some cohesiveness in an increasingly atomized city.

Rob Glushon of the Encino Property Owners Association, whose group favored Prop. F, felt a strong showing for the measure in the Valley could dispel some of the stereotypes about the area. "It is more than a vote on police reform," Glushon said. "If we get a sizable number of people who traditionally support the police to vote for F, that sends a powerful message beyond the implementation of the measure." He must be a bit disappointed. A majority of Valley voters did vote for Prop. F, but not in the same high numbers as voters in other parts of the city.

But Prop. F's margin of passage overall proves that the lack of funds and TV commercials, and the reluctance of white swing voters, was not enough to torpedo the most significant police reform in recent LA history. After the videotaped Rodney King beating, the trial and inexplicable acquittals of the four LAPD lawmen involved and the ensuing urban violence, LA voters knew it was time for them to reclaim their city. ■

Laureen Lasarovici is a staff writer for the LA Weekly, *where a version of this story first appeared.*

• • • • • • • • • • • • • • • • • • •

"To achieve full integration
[in Los Angeles],
over three-quarters of all blacks
and over half of all Chicanos and
Latinos would have to move into
Anglo neighborhoods."

(Source: Paul Ong)

Controlling the Cops

by Vince Bielski and Laura Proctor

I f any good comes of the acquittal of the four white cops who beat Rodney King, it's that police reform may be just around the corner. The long-fought battle to reduce police violence in San Francisco is gaining momentum following the widespread rebellion about the unjust verdicts. As protesters in Los Angeles sent a smoke signal of rage out to the country, Terence Hallinan became the first San Francisco supervisor to vow to stall the Police Officers Association's (POA) contract if it's not amended to lift the veil of secrecy at the Office of Citizen Complaints (OCC), the San Francisco police watchdog agency.

Hallinan, who chairs a Board of Supervisors committee that must approve the POA contract, said he has enough support to block the contract if the reforms aren't included. The reforms, a product of the mayor's Task Force on Police Discipline, are meant to increase the effectiveness of the OCC, whose secret investigations and low rate of sustained misconduct complaints have tainted the agency's reputation.

Hallinan argues that because the city has offered the police a generous pay raise in the middle of a severe budget crisis, the police union should swallow its medicine. "The POA is asking for a 28 percent raise," the supervisor said. "They can at least give us open OCC hearings."

At the same time, a similar political battle has unfolded in the state legislature, with two bills introduced after the King beating to curb police misconduct. From the beginning, however, the statewide reforms faced stiff opposition from California's numerous police officer associations.

These groups, like the innocuously named Police Officers Research Association, are among the biggest donors to political campaigns in the state. The California Correctional Peace Officers Association, for instance, poured more than $760,000 into Pete Wilson's gubernatorial campaign. Only the national Republican Party gave Wilson more money, the *LA Times* reported recently.

Both bills have been delayed in the Senate Judiciary Committee as a result of the riots that have shaken many California cities. SB 1335, carried by Senator Art

Torres (D-Los Angeles), is a sweeping reform measure that will increase the number of criminal prosecutions for police misconduct.

Currently, local prosecutors rarely bring charges against police officers, in part because these prosecutors and police work together closely on a day-to-day basis. Under the Torres bill, felony-level misconduct investigations would be handled instead by the Attorney General, thus removing the conflict of interest with local prosecutors. The bill would also create a citizen police-review board in all counties that don't have one.

Senator Bill Greene (D-Los Angeles) is carrying legislation to repeal a 1982 law allowing officers to file defamation suits against citizens who falsely accuse them of misconduct. The problem with the law is that it dissuades citizens from filing complaints against officers for fear of being counter-sued.

Opponents say police need such protection from malicious complaints, but currently the police are the only public employees in California who have the right to sue for defamation. Former Senator Alan Robbins, who's responsible for the 1982 law, was sentenced last week to five years in prison on political corruption charges.

Unsure of their constituencies' reactions to the contrasting TV images of police brutality and rampaging crowds, lawmakers are stalling both bills. "The timing might not make sense," said Greg Schmidt, chief of staff for Senator Bill Lockyer (D-San Leandro), who chairs the judiciary committee. "You don't make good policy in a crisis situation. We want something that works, not just to pass a law."

But Larry Morse, legislative director for Senator Milton Marks (D-San Francisco), disagrees. "There couldn't be a worse time for the opponents of these bills," he said. "We need to do everything we can to convince the public that there are not two different standards — those for police officers and those for everyone else." ∎

Vince Bielski and Laura Proctor contribute to the SF Weekly, *where a version of this story first appeared.*

Shattered Cities

by Jonathan Marshall

When White House spokesman Marlin Fitzwater blamed social programs of the 1960s and 1970s for the riots that followed the Rodney King verdict, he got his decade wrong. A more likely cause of the violence was a major social program that reached its height in the 1980s: the so-called war on drugs.

That war, fought daily on the streets of urban America, has been waged with good intentions and overwhelming public support. It has also benefitted from extraordinary resources: Federal spending on drug enforcement has increased 10-fold in the Reagan-Bush years.

Yet not only has it failed to stem the flow of drugs into American cities — the federal government just last week reported a rise in hard-core drug use — the "war" has magnified the sense of alienation and economic despair among inner-city residents, particularly minorities.

The drug war has wreaked havoc by treating whole classes of Americans as potential suspects, subject to harassment and abuse. By sweeping vast numbers of petty drug users and sellers into the criminal-justice system, the campaign has branded them as convicts, often destroying their hope of becoming productive citizens. In that sense — by arousing resentment against established authority and further impoverishing an already disadvantaged population — the war on drugs helped ignite the recent riots.

For many blacks and Hispanics, drug enforcement increases the chances of police harassment and even brutality. The narcotics police in America's cities (like American soldiers in Vietnam) have a hard time telling friends from enemies.

Novelist Ishmael Reed, for example, has described being stopped and searched last year by three members of the Burbank Airport Narcotics Security Force. "It was an ugly moment," Reed recalled in a recent article. "I thought I was going to suffer bodily harm." Given the frequency of such testimonials, it is no wonder that half of all black Americans surveyed in a recent *Time*-CNN poll said they risk being treated unfairly in everyday encounters with police.

The national crackdown on drugs in the 1980s "affected blacks much more severely than whites," says Troy Duster, director of the Institute for the Study of Social Change at the University of California-Berkeley. "Police went after dealers [in black neighborhoods], not after white buyers from Marin or Pacific Heights." Similarly, no resident of Los Angeles doubts for a moment that police are more likely to make drug busts in Watts than in the Hollywood hills.

Minorities also suffer because many states mete out much harsher punishment for crack than for ordinary cocaine, the drug of choice in wealthy suburbs. The Michigan Supreme Court last year ruled such an arbitrary distinction discriminatory and unconstitutional. But federal law still mandates a five-year minimum sentence for possession of five grams of crack, yet only a maximum one-year sentence for possession of any amount of powder cocaine.

By the mid-1980s, these factors led to a "dramatic, exponential growth in arrest rates for blacks compared to whites," according to Alfred Blumstein, dean of the School of Urban and Public Affairs at Carnegie-Mellon University. A recent report by the Edna McConnell Clark Foundation notes that, as of 1988, 43 percent of felony offenders convicted of drug trafficking in state courts were black, even though government studies show that black Americans make up only about 12 percent of the nation's drug users. In New York, 92 percent of people arrested for

Los Angeles: Ted Soqui

drug offenses in 1989 were black or Hispanic.

The number of Americans behind bars exploded more than 130 percent between 1980 and 1990. By the end of the decade, jails and prisons held more than a million individuals with another 3 million on parole or probation. The billions spent to target drug offenders explains much of this dizzy growth. In 1980, 25 percent of federal inmates were incarcerated on drug charges. By January 1992, they represented 58 percent of the federal prison population. Since 1987, according to the Bureau of Prisons, drug offenders have made up three-quarters of all new inmates.

Much the same story occurred on the state level, as mandatory sentencing laws clogged prisons with drug users and peddlers. In Indiana, selling three grams of cocaine can land you a sentence of 20 to 50 years.

For some minorities, these trends have had a truly devastating impact. According to a 1990 report from The Sentencing Project, a Washington-based reform organization, a quarter of all black American men aged 20 to 29 were behind bars, on parole or on probation — far more than there were black men of all ages in college. An astonishing 35 percent of black men of all backgrounds aged 16 to 35 were arrested at some point in 1989, according to calculations by Harvard economist Richard Freeman.

The Sentencing Project's report concluded, "Given these escalating rates of control, we risk the possibility of writing off an entire generation of black men from having the opportunity to lead productive lives in our society."

Prison amounts to an economic life sentence, not just a career detour. A recent study by Freeman found that men jailed before 1980 worked 25 to 30 percent less in later years than those who were never locked up. Fifty percent of those punished had held a job before incarceration, but only 19 percent did afterward. In view of these grim consequences, Freeman concluded, crime has become an intrinsic part of the youth unemployment and poverty problem, rather than deviant behavior on the margin.

Freeman did not try to pin down the mechanisms by which incarceration cripples job chances, but they are not hard to guess. A criminal record makes anyone much less desirable to employers. And the prison experience socializes inmates in ways hardly conducive to successful life on the outside.

Patricia Khan, a supervising parole agent with the California Youth Authority, notes that by the time young men leave that system, they will have spent most of their teen years in and out of custody, denied a chance to develop normal social skills and poorly equipped to think for themselves after taking orders every hour of every day.

"So now you have someone who is academically behind, socially backward and with little or no work experience," she says. "You have a man coming out who is 20 years old but functioning like a 13-year-old, who is expected to be self-sufficient. These are very serious hurdles."

In a truly vicious circle, the increasingly bleak job prospects for black men who do not get past high school make them more prone to selling drugs as a sideline; and that in turn raises their chances of imprisonment and thus a life of even worse poverty.

Discrimination has always held young black men back in the job market. But in the 1980s, the loss of blue-collar jobs, the huge erosion in real wages for low-skilled work and the weakening of industrial unions made legitimate work far less attractive for the poorly educated.

At the same time, drug dealing became much more profitable as stepped-up enforcement raised the reward for dealers willing to take risks. In 1989, 66 percent of young black men in Boston said they could earn "more on the street doing something illegal than on a straight job," an increase of 50 percent since 1980, when the economy was much weaker. More than four in five told interviewers that dealing drugs could be "a good way to make money."

• • • • • • • • • • • • • • • • • •

heal-ing pro-cess n
In a hypochondriac city like Los Angeles, the concept of healing has immediate appeal to people weary both of the King verdict violence and of having to watch it on TV. Coupling the word "process" also offers a purposeful, soap-opera-ish feeling of closure: After pain comes the balm. But will there be a genuine civic effort to heal the hurt of the communities outraged by the judgement of the Simi Valley jury, or merely an attempt to bring these communities to heel?

(Source: *LA Weekly,* 5/8/92)

Families and communities suffer no less than individuals from this vicious circle. A study last year by Anne Case at Princeton and Lawrence Katz at Harvard showed that the biggest family determinant of crime is growing up in a household with a family member in jail, confirming the assumption that prison breeds more crime across generations.

Experts offer no magic solution for this complex of ills — yet the cycle must be broken, lest the riots of early May be repeated in years to come.

Recent research points to a surprisingly strong potential for prison rehabilitation programs to turn convicts around. Carefully designed approaches can cut recidivism rates as much as 50 percent, according to Paul Gendreau, a psychologist at the University of New Brunswick.

Yet society has chosen to ignore this potential. "Rehabilitation is today considered the least significant corrections goal," notes Marc Mauer of The Sentencing Project. "In recessionary times, prison education and drug programs are the first to be cut."

The recent Clark Foundation report also advocates closely supervised residential drug treatment as a cost-effective alternative to imprisonment for non-violent offenders. Finally, for individuals at risk who have not yet turned to crime, investing more in education and training to raise the pay of legitimate work relative to crime should take precedence over building new prisons. The former may not be a sure-fire winner, but the latter program is a proven failure.

"In the 1980s, we conducted a great experiment," Harvard's Freeman observes. "We locked up huge numbers of people, but it didn't reduce the crime rate. So we know that doesn't work and had better try something different." ∎

Jonathan Marshall is economics editor of the San Francisco Chronicle *and co-author of* Cocaine Politics: Drugs, Armies and the CIA in Central America. *This story first appeared in* The Washington Post.

Los Angeles: Ted Soqui

The Color of News

by Erna Smith

*Riots are the voices
of the unheard.*
— Martin Luther King, Jr.

As South Central Los Angeles burned live and in color after the Rodney King verdict, no one old enough to remember could help but be struck by a sense of *déjà vu*. It was Watts, Detroit and Newark revisited, a tragic re-run of anger and despair.

Stories abound of parallels and differences between then and now, and many have looked at the root causes of such riots — poverty, unemployment, racial inequality. But journalism also would be served by turning the mirror on itself, because the press, with notable exceptions, has not done a very good job of covering the "unheard."

"The media report and write from the standpoint of a white man's world," a group of mostly white men wrote almost a quarter-century ago in the Report of the National Advisory Commission on Civil Disorders, popularly known as the Kerner Commission. Today, as numerous studies have shown, people of color still tend to make news when they do things that bring them into conflict with white society — like rioting — but otherwise they are largely ignored. As one editor told me, the traditional news format "tends to bypass minorities," and the effect can be startling.

For example, *What Color is the News?*, my 1990 study of local news coverage in the San Francisco Bay Area, found that people of color, Latinos in particular, were most frequently depicted in crime stories. Conversely, no Latinos were depicted in lifestyle stories, no Asians in business stories and no people of color of any stripe in obituaries. The results echo every study of press coverage of non-whites dating back to the 1950s.

Racial stereotyping is prevelant in media coverage today. Headlines using terms like the "Asian Invasion" on stories about Asian immigration to the U.S. are described in Project Zinger, a 1991 report on news coverage of Asian/Pacific Islanders by the Asian-American Journalists Association. The unconscious fears implicit in the "invasion" headline (published by a reputable Southern California newspaper in 1990) echo an insidious social theme found in newspapers more than a century ago: blaming Asians and other people of color for tough economic times. Most social scientists agree the media can influence racial attitudes by reinforcing racial fears. Recent studies suggest a link between news coverage and the modern racist, who believes discrimination is a thing of the past, and that any problems African-Americans and other non-whites face in American society are therefore of their own making.

The news media, wrote political scientist Robert Entman in a recent op-ed piece in the *Los Angeles Times,* inadvertently "stimulate modern racism" by reinforcing impressions of African-Americans as "threatening, overly demanding and undeserving." His analysis of 200 local television newscasts in Chicago showed blacks mostly got reported about when they committed violent crimes or asserted their political interests.

Ours is a society divided by race and class, and mainstream media, for better or worse, provide the only routine glimpse most folks get of people who aren't like them. It's a scary situation that is not of the press's making. But it is, nonetheless, one the press must find the will and courage to address. For everyone's benefit, the mainstream media must learn to cover issues of race and class on a routine basis, not just when the "unheard" scream so loudly they can't be ignored. ∎

Erna Smith is a former newspaper reporter who is currently associate professor of journalism at San Francisco State University. A version of this story first appeared in Muckraker: Journal of the Center for Investigative Reporting.

Los Angeles: Ted Soqui

As Our Cities Go, So Goes America

by Jeff Faux

America's economic fate cannot be divorced from the economic fate of our cities. The notion that a majority of Americans can live in suburban and rural prosperity while the center of our metropolitan areas decay is tragically wrong.

The nation as a whole can no longer afford the burden of large numbers of unemployed and under-employed people inhabiting the inner-city. When America dominated the global economy, one might have argued that such a burden was bear-

able. Now that the nation is engaged in fierce international competition, with productivity and living standards slipping, full use of the urban labor force is essential for our future.

Urban decay is dynamic: Poverty, crime and family breakdown in virtually all metropolitan areas have spread outward from the inner-city core. Yesterday's affluent suburbs are today's decaying inner-ring suburbs. Unless present policies are reversed, the process will continue, driving populations and businesses further out to peripheral areas, where the cost of transportation and constant rebuilding and relocating is making the nation's businesses less efficient.

The high density and variety that characterize the urban economy facilitate the innovation and rapid exchange of information upon which success in the global marketplace depends. This is particularly critical for the support of such high value-added activities as business services, product design and marketing, foreign trade, finance and insurance, joint ventures, education and legal services.

Instead of treating America's cities as social problems, we should treat them as economic opportunities. As the recent Economic Policy Institute report *Does America Need Cities?* points out, "Urban investment promises the highest return to the nation's economy, simply because such investment would be targeted where the greatest potential for growth now exists. Where are the most under-utilized people, the largest stock of usable or reparable infrastructure, and the biggest supply of conveniently located land? The answer, of course, is in America's cities."

The riots in Los Angeles and the recent flooding of downtown Chicago make it clear that the time has come for the federal government to reverse the policies of the last dozen years encouraging

what's to be done: economics

urban disinvestment. Federal aid as a share of cities' budgets was slashed by more than 60 percent in the 1980s. The reduction in aid, coupled with declines in direct assistance to the poor, changes in tax policy and additional federal mandates, forced cities to raise taxes and reduce services, putting further pressure on businesses and middle-class residents to move out of the city.

Reversing these policies will require a much larger shift in resources to urban problems than is contemplated by President Bush's proposals. The Economic Policy Institute has estimated that the nation must invest at least another $250 billion in education, training and physical infrastructure during the next five years in order to keep the U.S. from falling farther behind its international competitors in these areas. (This does not include the $60 billion in human- and physical-investment spending currently expected to be cut during the next five years by the existing budget agreement between the president and Congress.) About 80 percent of the additional investment needed — or about $200 billion — should be earmarked for metropolitan areas.

Under this program, priority should be given to:

•Rebuilding the infrastructure of the cities, particularly transportation and water systems. Such sustained public investment would not only reverse the crumbling infrastructure; it would also immediately create needed jobs that pay a decent wage for the unemployed — particularly unemployed young males — and it would create opportunities for new enterprise development and commercial industrial services to support long-term investment.

•A major increase in education and training for inner-city people. Every eligible child should be served by Head Start. Schools need to be upgraded — from the fixing of leaking roofs and the provision of books to the expansion of high-quality, innovative teaching methods. Anti-dropout and school-to-work transition programs

are needed to provide incentives for adolescents to stay in school. And we need a first-class apprenticeship-based vocational-training system.

•An emphasis on community-based neighborhood development. Job creation and education investments will return hope to the inner-city. The federal government should assist local governments in designing and implementing housing development, business creation and expansion, permanent neighborhood police anti-crime programs and other programs that have been developed and refined in communities throughout the nation in the last few years but starved for lack of funds.

During the next two years, the investment should be financed in a business-like way — by borrowing for investment. As the recent statement by 100 economists — including six Nobel Prize winners — stated in support of their proposal to spend another $50 billion per year on these investments through state and local governments, "The spending of these funds will help to stimulate the economy. Since the economy has idle resources of labor and capital available to meet additional spending with additional production and the threat of inflation is minimal, it is appropriate to let these expenditures add to the deficit, financed by borrowing."

In effect, the nation needs to make a long overdue distinction between government investment and consumption spending. Consistent with capital budgeting principles, this financing strategy would allow the operating deficit (reflecting federal government consumption) to continue to decline during the next few years and permit the appropriate use of borrowing for activities that will make the nation more productive.

As economic growth speeds up and funds from the peace dividend become available, the investment program should be financed by shifts in resources from defense and by tax increases. Thus, the program is also compatible with a gradual reduction in the overall deficit. ■

Jeff Faux is director of the Economic Policy Institute.

Musical Chairs As Economic Policy

by Richard Rothstein

When presidential press secretary Marlin Fitzwater, Attorney General William Barr and Vice President Dan Quayle blamed Los Angeles rioting on President Lyndon Johnson's Great Society programs, they repeated a sacred mantra from the never-never land of modern Republicanism. Along with beliefs that lower taxes would reduce the government deficit and that television sit-coms would inspire the poor to give birth out-of-wedlock, the Reagan and Bush administrations hold that welfare grants and food stamps cause poverty. In this view, the poor (meaning black people) develop an expectation of entitlement when they accept government "handouts." They are henceforth unable to hold jobs, motivate their children, plan for the future or, presumably, refrain from arson and looting when police aren't nearby. According to Quayle, responsibility for the Los Angeles riots can be traced to the Democratic Party, which has "practiced and preached the idea of dependence, and dependency has created inertia, lack of drive, lack of self-help."

In fact, recipients of most government handouts since the 1960s have not been the poor, but the super-rich: real-estate developers, agri-business investors, corporate executives and financiers. Their

141

what's to be done: economics

behavior confirms the Fitzwater-Quayle theory. In the post-Cold War environment, for example, defense contractors have found it difficult to shift to civilian production (like mass-transit vehicles) without seeking additional public subsidies. As Quayle's theory predicts, their habitual dependence on government giveaways permanently sapped their drive to do productive work in the private sector.

Yet Fitzwater and Quayle were not referring to these wealthy recipients of public aid. Nor were they referring to beneficiaries of successful Great Society programs like Head Start, the Women, Infants and Children (WIC) nutrition program or Medicare or Social Security cost-of-living adjustments. These programs are almost universally regarded, even by Republicans, as successful. Indeed, Social Security increases and Medicare are responsible for one of the great social achievements of our generation: the near abolition of poverty among the elderly since the 1960s. The true object of Republican ire is not in fact programs of the 1960s, but the 1930s New Deal welfare program that gives cash to single unemployed women with children. And, for welfare recipients, Quayle's dependency theory doesn't work.

In his 1984 book, *Losing Ground*, Charles Murray argued that, despite increased welfare expenditures since 1965, poverty has increased. He claimed that it had become irrational for young blacks to work or to marry, since it was now more profitable to collect welfare than to take a minimum-wage job. Though it became a staple of the Reagan administration, Murray's book was based on faulty data. Welfare benefit levels did increase in the late 1960s, but if Murray's theory were correct, this should have resulted in increased unemployment of young black males who chose not to work but instead lived off girlfriends' welfare checks. However, during the years welfare benefits increased, unemployment for young black males declined. Then, in the 1970s, most states slashed welfare benefits. Murray's theory predicts that this decline should

have propelled more young black males into the workforce. In fact, their unemployment rate increased in the 1970s.

Yet while welfare payments and food stamps, along with Great Society initiatives like Medicaid, Head Start, job training and federal aid to public schools, may not cause poverty, they haven't done much to prevent it, either. And it's a cop-out to argue, as many Democratic politicians have said in recent weeks, that if only these programs were fully funded they would be successful.

The reality is that most Democratic and Republican solutions to urban poverty miss the mark. The only workable solution is a full-employment economy that provides a job with good wages for every able-bodied American adult. Many Democratic programs — like job-training and apprenticeship plans, or more funds for reform of urban education — can only better prepare minority youth for jobs that don't exist.

There is, as Republican moralists like to point out, a strong relationship between the growth of single-parent (that is, female-headed) households and poverty. As the vice president pointed out in his "Murphy Brown" speech, married-couple families have a poverty rate of 5.7 percent, while families headed by single mothers have a poverty rate of 33.4 percent. But it is foolish to contend that illegitimate motherhood is caused by watching immoral television programs or even by some deeper deficiency in self-discipline and moral values. When young males cannot find jobs that pay wages adequate to support wives and young children, they become less attractive mates and marriage rates fall. Marriage rates normally decline in economic downturns, to rise again during periods of prosperity. But young men today, especially black men, find themselves in a permanent economic downturn. Average earnings of employed black men fell by 24 percent from 1973 to 1989. In the African-American community, expected fertility rates (the number of births a woman could expect during her lifetime) dropped dramatically — from

4.54 in 1960 to 2.29 in 1987. But without decent economic prospects for African-American males, marriage rates plummeted even more, resulting in greater poverty and welfare dependency of women and their children.

The Republican solution to the problem of black joblessness — enterprise zones — are offers of tax give-aways and freedom from regulation to induce plant relocations to the inner-city from more prosperous areas. However, absent a strategy for increasing the total number of jobs, enterprise zones, if successful, only succeed in shifting unemployment from the inner-city to less devastated outlying working-class communities.

Thirty-six states have established enterprise zones in the last few years (including California, which has 19 zones). Secretary of Housing Jack Kemp (lately joined by President Bush) wants to make the enterprise-zone program national by adding to state sales and corporate tax breaks for businesses that locate in a zone exemptions from capital-gains and income taxes for both investors and employees.

Perhaps the most dramatic application of what an enterprise zone tries to accomplish is the program the federal government established for Puerto Rico in a 1976 tax law. That legislation brought jobs to the island by exempting from income tax the profits earned by a mainland corporation's Puerto Rican subsidiary. Pharmaceutical companies especially have taken advantage of this tax incentive, since firms can also escape taxation on income generated by patents on drugs manufactured in Puerto Rico. As a result, pharmaceutical producers now receive an average of $71,000 a year in tax breaks for each of their Puerto Rican workers (who are paid an average of $27,000 a year in wages). These tax breaks, however, have not created net additions to the number of pharmaceutical jobs nationwide. More than 16,000 Puerto Rican workers now have jobs in the industry — but mainland employees of such firms as DuPont, SmithKline Beckman, Squibb and American Home Products lost employment when their plants moved to the commonwealth.

This musical chairs economic policy

— moving plants from location to location to tunes of tax breaks and deregulation — is the hallmark of U.S. government economic policy. It's the theme not only of enterprise zones and Puerto Rican development policy, but also of President Reagan's Caribbean Basin Initiative and of President Bush's plan for free trade with Mexico. There are now some 2,000 Mexican *maquila* plants employing half a million workers along the U.S. border. Since 1965, the *maquila* program has successfully used U.S. tariff waivers, Mexican tax concessions and a go-easy policy on Mexican labor and environmental regulatory enforcement to attract several hundred thousand manufacturing jobs previously located in the United States.

Supporters of free trade with Mexico and the Caribbean, like those promoting urban-enterprise zones, implausibly suggest that the zones' chief effect is the establishment of new firms that have no adverse effect on existing jobs elsewhere; their tax breaks and substandard wages will not undermine employment of firms outside the zone.

It is increasingly obvious that these claims have no basis in economic reality. Workers displaced by plant relocations suffer long periods of unemployment and generally find new jobs with far lower wages than the jobs they lost. In the 1980s, jobs paying less than poverty wages rose from 12 to 18 percent of full-time jobs for workers of all ages. Six percent of young (ages 25 to 34) male full-time workers earned wages below the poverty line for a family of four in 1979. By 1990, this number jumped to 15 percent. Twenty-three percent of very young (ages 18 to 24) male full-time workers earned less than poverty wages in 1979; by 1990, this number nearly doubled to 43 percent. The Caribbean Basin Initiative and expanded Mexican trade are among the policies responsible for the drop in average wages for all American workers from $11.43 an hour in 1979 to $10.99 in 1990.

President Bush has made opposition to racial quotas a cornerstone of his domestic policy. He appeals to the fears of white workers that they will lose good employment opportunities to minority workers given unfair preferences in hiring decisions.

Los Angeles: Ted Soqui

In a period like the present, when opportunities are scarce or even declining, such appeals are extremely effective. Yet enterprise zones are the ultimate case of reverse discrimination. Zones don't merely give hiring preferences to individual black applicants: Zones promise government aid if an entire plant moves from a white to a black community.

Enterprise zones' success, however, is not likely. In the state enterprise-zone programs that already exist, there is no evidence of significant job growth. Yet zone partisans, unwilling to face this reality, maintain that there is nothing wrong with enterprise zones that even greater tax breaks won't cure. Not understanding the continuity between domestic and foreign economic policies, they fail to see that firms willing to relocate solely to take advantage of tax and regulatory concessions are far more likely to move to Baja California, where wages average less than $1 an hour, than to South Central Los Angeles, where a minimum wage of $4.25 remains, for the time being, in effect.

When Lyndon Johnson planned a "War on Poverty," he overrode the recommendation of his Secretary of Labor, Willard Wirtz, that its core be a full employment plan to create new jobs for the poverty-stricken. Wirtz unsuccessfully argued that the "single immediate change which the poverty program could bring about in the lives of most of the poor would be to provide the family head with a regular, decently paid job."

Ignoring the pleas of Wirtz and his policy assistant (now Senator) Daniel Patrick Moynihan for a full employment program, Johnson proceeded with a menu of anti-poverty plans, based on the implicit assumption that poverty did not result from lack of opportunity but from the inability of poor people to take advantage of opportunity that was plentiful. This social-work, "blame the victim" approach characterizes many well-intentioned Democratic anti-poverty plans even today. These plans avoid facing the obvious fact that when the country's overall unemployment rate exceeds 7 percent (11 percent if workers are counted who have given up looking or have involuntarily taken part-time jobs), giving minority group members added tools to compete can only result in the limited, laudable, but politically dangerous goal of distributing unemployment more equitably.

Despite the limitations of this approach, the Johnson and Nixon administrations saw dramatic improvement in African-Americans' economic circumstances. From 1964 to 1974, the portion of all full-time jobs paying less than poverty-level wages dropped from 24 percent to 12 percent, and black workers shared in this prosperity. But except for the elderly, who benefitted from Medicare, diminution of poverty was not caused by Great Society programs. Most of the credit belongs to the war in Vietnam, which entailed such vast military purchases that total domestic employment opportunities increased. Military spending rose from 7 percent of the GNP in 1964 to 9 percent in 1968. After the Vietnam war, Pentagon costs declined to less than 5 percent in 1979, only to begin another rise under President Reagan. But 1980s military spending was never as great a share of the GNP as it was in the mid-'60s, and for African-Americans other countervailing economic policies — like the shift of manufacturing to low-wage nations, the weakening of unions and the loss of manufacturing jobs in corporate restructurings — more than offset the stimulative effect of 1980s military purchases. Los Angeles County, for example, experienced a net loss of 66,000 manufacturing jobs in the 1980s. In addition, many manufacturing jobs that remain are sweatshops in garment and other light industries; they have replaced high-paying jobs in LA's lost or shrinking heavy industries like automobiles, rubber and defense. Today, with military spending again in decline, we have the worst of all worlds: less fiscal stimulus from defense purchases, along with a deafening silence from both political parties on the subject of full employment in the civilian sector.

Studies show that, when young black men get good jobs, they are conscientious about keeping them. In jobs that pay well, for example, young black men have lower absenteeism rates than whites. A program to create new jobs that pay well, however, is the only urban program with a chance of remedying the conditions that caused the Los Angeles riots. It could not be a program specially designated to cure the problems of the disadvantaged, for in a mobile economy like ours, targeted policies are more likely to relocate opportunity than to create it. The only successful urban program is not likely to be "urban" at all, but a plan that includes monetary, trade and development policies reestablishing the United States as a high-wage industrial nation. In the past, large-scale wars have mobilized the work force, while wars on poverty have not been understood to require the same commitment of national wealth and human capital.

If we create new jobs, we won't have to use tax concessions to bribe companies to move jobs from one community to another. If jobs actually exist in sufficient number, we'll suddenly find less need for fancy training programs to qualify the unemployed to take them. And, once young men are again employed at jobs with adequate incomes, we may find that, no matter what television programs they watch, a significantly greater number will support their own children and marry their children's mothers. ■

Richard Rothstein is a research associate of the Economic Policy Institute and a columnist for the LA Weekly, *where a version of this story first appeared.*

• • • • • • • • • • • • • • • • • •

Plant Closures since 1965 in South LA
(Figures for total job loss are probably higher since additional layoffs usually preceded plant closures.)
American Bridge *(Commerce):*
closed 1979; 700 employees
Bethlehem Steel *(Vernon):*
closed 1982; 1,600 employees
Chrysler *(Commerce):*
closed 1971; 2,000 employees
Discovision *(Carson):*
closed 1982; 1,000 employees
Fibreboard *(South Gate):*
closed 1978; 250 employees
Firestone *(South Gate):*
closed 1980; 1,400 employees
Ford *(Pico Rivera):*
closed 1980; 2,300 employees
GM *(South Gate):*
closed 1982; 4,500 employees
Goodrich *(Commerce):*
closed 1976; 1,000 employees
Goodyear *(Los Angeles):*
closed 1980; 1,600 employees
Johns Manville *(Vernon):*
closed 1982; 200 employees
Lure Meat Packing *(Vernon):*
closed 1978; 500 employees
Max Factor *(Hawthorne):*
closed 1982; 1,000 employees
Uniroyal *(Commerce):*
closed 1978; 1,450 employees
Weiser Lock *(South Gate):*
closed 1981; 2,100 employees

(Source: Goetz Wolff, Labor Market Analyst; Keith Skotnes, UAW)

Democrazy
by Michael Ventura

The safest country in the world in which to invest money is the United States. The most dangerous industrialized country in which to be a human being is — the United States. Could it be that these facts are related? Somehow, right before our eyes, business and government have colluded to divorce the life of money from the life of people.

Statistics vary, but approximately one percent of the population now owns roughly one-third of the resources. Two things are clear about this one percent of fortune-makers: a) They don't give a fuck about what happens to the rest of us, and b) They own those people who call themselves Republicans and Democrats.

The One Percent needs these Republicans and Democrats in order to operate the mechanism by which they have separated the lives of American citizens from American money. That mechanism is called the "defense budget." But the only people being defended are the One Percent.

This purpose is carried out with admirable efficiency by Republicans and Democrats. It's a lie and an illusion that we have an inefficient government. If you look at our government as an anti-constitutional organization intended to deprive Americans of precisely the goals stated in the Constitution, then Washington, D.C., is in fact a marvel of efficiency.

The safest country in the world in which to invest money is the United States. The most dangerous industrialized country in which to be a

Los Angles: Anne Fishbein

than half would do nicely, since the Soviet Union no longer exists. In fact, without one major threat left to American security, you'd think we could afford to scale down.

We can't, though, because protecting America is not the purpose of the defense budget. The purpose of the defense — and, yes, I mean the intended, thought-out purpose of the defense budget — is to keep American resources out of the hands of average Americans.

How does that help the One Percent? It clears the field of any non-corporate competition. There is no suppport, no possible investment base, for any alternative to Big Business, Big Banking, Big Medicine, Big Insurance. All the resources that could support alternatives are consumed by "defense," but the only people being defended are the One Percent.

human being is also the United States. Could it be that these facts are related?

There's ample documentation for both statements. For the first, we can cite many an article from the *Wall Street Journal*. Let's pick the issue of May 4, written while the ashes of the Los Angeles riots still smoldered. "As the world's biggest — *and safest* [my italics] — economic power, the U.S. can attract all the capital it needs to finance its budget deficit as well as private investment."

Safest for whom? Not for individuals. Every day another statistic tells us that far more people are killed, wounded, beaten and robbed in the United States than anywhere else in the world. In urban America, we have almost no safe neighborhoods left — some places are merely in less of a state of siege than others. Rural America isn't that much safer. Medically, we're the disgrace of the industrialized world; environmentally, we pollute not only the earth but ourselves.

And, if all this weren't bad enough, on January 2, *The New York Times* confirmed in print what many have suspected: that most economic experts "predict that [American] job security — the comfortable expectation of being able to settle down

somewhere for life, at least by middle age — may be gone for good." Yet the United States is the safest place in the world for money. Somehow, right before our very eyes, business and government have deftly separated the life of money from the life of people.

These last 20 years in particular, most of the resources that might have sustained a decentralized, people-oriented economy — an economy that effectively supported small businesses as well as large ones; an economy, in short, more or less like we used to have when America was strong as well as rich — all those resources have been siphoned into the so-called "defense budget." When we are told there is no money for education, ecology, small business investment, research, medical care (no money, in other words for anything sane and productive), what is meant is that this money must be spent on weapons, on weapons research and on people who must operate weapons.

Must it? We wouldn't have had to fight Saddam Hussein if we hadn't armed him. As for the Soviet Union, now it's recognized that half our weapons would have been plenty to deter them. At present, less

I t is a dangerous fantasy — and I mean dangerous in the most urgent, personal sense — to believe that the Democratic Party, or any member of that party, is some sort of antidote to this situation. On Monday, April 27, two days before the Los Angeles riots, *The New York Times* reported as follows: "Democrats in Congress have backed away from their earlier plans to seek sharp reductions in the military budget next year, making it likely that the final figures will closely resemble those proposed by President Bush." The importance of this can't be exaggerated. This means that the Democratic Party, which has the majority in both houses of Congress, has doomed our children, doomed our cities, doomed our economy and doomed our environ-

Los Angeles: Ted Soqui

ment to another year of this refrain of "There is no money." The Republicans did not have the power to do this. They have no majorities in Congress. This defense budget is the result of Democratic power.

"But some Democrats didn't vote that way," you say. "*They* have integrity." I say: It's necessary that some Democrats don't vote that way. It's not only tolerated, it's encouraged. Those "good" Democrats make everything look like a political process — and most of them know it. If they had any real integrity, they'd quit the party.

To believe that the recent defense vote is some sort of mistake or aberration is to be blind to the last 20 years of our history — at the very least. Remember that it was Jimmy Carter who began the enormous arms build-up that Ronald Reagan continued and amplified, and it was Jimmy Carter who began the disastrous policy of mandating that states fund social programs without any federal money to back them. That policy is why, as the *Times* announced May 19, only three weeks after the riots, another $400 million was being cut from LA's school budget. This was the same day that the networks were full of stories about how Washington's save-the-cities fever, inspired by the riots, had stalled over the issue of where the money was to come for these programs — a question being asked by people who knew perfectly well where the money could have been found.

Then, on May 20, the *LA Times* reported that the House Armed Services Committee, controlled by the Democrats, is planning to give $1 billion to defense contractors to offset their losses. The same day, the *Times* reported that the Senate Appropriations Committee, also controlled by the Democrats, had added $1.45 billion to its Emergency Urban Aid Bill in response to the riots. The defense contractors, needless to say, didn't have to riot to get help.

Believing that a vote for the Democratic Party is an alternative to any of this indulges a blindness both to our recent history and to our present moment, a socially schizophrenic state of mind that allows one to vote for people in the hope that they'll behave as they have never behaved. I'm serious when I say that voting for Democrats or Republicans for national office is a form of madness, a panicky reflex to a decades-long crisis, an act of mass insanity that feels individual but that is goaded overtly by mass media and unconsciously by mass yearning. Which is why I find it healthy that so many people have stopped voting. They have decided not to be crazy.

It's unfortunate, however, that they don't vote at all. On local and even state levels, voting is still useful in America. It's even useful on a national level, if you want the political situation to remain as it is. But

the national situation teaches one lesson: There is nothing more important for the health of this country than the destruction of the Democratic Party. We must destroy the illusion that politics-as-usual offers any alternatives. Only then can the deep-rooted talent, energy and hope of the American people be employed in anything resembling constructive politics.

For while it's crazy to vote for these betrayers, it's equally crazy to give up hope. We've been conned into thinking that voting is the only sort of political action available. But politics is much more complex than pulling a lever. I just intended to type, "Democracy is in the streets," but what my fingers insisted on was "Democrazy." Well, democracy or democrazy, history teaches over and over that government only changes when the people make it change. And they usually have to get into the streets to do it. Franklin Delano Roosevelt and his Democrats did not give us Social Security; a decade of people peacefully demonstrating gave it to us, and the Democrats followed their lead. Peaceful demonstration has been the most effective political tool of our century. The question is, What do you really want? The next question is, Where do you have to go to get it?

Isn't it clear, for instance, that if the governor of your state awoke to find 100,000 parents sitting with linked arms around the governor's mansion, and the legislators came to work that same day and found another 100,000 parents sitting with linked arms around the legislature, and all of them, exercising their right of peaceful free assembly, refused to move until they were promised specific, drastic improvements in the education of their children — isn't it clear that the education of their children would improve, and quickly?

(And isn't it equally clear that if these hypothetical parents simply marched, waved placards and made speeches, they would probably not be listened to nearly as readily?)

Americans already know more answers than they want to take responsibility for. History shows that usually there's only one way people without money and guns can effect political (as opposed to social or cultural) change. Labor movements all around the world — Gandhi in South Africa and India, Martin Luther King, Jr., in America, not to mention the people of Eastern Europe, the former Soviet Union, the Philippines, China and, most recently, Thailand — have proved that peaceful, concerted action makes for change, and that the only way to learn it is simply to do it. It doesn't work all the time, and it doesn't work all the way (nothing does), but it works infinitely better than voting.

It's not that voting is useless or stupid. Rather, it's the exaggeration of the power of voting that has drained the meaning from American politics. Voting is a way in which we participate in the administrative power, in which we wield an administrative tool — nothing less, but nothing more. For a society that fundamentally agrees on its basic values, goals and functions, voting works out the dialectics and mechanics of that agreement. Even in such a society however, a vote without the threat of action to back it up is a vote all too soon taken for granted. And in a society like ours, a society that agrees now on next to nothing, a society struggling over which values, goals and functions will dominate its government, one that's arguing not only about how but about what that government will administer — in such a society, voting is never enough. Not even half enough.

Voting has become so unattractive, so dispensable, to so many Americans not because voting is too much trouble, but because it's not trouble enough. Nothing is at stake when you're voting for two parties as similar as the Republicans and the Democrats; nothing is at stake when you're voting for candidates who use the same words, who try to project the same images, and who are in fundamental agreement on the nature of power — what it consists of, who should have it and who should keep it. Voting in such a situation is a chore, not an expression.

To feel defeated by what you have been taught is a basic right is to find yourself in an (existentially, if you like) excruciating position, to find a contradiction at the heart of your political existence. It is to have power and yet to be completely powerless. It makes you, as a citizen, feel an awful emptiness in the heart of what is supposed to be your freedom. So you have the empty freedom to exert powerless power, and your emptiness fills you while your powerlessness overpowers you, you are caught in more contradictions than you can bear, so you turn off, or burst — or turn off until you burst. And when the only people coaxing you to vote are politicians, broadcasters, writers, editors — professionals who are, in short, caught up in the drama of the political game and who happen make their living from that drama, whether you vote or not — then the sane thing is to turn away, to refuse to play, to admit your powerlessness rather than hand over the tiny power you have (as a voting Republican or Democrat) to the coaxers. We coaxers make our living off the drama of your powerlessness, and to trust any of us, left or right, is a mistake.

I lose patience with anyone who suggests that I vote as a Democrat — especially if they intimate, however gently, that voting is my primary power, while action is secondary. They write so much about voting, and so little about action, that they transmit the inadvisability of action in the form of what they say — hence they can afford to talk about action every now and then, since it's plain by the space they give to the concept that they don't take it seriously. Are you really going to trust such people with the making of your history?

Because if you are — if we are — then we deserve the circumscribed history they allow us.

Ultimately, the "answers" are clear — and the tactics are well-known. It isn't a question of learning; it's a question of application. It isn't a question of somebody having to give us an answer; it's a question of applying what we know to problems nobody has to teach us about — they're staring us and our neighbors in the face. It's also a question of trusting our neighbors and reaching out to them. That's certainly the first and most difficult step. In the face of our day-to-day behavior, such trust is difficult; yet, every day, people rise above their day-to-day limits. Those who can't trust can't expect to be trusted. Grassroots political action begins with that truth.

As to the nature of the action, people demonstrate the society they want by the action they take. Gandhi, Martin Luther King, Jr., and the thousands with them demonstrated dignity, respect for themselves, respect for others (including those who disagreed with them). They didn't wait for society or a political leader to give them the world they wanted; they enacted that world, taught it, demonstrated it.

How you demonstrate *is* the world you really want, no matter what your rhetoric. The manner of your demonstration is the politics you teach, no matter what your belief. Belief is action. Action is belief. History teaches that the means never justify the ends, because the ends are never, ever, ever achieved — what is achieved, every day, are the means. The means are all we have, so the means must embody rather than merely justify the ends.

The choice is: Is your demonstration merely going to mirror your world, or does your demonstration truly seek to change it? Does this action demonstrate the kind of society you want? Does shouting down a public speaker because you disagree with him or her, for example, demonstrate the way you want to live?

Your life is your demonstration, there's no way around that. Whether it manifests itself singly or joins with masses, whether it satisfies itself with a vote or works its way in solitude, each life engages every day (as a matter of course, and whether or not one chooses to think about it) the deepest questions of conscience and courage — those old, burdensome and, finally, unavoidable words. To reduce this to a choice between Republicans and Democrats, to speak and act and broadcast and edit and write as though that were all there is to it, is to squander whatever resources of courage and conscience the general madness has left us. ∎

Michael Ventura is author of Shadow Dancing in the U.S.A. *and* Night Time, Losing Time. *He is also a staff writer for the* LA Weekly, *where a version of this story first appeared.*

A Call To Bold Action

by Jesse Jackson

Excerpted from the commencement address at Eastern Connecticut State University, May 24, 1992

Los Angeles: Cynthia Wiggins

Different Boats

My friends, as we struggle with the challenge of racial justice in our country, in the final analysis it goes beyond the question of ethnicity to the question of ethics. Ultimately, when family farms are auctioned off, when plants close, the jobs leave, when desperation sets in and the lights go out, you cannot use color or religion or gender for a crutch. It is then not a question of black and white, but dark and light, and wrong and right. As you enter the world as the interpreters and advocates of racial justice, social justice, gender equality, economic justice and world peace, our challenge is nothing less than learning to live together.

We all came on different boats. Some were captured for our labor, some were captivated by a vision of opportunity. We all have different histories, different dates to mourn and celebrate.

African-Americans have that defining moment in 1619, when the first slave ship arrived. In 1776, in the War of Independence, the first to die for American freedom was an African-American, Crispus Attucks. 1789: the writers of the Constitution declared African-Americans to be three-fifths human, declared women and men without property unfit to vote, declared Native Americans unfit to live. 1857: the Dred Scott decision, where the court ruled that an African-American had no rights a white was bound to respect. The jury in Simi Valley, blinded by racism and stereo-

types to the evidence of their own eyes and to the humanity of Rodney King — that jury handed down this generation's Dred Scott, that a black man has no rights that a white policeman is bound to respect.

In 1863, the Emancipation Proclamation. 1896: *Plessy v. Fergussen*. Then, in 1954, *Brown v. Board of Education*. 1992: the attack on 1954. We have come full circle in our boats.

We all have our boats, our dates, our moments of historic recognition. Hispanics have the Cinco de Mayo. Others the pain of 1492, when Columbus began the process of invasion and colonization, now called "discovery." Women have 1920, the year of the 19th Amendment and the right to vote. 1973: *Roe v. Wade* and the right to choose. 1990: Bush vetoes the civil-rights bill that would remedy historic discrimination against working women. 1992: the Thomas hearings, the Bush attack on choice. We have so far to go.

From 1840 to 1850, the Chinese were brought to America for cheap labor, sometimes in the same boats used to bring African slaves. 1818: the Chinese Exclusion Act. In 1924, the Asian Exclusion Act, shutting all Asians out. In 1942, 120,000 Americans of Japanese descent were put in American concentration camps.

Just three years earlier, in 1939, 900 Jews on the ship *St. Louis* fled to America. They got within eyesight of

Miami, but the U.S. government turned them back to Germany, where they were killed. Hitler called them a ship of fools, and said no one would take them. In 1938, *Kristallnacht* had already let loose a night of fascistic hatred and violence against the Jews. 1943: the Warsaw Ghetto uprisings, where Jews against all odds said no, and chose dignity and death over silent annihilation. In 1948 the founding of Israel. Now, 1992, we see a re-emergence of anti-Semitism, racism and fascism brought back into the center of American politics.

This has been an evil and mean-spirited year for America. The Bush Administration is still sending Haitians back into the arms of death, as we once sent Jews back to Germany in 1939, as we once put Japanese-Americans in concentration camps. It was anti-Semitic and wrong in 1939. It was racist and wrong in 1942, and it is racist and wrong in 1992.

Learning to Live Together

We all came on different boats, but it is not enough to say, "We're all in the same boat now." We must have an appreciation for each other's history, and learn to live together in one big boat.

We have been kept apart by law for purposes of exploitation and control. Black against white against yellow against brown, male against female, new immigrant against old immigrant. They erected legal walls to keep us from seeing our common interests. Now this generation must take the walls down.

It will take more than race survival and ethnic pride to rebuild this country. It will take education for the sake of learning and law for the sake of justice. It will take a coalition of Americans of conscience to demand new priorities for this country's great wealth. It will take mutual respect for other people, just because they are people. It will take character. It will take new leadership.

Vice President Dan Quayle has been giving a national demonstration in divisiveness and mean-spiritedness. He has shown the kind of leadership this country can no longer afford, the leadership of Ronald Reagan and welfare queens, of Bush and Willie Horton. Dan Quayle went to New York and called it the welfare capital of the world. He saw the riots in Los Angeles, and attacked the people who suffered the most. He attacked the values of poor people and the unemployed, yet he did not attack the morality of the corporate greedy who destroyed American jobs and businesses. Quayle attacked looters who took cans of dog food and kitchen appliances they could not afford to buy, but he did not attack the S&L billionaire thieves who looted billions of dollars from the national Treasury.

Dan Quayle called children born to unmarried mothers "illegitimate." I was born out of wedlock, and I am not illegitimate. Children born to single mothers are not illegitimate. At a time when half of all poor children live in households headed by a single woman where there is no man, when the stress of unemployment, lack of health-care options, homelessness, rising tuition costs, decreasing scholarships, inadequately paid teachers, is tearing families apart, we need leadership with broad vision and a commitment to bold action.

State of the Nation

We need a vision to renew this nation, and a long-term plan to rebuild. Today, the majority of America is economically insecure. There must be a plan for the locked

out — for forsaken farmers, for neglected children, for abandoned cities. Today, with 10 million unemployed and one in ten Americans on food stamps, 35 million in poverty, 40 million without health care, the nation's character is at stake.

What was unique — the aberration — about the Rodney King situation was the camera; there have been 47,000 police brutality cases reported to the Department of Justice in six years. Only 15,000 have been selected for investigation, and only 128 prosecuted. This is only the tip of the iceberg. That 47,000 does not include most cases which are reported to state and local police, or not reported at all. Without the camera, Rodney King would be in jail today, charged with assaulting a police officer.

Our cities and rural areas have been abandoned. In 1968, the Kerner Report warned of the emergence of two unequal nations, one white, one black. Now one is black, brown, yellow, poor and young. That analysis stands today. We do not need another commission or another study. We need corrective action.

What do we learn from LA, where the system of justice collapsed? The price of neglect is expensive. It costs less to invest in pre-natal care, day care and Head Start on the front side, than jail care, welfare and despair on the back side.

America needs a plan — a 20-year, long-term commitment to rebuild, renew and heal. Those who have missed the

• • • • • • • • • • • • • • • • • • • •

Percentage of South LA residents in overcrowded conditions, 1970:
14.4

Definition of severe overcrowding, 1970:
1.01 persons/room

Average living condition in South LA, 1991:
1.8 persons/room

Average living condition citywide [in LA], 1991:
1.3 persons/room

(Source: Report of the Los Angeles Community Reinvestment Committee; Community Development Department, 1970-1977 Report)

growing impact of racism, sexism, anti-Semitism, anti-Hispanic-ism, Asian-bashing, homophobia, those who have not heard the cries of children hungry and in poverty, the homeless, the unemployed, the abandoned — they have not yet heard the message. They are not just in a deep sleep; they are in a coma.

The country is reaping what the last decade of folly has sown. We have the strongest military in the world, but our economy is falling behind. We have gone from the world's largest creditor to its largest debtor in a decade. Of all industrialized nations, we suffer the worst infant-mortality rates, the most poverty, the highest high-school drop-out rates.

New jobs were created, but more than half were part-time, temporary or work-on-contract, with little or no health care or pensions. Of the net new jobs created, about half paid poverty-level wages; almost all the rest paid less than the average annual earnings of $23,000.

Those who were left behind — in the cities and poor rural areas, white, black and brown — have fared the worst. The federal government cut back aid to cities and support for family farmers. Cities and states now face the worst fiscal crises since the 1930s.

A Plan to Rebuild America

So far, the response to the crisis from both political parties has been limited to arguments about how to rearrange the furniture. We need *perestroika* — the restructuring of our economic priorities. We need *glasnost* — a new openness. Lack of openness led to the corruption and secrecy that created the S&L and banking scandals, for which our children will be paying far into the 21st Century.

America needs a 20-year plan to break the cycle of neglect and abandonment. It takes a 15- to 20-year commitment to develop a new weapons system. We need the same 20-year patience and commitment to pre-natal care, day care, Head Start, equal and adequate pay for urban and suburban teachers, tuition down and scholarships up. We need job training, summer programs and jobs after graduation to reclaim our urban youth. When a problem deteriorates into a condition, it takes longer to break the cycle of fear, withdrawal, pain, and for the restoration of hope, dreams and confidence.

The administration wants to revisit the idea of the enterprise zone. An enterprise zone is only valid if it is designed to benefit the people who live in the zone. If "enterprise zone" means building a development bank in the zone to provide local people with capital and end red-lining, if it means jobs and training for young people who live there, if it means that profits will be kept in the community, then an enterprise zone could be an effective tool. But we must not turn the ghetto into a tax write-off for outside investors. We must invest in the people of the area and create human opportunity, so that the community and businesses and schools and other institutions can flourish bottom-up.

Now is the time to build an American Development Bank and create a series of urban development banks around the country. A development bank is to our economic system what the heart and blood is to the human body. A brain and all organs depend upon a heart pumping blood. An economy and all its organs depend upon a development bank pumping capital. There is $1 trillion in public pension funds. Ten percent of that money, government-secured, leveraged during a 10-year period, is enough capital to build a series of urban development banks to invest in affordable housing, business development and training.

We have a plan for virtually every country in the world except ours. We have a plan for the Middle East, Kuwait, West and East Europe, Russia and the Commonwealth of Independent States, Japan — but no plan for LA, New York, Washington or other urban centers. After World War II, we sponsored the Marshall and MacArthur Plans to turn war zones into enterprise zones, centered around development banks — sources of long-term capital. We did not rely on tax incentives for American corporations to rebuild Europe and Japan. We provided massive long-term aid, trade, loans and grants for development. We called it long-term development in our long-term interests.

We invested in the resurgence of their independence, and in return we got markets, allies and increased world stability. The same principle of mutual benefit must be applied to our cities.

When West Germany and East Germany came together, the West German government made an investment to lift up East Germany. They knew that sustained inequality leads to resentment, and ultimately contempt and a weakened and divided nation. And so West Germany raised taxes, and put forth billions of dollars as an investment in unity and stability.

Why is Japan strong? Japan invests in Japan. Japan invests in Japanese children, paying teachers what we pay doctors and lawyers. Japan has a 10-year, $3-trillion plan to rebuild its infrastructure. We have a 10-year $3-trillion plan to defend them while they do it. Japan invests in research and development — in things people need. They have a 400-mile-an-hour train. If we built such a train, we could go from Washington to LA in eight hours. We could make the steel, lay the rails, build the cars and drive them, and reconnect the country.

New Visions, New Priorities

So often more is spent keeping dreams crushed and warehousing the souls of our youth in jails than is spent reviving, renewing or resurrecting dreams. In New York, one year at SUNY costs $6,000 — one year at Attica, $60,000. In California, state college is $5,800. One year at Central Juvenile Correctional Center: $34,000.

Students, you have the power to change this nation's priorities, and set a new course. But you must use the power that you have, and not cry about what you don't have. There are 26,000 unregistered high-school seniors in New York City alone, about 3 million nationwide, mostly unregistered to vote. There are 13 million college students nationwide, also mostly unregistered. Bush beat Dukakis by 5 million votes. You have the power to change the nation.

In the long term, the people of South Central Los Angeles need what every citi-

zen of this country needs: education, jobs, health care, affordable housing, business opportunities, security and a sense that their needs and rights are respected.

A long-term plan to rebuild our cities must include a full commitment to health and education — pre-natal care, day care, Head Start, equal and adequate pay for urban and suburban teachers and affordable higher education.

We need job-training programs, summer job programs and job opportunities after graduation to reclaim our urban youth. South LA lost 70,000 manufacturing jobs in four years.

Black-, Hispanic- and female-owned businesses must have access to resources and contracts to rebuild our cities. We need to end the many forms of red-lining, stop blocking urban entrepreneurs' access to start-up capital and provide new sources of capital.

Finally, we need anti-crime and drug measures. The most effective anti-crime program is providing alternatives to despair: education, jobs and hope. However, our cities now also require specific measures to combat an entrenched cycle of violence. On the supply side, we need to stop the flow of drugs and guns. On the demand side, we need instant access to drug-treatment programs for anyone who needs it. We need a real commitment to improved community-police relations and alternatives to incarceration for black youth.

Los Angeles must be the wake-up call for a national plan to reinvest in and rebuild America. The explosion last week could very well be the dawn of the reaction, not mid-day or twilight. To avoid our worst fears, we who have eyes to see with and ears to hear with must step forward and act.

Finally, it comes down to a question of character. How you treat the stranger on the Jericho road, how you treat the least of these. America needs you. Keep hope alive. ∎

Jesse Jackson is founder and president of the National Rainbow Coalition.

Index to Copyrights

the roots of conflict in LA

on the scene

same verdict: different location

making sense

covering the riots

in the aftermath

Contributing Photographers

Saul Bromberger

Ed Carreon/*Orange County Register*

Debra DiPoalo

Anne Fishbein

Harrison Funk

Gerard Gaskin

John Goubeaux

Maggie Hallahan

Michael Harrelson

Larry Hirshowitz

Sandra Hoover

Virginia Lee Hunter

Michael Schumann/SABA

Ted Soqui

UPI/Bettman Archive

Cynthia Wiggins